The signs of crime
A field manual for Police

Consulting Editor: **Philip John Stead**
Professor of Comparative Police Science
John Jay College of Criminal Justice

Some McGraw-Hill books of related interest

English and Houghton   *Police Training Manual*
Wilson and McLaren   *Police Administration* 4 edn
Edelstein and Wicks   *An Introduction to Criminal Justice*
Stead (Editor)   *Pioneers in Policing: an Overview*

The signs of crime
A field manual for Police

David Powis
Deputy Assistant Commissioner
Metropolitan Police

McGRAW-HILL Book Company (UK) Limited

London · New York · St. Louis · San Francisco · Auckland · Bogotá
Beirut · Düsseldorf · Johannesburg · Lisbon · Lucerne · Madrid · Mexico
Montreal · New Delhi · Panama · Paris · San Juan · São Paulo · Singapore
Sydney · Tokyo · Toronto

Published by

McGRAW-HILL Book Company (UK) Limited

MAIDENHEAD . BERKSHIRE . ENGLAND

Library of Congress Cataloging in Publication Data
Powis, David
    The signs of crime.
    1. Crime and criminals—Identification
    I. Title
    364.12   HV8073   77-30173

ISBN 0-07-084499-2

1234 JW 7987

PRINTED AND BOUND IN GREAT BRITAIN

Dedication

This book is respectfully dedicated to the following *unarmed* English police officers who, within the past eleven years and while in the execution of their public duty as peace officers, were murdered by persons whose names are unworthy to appear here.

PS CHRISTOPHER HEAD, aged 30,

PC GEOFFREY FOX, aged 41,   and

PC DAVID S. WOMBWELL, aged 25, all murdered on 12 August 1966, at Shepherd's Bush, London.

PC BRIAN ARMSTRONG, aged 31, on 12 September 1966, at Gateshead.

Inspector JAMES R. BRADLEY, aged 31, on 3 December 1966, at Banbury.

PC MICHAEL DAVIES, aged 23, on 18 August 1969, at Wimbledon Common, London.

Inspector BARRY TAYLOR, aged 30, on 13 February 1970, at Farsley, Yorkshire.

PC IAN COWARD, aged 28, on 27 June, 1971, at Reading.

Superintendent GERALD RICHARDSON, aged 38, on 23 August 1971, at Blackpool.

PC PETER GUTHRIE, aged 21 years, on 22 July 1972, at Coventry.

PC MICHAEL WHITING, aged 21 years, on 5 May 1973, in Oxford Street, London.

PC DENNIS A. SMITH, aged 44 years, on 21 December 1973, at Torquay.

PC JOHN SCHOFIELD, aged 27 years, on 6 July 1974, at Caterham.

PC STEPHEN TIBBLE, aged 22 years, on 26 February 1975, in West London.

PC DAVID C. GREEN, aged 20 years, on 17 July 1975, at Birmingham.

PS BRYAN DAWSON, aged 42 years, on 1 September 1975, at Leicester.

PC NORMAN GARNHAM, aged 25 years, on 2 March 1977, in North Yorkshire.

Contents

Foreword

by SIR ROBERT MARK, GBE, QPM

Commissioner of Police of the Metropolis,
17th April 1972–13th March, 1977

It is unusual for a Chief Officer of Police to express formal approval for a publication by one of his officers and still more unusual that he should exhort his colleagues and the public generally to read it. It gives me no qualms of conscience, however, to follow that course in support of this book. I have often complained during a long police career that of all the mountains of printed matter about the police almost all consist of fiction and that there is virtually nothing that contains anything of any merit. This book is a noteworthy exception.

The author has had many years of practical experience in dealing with ever kind of police problem in the Metropolis and has dealt with them all with a thoroughness and fair-mindedness and an effectiveness which has gained him not just a high reputation but the confidence and trust of his colleagues in every part of the Force. He does not write to impress. He writes from a desire to impart the results of practical experience to those serving with him and to all those who are to follow him, and I can pay him no higher compliment than to say that from the point of view of a serving police officer, his book is value for money indeed. I hope warmly that it enjoys considerable success because I think it contains much that will benefit serving and future members of the Police Service.

26 November 1976   ROBERT MARK

Preface

Vigilance, or watchfulness, is a primary police quality, without which the other essential elements of the police officer's mental apparatus cannot function properly. Knowing what to watch for, however, is something that has to be learned.

We learn by being taught by others and we learn, often awkwardly, sometimes painfully, by experience. The present manual is based on the hard-won experience of a seasoned and successful police officer, now in senior rank at Scotland Yard, who has also taken a distinguished part in the instruction of the Service at the National Police College, Bramshill and elsewhere.

His book is a selection from his knowledge of crime-fighting, made specifically for his younger colleagues, with the aim of helping them to avoid the more wasteful ways of learning and to profit from the practical skills which he and those with whom he served have built up over the years in their confrontation with crime. Mr Powis does not, of course, expect his work to obviate his reader's need for personal, actual experience: he intends it rather to make that individual experience, in the process of being gained in the formative years of the police career, more meaningful and more productive. He has sought to share what he knows, so that vigilance may be sharpened and directed with greater awareness.

When I first read the manuscript of the book—and the impression has become stronger with each re-reading—I found it very heartening to realise that here was something written in the light of a conception of police work which is at once not only keen, positive and expert but also compassionate. The author's realism is tempered by his innate recognition of the fact that the police are fellow-citizens equally of those whom they protect and of those who break the law. He writes with a healthy scepticism, certainly, but without cynicism. Long acquaintance with the crime and confusion of our society has not undermined his belief in human nature nor impaired his sense of humour.

The whole approach of the book is frank and down to earth. Its style is plain, exact and blessedly free from the 'official' tone. The author has been at pains to emphasise his more important points, and he has not been afraid of repeating some of them in order to drive home the lesson.

The glossary of slang which is appended needs little justification. The newcomer to police work has to contend with a linguistic jungle of terms of art and also with a bewildering variety of expressions on which it is often embarrassing to seek enlightenment from others. Argot in this sphere is often obscene and perverse but it is a part of the living language and a key to the better understanding of people.

The front line of police work is patrol, the basic police function. On patrol the officer learns the job's true nature, in the demanding presence of the public, getting the first professional insights amid the endless surprises of the street. At this time the officer, whether on uniformed or detective duty, should be growing in ability and confidence.

This manual is meant to assist in that development of police quality. Books of practice are rare in police literature and this present one makes a salient contribution to this much-neglected field.

P. J. STEAD

Discrimination between the sexes

In a book on the subject of police work and crime, featuring well-established police terminology and colloquial expressions associated with crime, it is impracticable to eliminate completely the use of genders and retain a fluent and readable text. The reader is asked to accept that in the great majority of cases a deliberate distinction between the sexes is not implied.

Acknowledgements

All those who have the presumption to write training manuals receive much help, whether they realise it or not. This contribution is no exception. In thirty-one years of police service in Portsmouth and London I have learned from many fine officers, all with considerable skills as thief takers. It is their techniques I have tried to set down in plain terms, and which I now acknowledge.

Detective Constable 'Trotsky' Wilton, MM, Detective Sergeant Jesse Hughes, and Detective Superintendent Harold Payne, once officers with me in the old Portsmouth City Police, deserve repeated mention in this connection, as do the then Detectives Ian Forbes, John Morrison, QPM (both later Deputy Assistant Commissioners), Thomas 'Tommy' Butler (later head of the Flying Squad, now tragically dead) and Laurie Helstrip (later Chief Inspector), all of whom served at Paddington Green CID Office in my years there as an 'aid' and detective constable.

For making valuable suggestions, giving encouragement and reading manuscripts, I am under obligation to many people, particularly Sir James Starritt, KCVO, lately Deputy Commissioner of Metropolitan Police, Professor P. J. Stead, OBE, Mr. D. W. Warran, Mr. W. A. Ratcliffe, QPM, lately Assistant Chief Constable of Glasgow, Detective Superintendent Francis Holt, Metropolitan Police, Miss Rose Sabatini and Mrs Joan Hobman. For allowing certain of the illustrations I thank The Commissioner of Police of the Metropolis; also Mr Douglas Jordan, Chief Investigation Officer, Her Majesty's Customs and Excise; Mr Edward M. Davis, Chief of Police, Los Angeles Police Department; Mr P. J. Matthews, OBE, QPM, Chief Constable of Surrey; and Dr M. H. Hall, Consultant in Charge, Emergency and Accident Department, Royal Infirmary, Preston. I am grateful to my wife, a senior nursing officer, and to many of her colleagues, for advice and help with the 'battered baby' chapter, as I am to Dr Hall, already mentioned.

G. J. Kelland, Esq, QPM (currently Assistant Commissioner in charge, Criminal Investigation Department), Chief Superintendent Atkins, Airport Division, Detective Superintendent David Prentice of New Scotland Yard, and P.C. Frank Pulley of Notting Hill, more than merit special mention concerning their exceptional and humane skills in the prosecution of London's violent motor thieves, fraudsmen, pickpockets, and the traffickers in corruption and prostitution.

DAVID POWIS

New Scotland Yard,
21 April 1977

Primary objects of police

'It should be understood at the outset that the principal object to be obtained is the prevention of crime. To this great end every effort of the Police is to be directed. The security of person and property, the preservation of public tranquillity, and all other objects of a Police establishment will thus be better effected than by the detection and punishment of the offender after he has succeeded in committing the crime. This should constantly be kept in mind by every member of the Police Force, as a guide for his own conduct. Officers and Police Constables should endeavour to distinguish themselves by such vigilance and activity as may render it extremely difficult for anyone to commit a crime within that portion of the town under their charge.'

(From the original instructions to Metropolitan Police in 1829.)

1. Fundamental principles

Essential facts you must know about the behavioural patterns, attitudes and life-style of thieves and successful thief catchers.

Every police organisation has a few men and women who seem uncannily successful in recognising and arresting criminals in the street. Their abilities are frequently shrouded in an air of mystery not discouraged by the persons concerned. Many of the officers themselves are reluctant even to discuss the reasons for their successes, especially with younger men and women. This may be understandable, for effectiveness in practical duty brings envied reputation; nevertheless, it is overwhelmingly in the public interest that these abilities are recognised for what they are, *acquirable skills*, and not innate detective ability or mysteriously recurring luck.

Every police officer, however young in service, can develop and improve aptitudes in this direction, provided old principles and techniques of taking thieves are analysed, brought up to date and patiently examined. Any belief in luck is foolish and, in the context of practical street work, officers will to a large extent make their own luck. It is an error that these skills are regarded as the province only of a favoured few, and it is certainly very wrong indeed that little attempt has ever been made to teach or even accurately describe them.

Many officers who are successful with street arrests of criminals do not themselves fully appreciate why. People assume they operate intuitively, without knowing what this means. Intuition is the power of knowing or understanding something immediately, without having to reason it out. The mind, however, can work only with acquired knowledge. The first fundamental is to learn to distinguish between normal and abnormal conduct of members of the community. This acquired knowledge will sink into the subconscious mind and, when unusual conduct is observed, suspicion will rapidly register without conscious rationalisation of cause and effect.

1

Young men and women must get clear in their minds that thieves do convey stolen property and incriminating articles through the roads and streets of any large city, and they do so hundreds of times a day; they have no occult power of spiriting objects away from buildings and vehicles. Therefore, opportunities will arise at more than one stage for an alert officer to detect the thieves in possession of incriminating articles. This may be taken as an obvious comment; however, it needs to be made because many police officers become discouraged by lack of success in the early stages of their careers and begin to look upon street interrogations, or 'stops' of suspected persons, as academic aspects of duty, supposing again that luck rules success. Nothing could be further from the truth. Over the years there have been innumerable cases of expert thieves being taken red-handed by intelligent stops. But, as with all worth-while things, consistent success comes only with practice, knowledge and persistence, and the greatest of these is a determined persistence.

Repeatedly study and observe in all circumstances the behaviour of ordinary, innocent people, as well as the behaviour of criminals. Once differences have been analysed, there will be development towards instant recognition. Try not to be over-reluctant to act upon 'hunches', for they are probably based upon quite sensible prior observation, taken in and registered by your brain within a minute fraction of a second.

Remember, we live in the motor-car age. As the internal combustion engine dominates the economy and daily life of our country, so it dominates crime and criminals. It is rare for a crime of real consequence, committed by persons over 17 years of age, to take place without a motor vehicle or vehicles forming some part of the transaction. The car has become the common denominator of crime.

Although thieves usually make use of stolen vehicles to commit crimes, the majority of them these days possess vehicles of their own. These are used to reconnoitre intended crimes and to convey stolen property some time after a crime. It has been noticed repeatedly that persons of bad character, even if financially successful, seem reluctant to tax their own vehicles and are found frequently to have had dealings in stolen or fraudulent excise licences. Similarly, experience has shown that persons of bad character frequently fit stolen accessories to their own cars. There is statistical evidence available (*The Criminal on the Road*, by Dr Terence Willett) indicating that persons of bad character are far more likely to commit serious traffic offences, and are more likely, therefore, to be disqualified from driving.

Few criminals are caught actually committing serious crime, because they take sensible precautions and have tactical surprise in their favour, but there are four general situations where 'vehicle-orientated' criminals are extremely vulnerable to alert uniformed police:

1. When, as has been said, they are reconnoitring intended crimes in their own vehicles, or when driving to the scene where they propose to steal a suitable vehicle for such a crime, or when in a stolen vehicle going to the scene of a crime; or
2. later, when conveying stolen property in their own vehicles to a place of concealment or to a receiver; or
3. when driving their own vehicles with stolen spotlamps, radios and similar accessories fitted, or bearing stolen or fraudulent excise licences or plates; or
4. when driving generally, despite the fact that they are disqualified.

Uniformed police have an advantage over their plain clothes colleagues in dealing with thieves using motor cars because they can legally compel drivers to stop by signal, and they alone have the general power to arrest for 'driving whilst disqualified'. They can also interrogate drivers concerning road traffic matters without arousing suspicion and resentment, and without revealing their original suspicion.

It follows that every uniformed officer should do his utmost, at an early stage of his service, to become as skilled as he can in the techniques of successfully searching suspect vehicles and in interrogating drivers. First, he must know precisely his powers of stopping and searching vehicles, and secondly he must develop, both by experience and study, the real skills required. It is not an easy task, but it is nevertheless within everyone's capability.

Always bear in mind that a substantial proportion of detectable crime (well over 50 per cent) is committed by persons between the ages of 17 and 30, especially by those under 21, so it is reasonable to be more suspicious of very young drivers or their companions.

Rough classifications

People who steal motor cars can be divided conveniently into six main categories. When persons are in custody for offences associated with the theft or unlawful taking of motor vehicles, try to see them at court and learn the facts of the case. See to which category they belong. This will

3

help you to slant your mind to the general type of person you must watch for when patrolling.

These categories often overlap but, placed in order of importance, they are as follows:

1. Professional and violent thieves who take motor cars to use in other serious crimes. They are rarely accompanied by females and usually have car-theft instruments with them. They frequently have offensive weapons concealed in their vehicles. They steal powerful cars or vans, and usually select the more common of this class, e.g., Jaguars and the larger Fords and Vauxhalls; Ford Transit vans and Dormobiles are increasingly used. They often travel to the scene of the vehicle theft in their own cars or vans.

2. The professional car thief who steals the vehicle for subsequent sale. Both road-engineering and large commercial vehicles are occasionally stolen by this class of thief, usually as the result of orders received rather than 'on spec'. He often has the most sophisticated of car-theft instruments with him. He may be accompanied (sometimes by a well-dressed female), but is often alone, and steals vehicles currently popular with a good resale price.

3. The professional thief who takes motor cars with the intention of stealing the contents or accessories and then abandons the vehicle. He usually has sophisticated car-theft instruments with him, and rarely works alone. He will take any vehicle if it has quality accessories or valuable contents. Like the first category, such a person often travels to the scene of the theft in his own car or van.

4. Young males who take motor cars, motor cycles and scooters for 'joy-rides' and abandon them within a few hours. They are often accompanied by young females, and frequently have elementary car-theft instruments with them. These youngsters will take any type of vehicle, but prefer something flashy and popular.

5. Adult males, often of reasonably respectable background, who are stranded a considerable distance from their homes or destinations but without train or taxi fare, and who are thus tempted to take vehicles. They are only rarely accompanied by females, and seldom have car-theft instruments with them. They will take any driveable vehicle, but prefer the older popular types as generally these are easier to start without an ignition key and, of course, they have no steering locks. Stranded servicemen sometimes come into this category.

6. Adult males under the influence of drink, usually alone, and with no car-theft instruments. They will take any vehicle that can be started, even large trucks and public service vehicles. No wheeled object is too bizarre for their attentions; huge cranes and earthmovers have been taken in the past.

2. The moving suspect and his vehicle

Proven ways to recognise and take the moving thief—by means of his vehicle.

Bearing in mind the general classifications of vehicle-orientated thieves just mentioned, when patrolling you must:

Watch for

▷ Persons, especially those in the suspect age group, who appear un-familiar in any way with the mechanism or controls of the vehicle they are using. Switching lights on in daylight or windscreen wipers on in dry weather, without realising which switch has been used, is very suspicious indeed. In some vehicles inexpert shorting of the ignition to start the vehicle without a key can cause the windscreen wipers to operate and, more important, refuse to stop! In dry weather, windscreen wipers seen operating for more than a few seconds are *always* worth prompt in-vestigation.

Watch for

▷ Persons, again especially in the suspect age group, not properly dressed for motor cycling, riding motor scooters or motor cycles in cold or wet weather, especially when public transport has ceased. Crash helmets that are too large, too small or even just awkward-looking are suspicious.

Watch for

▷ Persons, especially those belonging to the indicated groups, driving new vehicles of a class, make or type not usually hired by hiring companies, e.g., Jaguars or Rovers. (Remember that insurance premiums on power-ful sports cars are quite prohibitive and well beyond the means of most young persons.)

Watch for

▷ Persons, particularly of the described groups, loitering near motor vehicles in warm summer weather, who are wearing leather gloves. Many thieves have a quite unreasoning fear of leaving finger impressions behind, and take more than adequate precautions. The unnecessary wearing of gloves is a manifestation of this fear. Wiping the rear-view mirror or the door handles with a handkerchief or cloth is another suspicious action, particularly if the driver walks away afterwards. Also, be suspicious of young men wearing gloves whose general appearance, class of life or other clothing make the gloves seem out of place. Rubber gloves, of the sort sold to housewives for washing up, are particularly incriminating if found in a man's pockets. If they are neither oil-stained nor brand new, what possible explanation can there be? You may well have a clever and careful housebreaker in front of you. In this context the wearing of outer garments inappropriate to the weather is sometimes a pointer. Many thieves are fundamentally greedy and, even in mid-summer, cannot resist stealing a good-quality winter overcoat from the scene of a housebreaking. A man or woman wearing an overcoat of good quality in a motor car in summertime, therefore, and people wearing a mixture of shabby and smart clothing, are always worth gentle inquiry. Learn the difference between expensive and inferior fur coats and capes. Sable and mink do not 'go' with paste jewellery, tawdry make-up, cheap spectacles or sunglasses, and low-priced mass-produced cars.

To express a couple of personal prejudices. First, I have never seen street or motor thieves, no matter how financially successful they might be, wearing well-polished and well-repaired shoes. They may be 'snappy' or 'flash' dressers, their shoes may be of good quality, even new, but almost certainly they will be scuffed, dirty in the welts and down at heel. You can be certain they will not have been cleaned underneath between sole and heel. Second, I have never known such characters to smoke pipes, or rather to smoke pipes in that slow reflective way that real smokers do. Some flash confidence thieves may have a pipe in their mouths for effect, but they still will not look like pipe-smokers.

Watch for

▷ Groups of young men dressed in 'scooter-type' clothing, e.g., green anoraks or 'combat jackets' with the usual badges and ornamentation, who are on foot or travelling by public transport. Young motor thieves dress like this when on foot so they will not look out of place on a stolen scooter. The unusual absence of young women of a similar class from such groups of males may indicate an intention to steal.

Watch for

▷ Persons of the indicated groups pushing apparently undamaged vehicles or fixing some form of towing gear to such a vehicle. Remember that thieves sometimes dress in clothing that gives the impression that they are motor mechanics properly engaged on repair or recovery work. Remember, too, that thieves may have legitimate employment as mechanics and may be using their employer's recovery gear without permission.

Watch for

▷ The safety of your comrades and yourself. Policemen must bear in mind that there is latent in many criminals a violent, even ferocious, streak of character. This applies particularly to thieves engaged in robbery, and to travelling housebreakers. If these thieves are also users of dangerous drugs, particularly the hallucinatory drugs, this natural propensity may be heightened because you may have come across them in abnormal condition. The same applies if you have crossed their paths when they have taken too much hard drink, perhaps after a celebration. If they are in company with their womenfolk, there will be a temptation for them to show off their masculinity, their contemptuous disregard of the law and their hatred of policemen generally. Violence is near the surface in such a situation. If these are the conditions when you interrogate them in the street, at the wheel of a powerful motor car, realise that they have a weapon they can use against you—the car! It can be driven at you or the driver's door can violently be opened and banged against you. Thus, a primary consideration when stopping a suspect car is to find a safe and well-lighted place to do so—safe for the occupant(s) of the car you intend to stop, of course; safe, too, for public traffic using the thoroughfare concerned; but fundamentally safe for you. Lonely places should be avoided, if possible. Never approach the vehicle walking towards its front. Trained policemen are an expensive commodity and not easily replaced.

Watch for

▷ Signs of recent injuries about the face or hands, or dishevelled or blood-stained clothing, on persons passing you, whether on foot or in vehicles.

They are worth inquiry. Such a person may have been the victim of a road accident or assault, but may alternatively be a guilty driver or a person who has just previously been engaged in some form of violent crime. Beware of such a person who suddenly becomes quiet after arguing loudly with you. This is the classical behaviour of a man about to strike you. Visible injuries to members of the public should always be investigated promptly. Be wary—I emphasise that you may be tackling a violent thief or psychotic person, not a passive victim.

Watch for
▷ The violent driver who leaves the driving seat and faces you. Keep to the left of him. Most people are right-handed, and it will be easier for you to block or parry a blow or an attempt to strike you with a weapon if you keep your right shoulder slightly to the right of his right shoulder. It need not look unnatural. A man usually wears his wristlet watch on his left wrist, showing he is right-handed. If he wears it on his right wrist he may hit you first with his left hand. First blows are nearly always struck with the dominant hand. Weapons, whether firearms or bludgeons, are invariably grasped in the ascendant hand. Beware of the man butting you in the face; do not let him get too close and *keep to the side of him.*

Watch for
▷ The suddenly swinging driver's door already mentioned : I know I repeat myself but it is so important. The door can easily knock you to the ground. Twenty years later, marked leg discomfort from such an injury can still be a real nuisance. Stand by the offside centre-post of the vehicle, very slightly to the rear of the driver. It puts him at a psychological disadvantage and makes him adopt an unbalanced position to speak to you. He must crick his neck to the right and backwards even to see you, but most important of all—he cannot swing that door. You can also unobtrusively look down into the inside of his inner jacket pocket in this position. You may see him pull out something incriminating as well as his driving documents. Two driving licences for example! Never go to the front of the suspect vehicle unless the engine is switched off. If you are suspicious of the occupants, look for the opportunity to get hold of the ignition keys. A thief's key-ring shouts 'Thief!' to a discerning officer. Usually there will be too many keys for legitimate use and most will not be the original factory keys. Be suspicious of several duplicate ignition keys if their newness and brightness are obvious, particularly if jumbled up with old, worn or filed keys.

When I served with teams manning London 'Q' cars (disguised saloon vehicles with a crew of three plain clothes officers) in the 'fifties, we made it a drill, when intending to stop vehicles, to have the police vehicle driven to the offside, parallel to but slightly to the rear of the vehicle in question (remember, we were in plain clothes). Your Force may supply you with a suitable sign, but you can easily have made up, by index plate manufacturers, two index mark blanks, one reading 'Police', the other 'Stop', in the celluloid letters used on these plates. The plates can be bolted one above the other on a piece of three-ply, with a simple metal handle at the back. This is convenient and effective, and can easily be read by another driver, even at speed. Now that reflective number plates can be obtained, such a sign would be even more effective, especially at night when a torch can be shone on it.

The horn and gong of the police vehicle would then be sounded sharply twice, and the made-up sign shown to the driver by the officer in the front passenger seat of the police vehicle. After ensuring (by the mirror) that it was safe to do so, the police vehicle would drop back behind the suspect vehicle, the distance between the vehicles being dependent on the joint speed; roughly one vehicle's length for every 15 m.p.h. (24 km per hour). When the suspect vehicle had stopped, the police vehicle would pull up some 10 ft (3 m) behind, offset about 2 ft (0·6 m) to the offside, but with its front inclined some 15 degrees to the right. Thus, when the officer from the front passenger's seat left to go forward to speak to the suspect vehicle's driver, he was shielded from the overtaking traffic flow, so important on a fast-moving road.

However many routine checks of vehicles you make, in which no real incident occurs, persistent officers will eventually come across armed and violent men. Remember the Shepherd's Bush case, where the entire crew of a 'Q' car, three fine officers, were shot dead by cowardly thieves found in a suspicious delivery truck. With a crew of three men, carefully thought-out tactics should include the best possible survival patterns for everyone in the crew, but one man must always be able to leave the scene rapidly for help or to block the escape of the thieves, or both of course. The driver of the police vehicle is the person best able to do this, and he should invariably remain in the police vehicle, with its engine running. He can survey the incident and take action according to the way it develops. I thoroughly urge and recommend you to think through tactical plans, and to stick to them. These routines will save both injuries and fatalities.

Sooner or later you will meet with male drivers, not necessarily of bad character, who dislike police intensely because of some real or imagined slight in the past. If you signal such a driver to stop, when patrolling in an unmarked police vehicle, while you and your colleagues are wearing plain clothes, and when you do not have in your car a 'Police—Stop' sign, he may—in a perverse and mischievous pretence of not realising who you are—think to himself, 'I'll lead them a wild goose chase! There is nothing in the car or on me I need worry about, and I can always say I thought they were criminals after me!' Off he goes and, without that sign, you may wave your warrant cards at him, flash lights, sound the horn and gong, all with no effect upon him. In the excitement that comes so easily in such a situation you may find yourselves driving to the very limit of safety, only to be made to look fools when he does eventually stop. Get yourself a proper sign; it will at least preclude this style of behaviour.

At night time, the use of full headlamps to illuminate the suspect car and its occupants should be within the discretion of the police driver. The man who first goes forward to speak to the occupants should take with him a stout wooden clip-board. It has several advantages: it looks official; it is very handy to write on when standing; the officer's warrant card can be clipped to the top of it so there need be no fumbling in pockets when police identity is stated or challenged; and it provides a shield for the face and eyes if blows or objects are aimed at you. Lastly, it is itself an excellent weapon immediately to hand if you are suddenly attacked.

Watch for

▷ Signs that a vehicle is being lived in. Food wrappers, crumbs and other food scraps, also dirty clothing, particularly soiled underwear, sleeping bags and blankets are the pointers. Of course, it may indicate only untidy, honest travellers. It may also indicate a nest of travelling 'no fixed abode' housebreakers, a wanted man or other thieves. Be a little careful; violence may be near the surface with such characters, especially if they are prison escapees. A good look around vehicles parked in the waiting bays at motorway* service areas, and outside roadside cafés, is a drill you should always carry out to catch this type of thief. If you have a plain clothes member of your car crew, he is the one to do it. If you find a car so parked and are certain that recent occupants are either 'wanted' or actively engaged in crime and are away eating or washing, park the police vehicle in a way totally to obstruct any escape. Sometimes it is sensible to immobilise the suspect vehicle by removing the rotor arm or

* English term for a freeway.

disconnecting the low-tension cable inside the bonnet,* if this can be done unobserved. Keep an eye out for the suspects; they may come out of the building they are in, see you and pile into another vehicle they control and which you know nothing about. They may even steal another vehicle from the parking space and drive violently away. When you park the police vehicle so as to obstruct the original suspect vehicle, do not put it in a position where you cannot quickly follow them if a chase of a second vehicle is called for urgently.

Watch for

▷ Criminals using vehicles who, although not dishonest in the ordinary sense, may, owing to extreme political views, intend to harm the community you have sworn to protect. While there are subtle differences between these types of extremists and thieves, it is difficult to put one's finger on material distinctions. However, they seem to have a motivation or dedication, whatever their appearance (they are usually scruffy and, occasionally, personally dirty), markedly dissimilar to the cynicism of the greedy and dissatisfied thief. Most thieves are reasonably conservative in their style of dress. Their unusual appearance would be towards flashiness rather than a 'don't care' casual look. You see, political immoderates consider themselves soldiers, rather than 'smart operators' who think the world owes them a living. This will show in their ordinary conversation, where almost unconsciously they will use the jargon and phrases of their beliefs. This intense and extremist gabble, if spoken with a cultured voice, particularly if the speaker is a woman, should make you pause and think through the likelihood that you may have stumbled over an important matter. Is there anything else in the car to confirm a suspicion? Politically motivated activists are usually a little naïve in the ways of professional criminals and are therefore (as Special Patrol Group experience has shown) more likely to make obvious mistakes when making up false index plates or using counterfeit licences, both of which will be quickly obvious to a keen police eye.

Anyway, bear the suggested contrasts in mind and use your nose—yes your nose—as well as your eyes and ears, when speaking to suspect drivers in their vehicles. An additive commonly used to make the shattering effect of home-made explosive more efficient has a pungent smell like boot

* English term for hood.

polish. Ether, which is used in the manufacture of LSD, has an unmistakable smell, and this odour can permeate clothing for a long time. A pine-like smell, similar to sandalwood soap, may indicate the presence of cannabis in the car. Commercial explosives vary in odour but a frequently used one smells like marzipan. Any unusual chemical odour emanating from a vehicle should be investigated thoroughly.

The smell of semen is very distinctive. If you are trying to make up your mind whether or not the persons you are interrogating are motor-wandering thieves, fugitive escapees living and sleeping in their clothes or merely honest travellers, this smell in the vehicle, especially if stale, can be a pointer to a depraved style of living consistent with a life of thieving, prostitution or political 'drop-out' activity. I am not presuming to judge these types of people, but merely indicating useful, detectable and objective factors which a worldly policeman should consider when deciding on action that needs to be taken at the scene of a traffic 'stop'. It goes without saying that no females need be present for such an odour to be detected about the clothing, sleeping gear or general belongings of such unfortunate people. Prostitutes can be male or female, remember.

Those pressurised cans that spray deodorant or 'air freshener' have themselves a slight but distinctive odour, slightly differing from brand to brand. Over-use of these pressure-can sprays, in a vehicle that is otherwise dirty and untidy, can be very suspicious. Are the occupants trying to mask the smell of cannabis or other pungent chemical odour ? Bear this in mind on those motorway stops.

There is a marked difference between the odour on the breath of a driver who has had beer and one who has drunk spirits. This is important as, no matter what his external conduct is like, the man smelling of spirit is most likely to be the more intoxicated. Large men, over say 16 stones* (102 kg), can be quite drunk but externally appear only mildly 'merry'. In such a case the latter odour can be a valuable consideration for you in deciding what to do.

Watch for
▷ Any person who seems nervous of you, especially one who avoids passing you on the footway and crosses the road. Such persons sometimes can be seen to have flushed faces or to be perspiring unnaturally. Conversely, suspicion can be aroused by a person who either shows an unnatural lack of concern for your sudden presence or who is unusually

---

* 224 lb. A 'stone' is a commonly used English measurement for 14 lb.

over-friendly or fawningly servile. Some will also adopt a bold approach, such as walking up to you and asking for a light for their cigarette or 'the correct time'. Any person who attempts to abandon any article, however seemingly unimportant, as you approach is worth questioning. They may have a stolen vehicle nearby, or one that contains stolen or incriminating gear. They may be a look-out for a crime actually occurring nearby.

Watch for

▷ A person who half-runs or noticeably hurries in deserted side streets and alleys, and who, when in a street where foot passengers are walking along the pavement, changes his pace to that of the people in the street. He may well be worth questioning. This is the classic behaviour of a thief who has just abandoned a previously stolen car. Supposedly drunken persons arrested by you, who suddenly become sober when nearing the station, may be worth investigation. It may be prudent to hurry back to the scene of the arrest after handing your prisoner over to a superior and telling him of your suspicion.

Watch for

▷ Men in vehicles who are watching you. If two or more are looking intently at you in this way, you are the subject of interest and conversation. Why? This applies with added force if you are in plain clothes. When you are patrolling in a car, keep an eye open for unusual behaviour by other drivers when they become aware that you are a police officer. Are they reluctant to overtake you? This may be more than just a wish not to exceed speed limits. As soon as your eyes meet with another driver's and 'lock on' does he jerk his head away? Does he hold a hand up in an unnatural way? He could be endeavouring to obscure your view of his face. Is he a wanted man or a disqualified driver? Does he stop and make a U-turn or suddenly and unexpectedly turn into a side road? Remember this, however. People other than criminals act guiltily. A man carrying on an illicit love affair may, when in his car or when near the address at which he intends secretly to meet his friend (male or female, remember), act very suspiciously. He may think (if you are in plain clothes) that you are a private inquiry agent and are following him to obtain divorce evidence. Private detectives themselves almost invariably act in a suspicious way when carrying out their duties. Other policemen or security men, whom you do not know, may also cause confusion.

Watch for

▷ Those drivers, otherwise of natural appearance, who stiffen perceptibly as they pass you. This may not be so significant as it seems—perfectly respectable persons' expressions and attitudes 'stiffen' when they are passed by police vehicles driven by traffic patrol officers. There are subtler signs for the discerning policeman in these circumstances. To develop the point, a significant number of mature criminals have become 'institutionalised' because of the years so many of them have spent in approved schools, Borstal institutions and in military or civil prisons. One of the signs of being institutionalised is the strange glance such people use towards those in authority—masters, magistrates, prosecuting authorities, prison officers, non-commissioned officers and policemen. This is noticeable, most especially when they are not actually being spoken to directly. They will look right through such persons, for all the world as if these persons were not even there. Their glances are quite normal towards people not 'in authority', however. Very occasionally, for a fraction of a second, there may flash over such a contrived blank expression an intent and sharp glance, but the unnatural, almost impertinent, blankness of the glance is the main feature to look for.

The same phenomenon applies to institutionalised criminals when they see a police car, while they are themselves driving or are a passenger in another car. Unlike the mildly interested unaffected glance of the honest person towards any police car he sees (in just the same way that he would show a slight interest in a passing ambulance or fire engine), the institutionalised criminal will glance right through any police vehicle as if it was not there, as if it did not exist. These signs are unmistakable once seen and identified in your mind.

Watch for

▷ and recognise the reactions of less experienced thieves—the ones who have never been in prison. There is always a first time for them to commit serious crime. The visible reactions of young thieves and unworldly political activists are quite different from those described immediately above. Recognition of you will be obvious—the driver will give an apprehensive and then suddenly frozen glance and, if he is the first to see you, will tell his companions in the car. Straightaway, similar apprehensive expressions will be seen on their faces. Some may even point out with their fingers your presence to other members in the car. They may

15

look at you with an apprehensive even frightened expression, or a certain trace of arrogant cheekiness, but never the 'You aren't there' look that old 'broken-in' thieves cannot shake off.

In those areas where street robberies or 'muggings' are a problem:

Watch for

▷ Four or more young men, perhaps very young men indeed, who are passengers in a dilapidated motor car or van. The very word 'mugging' connotes something vaguely derogatory about being such a victim. Aggrieved persons are aware of this and the implied contempt in the phrase operates on their minds and, in turn, they exaggerate the age and size of the persons who robbed and assaulted them. It is, it seems, less reprehensible to be robbed by two strapping men of 25–35, than it is to be 'taken' by two or three 12-, 15- or 17-year-old youths. Bear in mind, too, that white victims have difficulty in establishing or estimating the age of young black thieves. Again they greatly over-estimate ages; another contributory factor to this inaccuracy is often their unfamiliarity with black society generally.

If the radio report you receive indicates that only two or three thieves are concerned, still keep your eyes open for groups of as many as fifteen. In South London and Notting Hill I have observed, over the years, that groups of young persons of up to fifteen or twenty in number, black or white, who are intent on violent thieving, tend temporarily to detach themselves into small aggressive groups of three and four. Subsequently they quickly regroup into the principal large conglomerate. One or two dilapidated but operable vehicles, including vans, may well be a central feature of such a large group of youths, as will be derelict or near-derelict dwellings and shop premises.

Watch for

▷ Stationary vehicles with either windows tightly closed or fully open. Among the groups just described—young persons intent on stealing in the mugging manner—there seems a cult desire to smoke cannabis. A group of youngsters in a car or van in a back street, with the windows closed, may indicate that they wish to smoke privately and keep the smoke within the car. There is, anyway, a 'conspiracy feeling' when indulging in drug taking, and closed windows add to this atmosphere of

16

mutual and comradely secrecy. Conversely, they may have become aware that police are in the vicinity, and have just opened windows fully to dispel the unmistakable smell of burning cannabis. Similarly, but in more concentrated form, this suspicious behaviour can be heightened in summer and winter, i.e., windows closed in summer or windows open in winter.

As an observer or radio operator, it pays to look carefully at every car that passes you as you drive towards the scene of crime recently committed. The driver must drive, whereas you must observe intently and intelligently. In the matter of reported robberies at banks and post offices, and indeed on the way to the scene of violent street assaults or heavy breakings, it is worth while noting down if possible the index mark (licence plate) of every vehicle that passes you, but especially the ones that look slightly unusual in any way. The statistical chance of noting a useful and traceable index mark of the offenders' car is, of course, quite remote but not impossible. However, if the crime is really serious, witnesses will be wanted, and the index marks you have taken will be valuable follow-up clues in the seeking out of such witnesses. Additionally, to identify promptly and positively the stolen cars used can concentrate and speed up the search for hidden fingerprints.

The chances are that you will often be the second, third or fourth police vehicle arriving at the locus of crime. There is frequently temporary disorganisation at the scene and, when you have made an assessment that there seems to be little object in pursuing probable paths possibly taken by the escaping thieves, and where injured persons and principals concerned are already being dealt with adequately by the crews of other cars, you should take up without further instruction the vital role of getting eye witnesses. Remember, they may not be in the immediate vicinity of the crime. While the matter is 'hot', witnesses usually come forward upon sensibly phrased inquiry and polite request. Two or three days later they may be reluctant to be involved. Use a phrase like, 'Can you help us out of a difficulty, sir? We can't work out how many there were and which way they came up to the post office . . .'. This lead-in phrase is so much better than saying, 'Anybody witness anything?' Even the use of the word 'witness' can put people off—it has undertones of the frightening witness box and long waits in the corridors of courts! Simple 'pavement psychology' has its uses in getting genuine witnesses.

At the time of the violent crime there are feelings of outrage, even hatred, towards the thieves concerned, and you will get accurate frankness.

17

Later, it 'ain't necessarily so'. In particular never, *never* ask for names and addresses until *after* the person has told you, in the form of general discussion and comment, conducted in friendly conversational tones, what he has seen. Then get *every* address and telephone number he has; work, home and close relatives—even a neighbour's telephone number, where appropriate.

Scan the crowds and look for persons who are explaining the incident to others. Bear in mind that they may be giving hearsay versions to their listeners, but 'know-it-all' explainers are often original witnesses.

Back now to the moving suspect in his vehicle:

Watch for

▷ Rapid U-turns being made by any vehicle. Even slow U-turns are worth thoughtful consideration, but any unusually sudden change of direction across existing traffic flows, especially unexpected right-hand turns,* or backing into side roads preparatory to travelling in a direction opposite to that originally taken, must always alert you. You will know well the 'rat runs', or short-cut side streets, of your police area. These will, of course, be used by escaping thieves, especially those raised and schooled in the district, but more subtly—

Watch for

▷ Any vehicle turning into a side street which does *not* form part of a well-known side-street through route, especially by a vehicle driven even slightly above the average speed of traffic at that time.

This can be an overwhelmingly suspicious incident and a plain sign of stress causing panic selection of an unsuitable route. Any vehicle driven into a 'no through road' should also be regarded thoughtfully, especially if you know that at the blind end of the roadway there is a footpath across waste land or playing fields, or through buildings, play streets or pedestrian shopping precincts. It is a fact that innumerable escape routes traversed by thieves, where vehicles are to be switched, have passed through such interrupted terrain.

Watch for

▷ The very least manifestations of unfamiliarity by a driver with the vehicle he is driving. This is repeated because it is so significant. A thief

* Left-hand turns in the USA.

18

can be an experienced driver and still show clumsiness. Remember the likelihood that an escape vehicle used by thieves is one recently stolen for the express purpose of driving away from the scene to a place where they can switch vehicles, perhaps to their own vehicle, or to another stolen one.

During the intense nervous strain operating on thieves at the time of the commission of crime, it may well be that, even if experienced drivers, they will have difficulty with the simple operation of the vehicle. Whereas they may be generally familiar with the model stolen, they cannot know the idiosyncrasies of the individual vehicle concerned. There may be difficulty in as elementary a procedure as starting, for at times of strain and tension, flooding of a carburettor is easily done. If these observable difficulties are accompanied by excitement and agitated movements, *particularly by persons other than the driver*, you may well have come across the thieves vulnerably placed at the time of their first or second change of vehicle.

Watch for
▷ Other manifestations of unfamiliarity with a vehicle; mistaken switching on of windscreen wipers during fine weather, for example. This has a comic aspect which should not deflect us from the knowledge that it has been a frequently observed and significant over-nervous response by thieves under stress. Bear in mind, too, that with Continental, American or Japanese cars (which are increasingly being used in crime) having had their steering systems moved from left to right for import into this country, certain controls attached to the sides of the steering wheel or column are not necessarily similarly changed over. Thus a thief used to having his left and right indicators on one side, suddenly may find them on the opposite in such a vehicle. He may have got used to a foreign car of his own and is then awkward at the controls of a stolen English vehicle. Again, in such circumstances, the needless sounding of a horn or the flashing on of headlights (particularly in a Rover V8) may be a manifestation of this marked and suspicious unfamiliarity. Remember the invariable rule—aberrant behaviour increases significantly at times of stress. Escape from the scene of serious crime is always a stress situation and one of particular intensity.

Watch for
▷ The set of circumstances where only one or two of the thieves manage successfully to get away in the escape vehicle. A witness may shout to

19

you, 'Two of them ran down there!' They may be criminals who, in the excitement, were left behind. In central urban areas there seems to be an inclination for thieves, findings themselves in such an unexpected situation, to enter multi-exit departmental stores, so they can mingle and be lost within the crowds constantly flowing in and out. Similarly, there is some evidence to show an inclination for such persons to run or even drive into the precincts of estates of flats,* particularly local authority estates. As an interesting aside, it has been noted that while subject to tension, stress or injury, men tend to seek familiar places and, if thieves were raised in such housing estates, there is operating upon them powerfully at this time of strain a desire to hide themselves in familiar surroundings.

Watch for
▷ The wearing of boiler suits by occupants of vehicles approaching you, especially if these boiler suits or overalls are of new or freshly laundered appearance. The chance of three or four men in a saloon car, all wearing new overalls, being engaged in lawful pursuits, is sufficiently unlikely to justify the vehicle being stopped there and then.

Watch for
▷ Any changing of clothing inside a moving vehicle—the removal of wigs is, of course, massively suspicious, but so is the removing of shirts, perhaps showing another one underneath. Even when the vehicle is stationary at the side of the road, any removal of overalls, particularly if hurried or where it is seen that the persons so changing have better class or very trendy 'non-working' clothing on underneath, is suspicious. Woollen ski caps, fabric ski masks, woollen watch caps, Balaclava helmets, in fact any headgear that can be pulled over the face, is worth consideration, especially if worn during moderate or warm weather.

Watch for
▷ A vehicle passing you at normal or slightly advanced speed, with a leaking radiator. Indeed, any newish car moving with unmistakably recent damage visible is worth considering. Proud owners have repairs done as soon as possible, thieves do not care. Stress brings accident-proneness to motor thieves just as it does to anyone else, but with violent

* Apartment houses in the USA, especially Government-funded housing.

thieves there is a fierce intensity about the stress just after the commission of violent crime which goes hand-in-hand with 'side swipe' or 'Fry's sandwich' collisions occurring when they accelerate through narrow gaps in traffic. Entering a roundabout in top or third gear gives a sign obvious to every traffic patrol officer—it may not be inexperienced driving or bad steering, it can be another manifestation of the stress present when escaping thieves cannot concentrate on the skills of driving.

Watch for

▷ The clever confident thief, the man of strong personality, who sits calmly with stolen property openly on the seat beside him in his motor car. Not all thieves are apprehensive or nervous when spoken to by policemen. The signs showing that such a man is a 'wrong 'un' are more subtle, but are still there for shrewd policemen. Look for small inconsistencies in conduct and explanation.* Remember, liars require good memories, so ask again the questions you posed quietly at the beginning of the interview. These answers may still betray the cleverest of thieves.

Watch for

▷ Vehicles well down on their rear springs. It may be that oxygen cylinders or a stolen safe are in the boot† or in the back (Fig. 2.1) or that a large amount of stolen lead or printers' metal is being carried. Vehicles exchanging loads are worth inquiry always, but especially if back to back in a side street or on waste land. Thieves often abandon unwanted stolen property which they consider valueless, difficult to negotiate or embarrassingly bulky. If you see an unusual abandoning of suitcases, carrier bags, parcels or clothing, especially if taking place in a lonely spot with a vehicle nearby, investigate at once. Any incident where objects are thrown into a canal or river by adults, especially at night, calls for energetic and immediate inquiry. Any loitering on bridges deserves gentle inquiry.

Watch for

▷ The possibility that male or female loiterers in plain view may be lookouts for other criminals currently at work.

* Such confident thieves will answer fluently, questions not even asked!
† English term for trunk.

21

Acetylene cylinders. Oxygen cylinders. Calor-propane gas cylinder. Thermic lance rods (long and short). Thermic lance holder, valve and tube. Acetylene and oxygen regulators. 'Suffine' cutting torch with hoses. Thermic lance holder, rose, valve and T-piece. One length of hose. Five gas-cutting nozzles. Three regulator keys. Five O-clips. Thermic lance adapter. One pair of welding goggles. Two screwdrivers. One hammer. Two wrenches. One pair of grips. Two bolt cutters. Two short jemmies. Two long jemmies. One torch. One pencil torch. One tape connector. One ball of string. Two torch batteries. One bundle containing five green canvas bags. Three dust masks. Quantity of cotton wool. Two caps. Two pairs of overalls. Two lengths of rope. Two pairs of gloves. Quantity of nails. One canvas holdall. Four coshes. One small canvas sheet. One large canvas sheet. One bundle containing 10 white canvas bags.

Fig. 2.1. Incriminating tools and equipment found in a van.

Regard with real suspicion any 'blinking' of headlights from cars parked near vulnerable premises. This applies day or night. Remember, too, that home-made electrical battery alarms have been used by criminals, wired from the lookout to those inside premises. Unusual wires near stationary vehicles should therefore be regarded with suspicion. VHF radio has also been used. More than one lookout may be employed at different points.

Lookouts in vehicles often pose as courting couples. Newspaper sellers who shout their wares over-loud when you appear, or who wave a newspaper with greater energy than usual, may be giving warning signals.

Watch for

▷ The opportunity legitimately to use bluff with car thieves. Elsewhere I have said that it is of paramount importance always to be fair and open in your dealings with thieves, and I stand by this. Nevertheless, there are occasions when the use of a ruse is justified, provided your senior officers and the court are later told exactly what the bluff was.

Thus, in situations when you are in plain clothes and are either alone or, if with a companion, well outnumbered, it is sometimes in the public interest to expedite inquiries and preclude having to investigate a complicated, lying tale of explanation by saying (in suitable cases, of course, i.e. when you really suspect persons of having stolen the car they are in): 'What are you doing in Dr Mervyn Phillips's car?' The name you selected must be fictitious but genuine-sounding and, if the persons you are speaking to have stolen the car, you will immediately induce some form of incriminating answer or behaviour from them; for example, 'He said we could borrow it', 'He told us to collect it for him', etc. They may even make a run for it, but you will at least bring things to a head.

When alone and faced with three or four sturdy-looking thieves, the use of the trick question may get you all the information you require, i.e., that the vehicle is stolen. A wise course is then to act 'wet'—retreat and allow the thieves to go, as if you accepted their explanation, then either covertly follow them to a place where there are other officers at hand or go to where you can telephone or radio a 'thieves in sight' message.

Respectable people will answer in such a way as to show clearly that you are mistaken. Make your apologies and no harm has been done. Similarly, a trick question can be phrased around a non-existent dent in the rear bodywork of a vehicle. By the way, cars are frequently stolen at night under artificial light. Sodium and other similar street lighting can distort colour

23

appreciation, so a thief may not know the colour of the car he has stolen if you stop him shortly after the theft. Your headlights or a torch (flashlight) should show you the right colour, and the question 'What is the colour of this car?' can produce a revealing answer in these circumstances!

Watch for

▷ Another sort of dishonest motorist, usually well-to-do, who has no need to cheat but does so just the same. I mean the man who defrauds ratepayers and local authorities by tampering with parking meters. Some merely search for a meter out of order or leave a note on a working meter falsely stating they found it out of order. This minor cheating is difficult to prove and no great menace, but some motorists insert a coin and then deliberately jam the mechanism by some means. Beer-can rings, foreign coins, pieces of cardboard, electrical junction box pushouts or deliberately bent current coins and the like are inserted so as to cheat. A sharp-eyed policeman can catch and prove offences against such motorists. Ask your wardens* to show you the things they have found and to indicate the men and women they suspect.

Charges to consider are, 'dishonestly obtaining pecuniary advantage by evasion of payment' (Section 16(1) of the Theft Act 1968) or an attempt to do so (common law) and 'going equipped to steal or cheat' (Section 25, same Statute), quite apart from the offences against Section 42(4) of the Road Traffic Regulation Act 1967. The advantages of the first three charges are that they carry 'arrestable offence' powers. If the meter is intentionally damaged in the course of such cheating, an arrestable offence under Section 1 of the Criminal Damage Act 1971 has been committed. There would have to be an intent to steal for a Section 25 offence to be made out.

Watch for

▷ Clandestine or furtive movements inside a moving car. As previously emphasised, males removing or changing shirts or jackets, or taking off woollen Balaclava helmets or knitted ski caps, in a hurried manner, while the car is moving faster than the general flow of traffic, is definitely suspicious and 'worth a pull' (worth investigating) promptly.

Similar movements by females are not so suspicious, but if a woman is seen removing a wig in a car, particularly with males present, that would be sufficiently questionable to merit a stop and inquiry there and then.

* English term for meter attendants.

24

Sunglasses can be suspicious. On a sunny day, a driver and front passenger are likely to wear them, but if every other person in the car has them on, especially if the weather is not over-bright, they may be using them as a form of disguise.

There is a 'head in the sand' belief, really quite unjustified, that sunglasses are an effective mask. Many thieves seem to wear them when weather conditions never justify their use. Sunglasses are also, in some strange way, part of the subculture of drug addiction. As has been said elsewhere, addiction and thieving are closely related. Be reasonable and sensible about it, of course, but look carefully in these circumstances. Gentle and well-mannered inquiry may be called for to decide, when you see over-use of sunglasses, whether you are dealing with exuberant harmless youngsters (who dress so as to be thought of as up-to-the-minute 'swinging chicks' and 'cool cats') or interrogating criminals and addicts, who rationalise and excuse vile and greedy behaviour by pretending to be part of a 'new movement' to 'liberate humanity'.

When you are alone, either in plain clothes or as the driver of a one-man 'Panda' car, and you decide it is necessary to speak to a group of hard-looking characters, or even when approaching one rough-looking man, get into the habit of saying as an opening gambit, 'We are [not, "I am a"] police officers . . .' or 'My colleagues and I are police officers . . .'. The persons you speak to cannot be sure whether or not you have help very close at hand, perhaps watching them from across the street. These simple words will very much reduce the likelihood of your being assaulted.

3. The stationary suspect vehicle

Points of vital knowledge

When you are beside a stationary suspect vehicle, pay particular attention to the following 10 points:

1. Your own safety. Never lean on or into a vehicle when speaking to the driver. Severe injuries to policemen, some resulting in death, have occurred in the past when a thief has suddenly accelerated. If you feel suspicious, ask for the engine to be switched off. You can say quite truthfully that you are having difficulty in hearing because of the noise.
2. The windows, particularly vent windows. Look for evidence of tool marks on the frame surround, or signs that the rubber waterproofing has been damaged by a sharp-pointed instrument.
3. Index plates* insecure. Look for recent tool marks on the bolts securing the plates. If the securing bolts are rusty this may indicate irregularity; thieves rarely paint over the bolts when fastening false plates. Rust occurs within a week. Clean index plates on a dirty car or muddy plates on an otherwise clean vehicle may be worth inquiry. Were the plates intentionally muddied to avoid someone recording them?
4. Index plates slightly altered. Look particularly at numbers containing the letters B, P or R. The numeral 1 can easily be changed to 4. An O can be blacked out to represent a C.
5. A badly fitting index plate or one that is the wrong type for the car, e.g., a cheap mass-produced plate on a new Rover or Jaguar. A gap between the plate and body of the car is worth investigating. An expensive plate on a Ford Transit or other van is suspicious.
6. Any suspicious holes in the body metal near or under where the plates are fixed. This can indicate that a false plate of different size has been fitted. These holes are sometimes plugged with rubber or compound.

* English term for licence plates.

7. Plastic stick-on letters and numbers. The possible misuse of this type of index mark is obvious. Look for inconsistencies; a 6 can be turned upside down to form a 9 and vice versa, but in some plastic sets these figures are not exactly similar.

8. Motor vehicles being used with trade plates* in the evening or at night, especially if there is more than one occupant of the vehicle. Know the offences with regard to trade plates and invariably report offenders. A trade plate being used on a Sunday is always worth investigation. Bear in mind that thieves may be using their employer's trade plates without permission for their own illegal activities.

9. The vehicle excise licence.† Question a suspected driver as to the date of expiry, where obtained, date obtained, etc. Make it a routine always to check the registration number with the number on the index plate. Look for evidence of alteration—a smudged or suspicious date stamp. If bleach has been used on the licence, there will be a characteristic absence of paper shine where the bleach was used. Remember that thieves sometimes write the index mark of the stolen vehicle, with a ball-point pen, on a convenient place inside the vehicle, e.g., on the sun visor, so that they can accurately answer your question, 'Do you know the number of this car?' The presence of such writing inside a vehicle should make you very suspicious indeed. Remember, a genuine owner usually knows the mileage on the 'clock' and the contents of the dashboard pigeon-holes and boot. He may know the makes of his tyres. Ask a suspect to operate the windscreen wipers and the head-lights. Unfamiliarity with the position of these switches may confirm your suspicions. Catch a thief out with questions on these points.

10. The ignition. The absence of an ignition key in a vehicle with the en-gine running usually means a recently stolen vehicle, in which the ignition system has been short-circuited. Thieves sometimes 'short' the ignition, get the engine running and then place a key, suitably bent to give an 'on' appearance, in the ignition lock. With suspect drivers, make sure it is the right key. This can be done by removing it—if the engine still operates, the key is false. Where there is a high noise level from other traffic, it may be necessary to place your hand on the bonnet of the vehicle to feel for vibration to be certain the engine is still operating. When you are generally suspicious of a vehicle, have a look

* English system of licensing automobile dealers who have licence plates painted red on white.
† English system of showing that tax has been paid on a vehicle.

at the key. Some serials can be filed to fit a number of car locks. If the key is on a ring, are there several other ignition keys there? What is the explanation for this? You may find a brand-new key in the lock of a car several years old. Is there a good explanation for this? Similarly, older vehicles fitted with either expensive or brand-new accessories require explanation. Where has the money come from to purchase expensive accessories?

Thieves who specialise in stealing one type of expensive car, occasionally purchase (or steal) a whole ignition switch, complete with key. They steal the car of their choice by shorting the ignition with a 'jumper' wire (Fig. 3.1) and, at their leisure, replace the existing ignition switch system with their own. Thus a man found in possession of a spare ignition switch complex should be regarded with real suspicion.

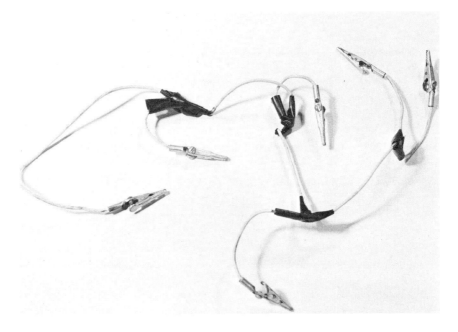

Fig. 3.1. *'Hot wire' set or 'jumper' wires.* This apparatus is used to bypass ignition systems. Once entry has been gained, a skilled motor car thief can 'hot wire' the older style of car in less than 2 minutes. Possession of such an implement is massively incriminating. (Courtesy Edward M. Davis, Chief of Police, Los Angeles Police Dept.)

As more and more cars in Britain are equipped with combined steering and ignition locks, stealing this style of car will increase if Swedish, German and American experience is anything to go by, as it so often is in criminal *modus operandi* patterns. Several tools have been adapted to pull out the cylinders of the locks concerned. One, called a slam hammer or slam puller (Fig. 3.2), consists of a hardened steel miniature corkscrew-type bit

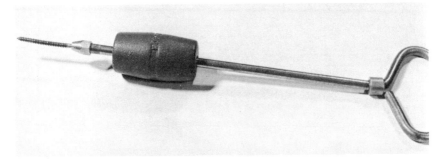

Fig. 3.2. *Slide hammer.* Sometimes called a 'slam hammer', 'slam puller' or 'Yankee'. The threaded end of this tool is screwed into the ignition (or any other similar) keyway. The weight is then pulled briskly toward the handle, forcing out the ignition switch or lock core. The tool has a legitimate use in the motor trade in removing dents in wing and bodywork of vehicles. Nevertheless, possession of such a tool in the street, in the boot of a vehicle, in a brief case, or concealed in a bedroom or living room drawer, is massively incriminating. You must be able instantly to recognise such a tool or, more likely, home-made equivalents fabricated by the thief concerned. (Courtesy Edward M. Davis, Chief of Police, Los Angeles Police Dept.)

at the end of a rod-shaped tool resembling an Archimedean-principle screwdriver (these types of 'push and pull' screwdrivers are often called 'Yankees' by English tradesmen). The bit is screwed into the keyway and the tool sharply pulled backwards, thus exerting tremendous mechanical advantage, tearing the whole cylinder out of the lock. It is a simple matter now to free the steering and start the car. Another lock, with key, can be inserted later.

A spring-loaded centre punch, ordinarily used by metal workers to mark metal, is a useful tool for a car thief to break quarter-light windows quietly. Such a tool in the possession of a man in the street is very suspicious.

Another tool, of Scandinavian origin, is much smaller and resembles a mechanical wine corkscrew with a screw thread and lever to exert increased pressure. All these tools are adaptations of the skilled housebreakers' 'Ingersoll tool', used for many years since the early 'thirties to force out

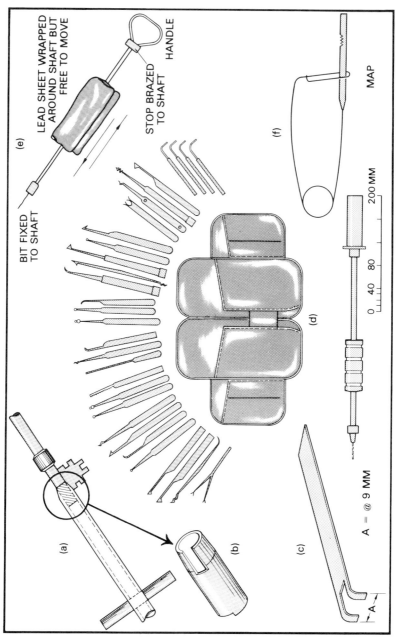

Fig. 3.3

the cylinders of front door cylinder locks. Any such instrument *or any adaptation* seen (Fig. 3.3) should be regarded with great suspicion and seized at once to prevent it being abandoned in circumstances where you cannot evidentially connect it with your suspect. *Any strange-looking home-made tool, not quite of the principle already described, but which has a bit with a device for increasing pressure by mechanical advantage, should always alert you,* as should a device again with a bit but also a circular travelling arm having a cutting blade at its end. Most of these tools are small in size, but some—for example, those adapted to cut a circular hole in the side of a safe—can be very large, perhaps as big as a dinner plate. Anything that looks like a giant tin opener (Fig. 3.4), of the older sort, is very suspicious.

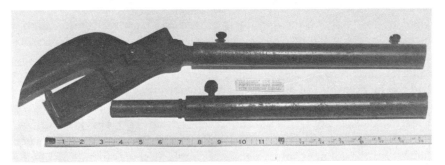

Fig. 3.4. *Tin-opener type tool.* Used to take off the back of a safe. Shown with extension handle. This style of heavy tool may be found wrapped in oily cloth and plastic sheeting, buried in a garden or under floorboards. There is no reasonable lawful use for such an implement, and if found in a motor vehicle is totally incriminating. (All rights reserved.)

Fig. 3.3. Police officers must be able instantly to recognise the more sophisticated thieves' implements, even when they are mixed with hammers, screwdrivers and the like in a toolbox or bag (see parts (a)–(f)). (a) Hotel and 'back-door' thieves' tool used to turn keys left in locks. Used from the outside. Made from narrow-gauge aluminium tubing. A dishonest ponce (one who steals from his prostitute's client in a 'locked' room) might have such an implement. (b) Enlargement of the bit of the tool described in (a). (c) Tool inserted into the keyway of Yale-type cylinder door-locks to provide turning tension during the time a lock-pick (such as in (d) or (f)) is inserted. (d) Leather zip-fastened case containing tension tools and lock-picks of the very first quality. (Commercially available in foreign countries.) If found, indicates you either have a skilled locksmith or a top-quality hotel, car or house thief. (e) A home-made slam puller. Bit is screwed into soft metal of pin tumbler keyway, then lead weight is vigorously moved towards the handle. The sudden 'bump' against the stop is enough to shear the cylinder out of the lock. (f) Home-made lock-pick improvised from a large blanket pin. Inserted bit is 'jiggled' in keyway of pin tumbler lock. Used with a tool similar to (c).

31

It is used for 'rip jobs' when opening cheaper safes. Be suspicious if a car's jack, often carried in the boot or trunk, has been adapted in any way, possibly by the addition of a stout chain with a flat hook at one end. This is a common device to force open or 'spring' the locked boot of another car so that the spare wheel can be stolen.

The small-scale road block

'In the field of observation, good luck favours only those whose minds are prepared.' (Louis Pasteur.)

Here are my views on the usefulness of road blocks, when considered as a tactic of catching motor thieves. These views are based upon experience gained with the Metropolitan Police Special Patrol Group's many thousands of 'mini road blocks', held in the late 'sixties when, as now, the group had the highest ratio of direct street arrests for crime in London.

Road block systems are worth careful thought and evaluation. The occurrence of serious crimes and escapes from HM prisons calls for immediate major road blocks upon main roads. Success, however, when judged by the number of arrests, is not high, despite our unquestioning acceptance of the system as a realistic tactic of ordinary thief-taking practice. I have my own view on the lack of success of the major road blocks, and fundamentally it is to do with the subconscious behaviour of thieves.

Let me illustrate it like this. You have lived in, say, Leeds or Philadelphia all your life, and your relatives and long-standing friends also live in these great cities and their suburbs. From schoolboy days you have travelled the city by walking, cycling, driving and public transport and a combination of these. Now ask yourself—if you intend to drive in a car across your city to visit a relative do you, as a lifelong Leeds or Philadelphia man, use primary routes to get there? *Only when you have to*, I am sure. Out of your earliest memories you will take short cuts into side roads whenever possible, and go through those sometimes indirect minor roads that are free from heavy traffic. Your time on main roads will be minimal. It is a matter of local pride to know the 'back doubles' and 'rat runs' well.

Now I suggest that a city's thieves, driving to and from their crimes, to and from their meetings and conspiracies, are exactly the same and endeavour to use secondary and tertiary roads whenever possible. It is the through traffic and outsiders generally that use primary roads. You are thus far more likely to catch local thieves with incriminating gear, or in incriminating company, by small road blocks in side streets than with massive road blocks on primary routes with all the confusion and complaints they bring. There are other advantages. You can 'run' such mini road blocks with one vehicle and three officers. There is no pressure upon you in a side street to deal hastily with persons stopped because of noisy traffic piling up behind you, as in a main road. A team of motor thieves comes on a mini block unexpectedly and suddenly, unlike the self-advertising major road block, and its members are thereby less prepared for questions, having surrendered the initiative and surprise to you. Anyway, upon a realistic assessment of the cost of police man-hours, the major road block seems so wasteful as to be unacceptable in other than emergency situations.

Speaking now particularly to young inspectors and sergeants and those in charge of late and night reliefs—if you can muster four vehicles and 12 men, with four mini blocks in side roads, carefully selected as likely secondary and tertiary routes across your city or built-up area, *each road block lasting no longer than* 30 *minutes,* but each team of three officers conducting four consecutive blocks, you are casting a finer meshed net. On the plain statistical evidence available, you are about 37 times more likely to produce a plurality of arrests of quality than by using the same resources for a major road block on a main road. *Brief your fellows well beforehand and emphasise fluent and sincere good manners.*

Consider, too, a South African policeman's (Lord Baden-Powell) advice: 'The secret of getting successful work out of trained men lies in one nutshell—in the clearness of the instructions they receive.'

Good briefing and clear instructions include telling men the philosophy or the thinking behind the orders they receive. They need to know the 'reason why', so explain that there are good, hard-nosed practical reasons for the carrying out of mini road blocks, of short duration, in minor streets. A man who understands will work with greater depth of perception than a mere obedient subordinate, however well disciplined he may be.

4. Motor expertise and searching suspect vehicles

Know more about 'auto crime' than the cleverest motor thief, and learn the hiding places of drugs, which are often concealed in motor vehicles.

If you are not 'motor-car minded', get one of your colleagues to explain how the ignition of a car can be 'shorted'. Wired crocodile clips, coins, silver foil (chewing gum foil is a favourite), Brillo pads* and safety pins can be used. Chewing gum itself has been used, chewed up with metal foil, around the rear of the ignition switch complex.

Clever young thieves, adaptable and mechanically minded, have even constructed a proper switching system, complete with push-button starter, mounted on a piece of flat wood about 3 in (75 mm) square, with stout 'crocodile clips' attached by medium gauge wire, so they can conveniently bypass the combined ignition and starter switching of the car.

Familiarise yourself with the electrical systems in the various makes of commonly used motor cars, so that you will know what to look for quickly in a suspect vehicle. Visit car-breakers' yards and see for yourself the detail of various electrical systems—they vary from model to model. Invariably examine closely any car coming into possession of police that has had an electrical system 'doctored' by thieves. Do not be ashamed to seek after such knowledge; you probably know more about another aspect of police duty than your colleague. Share expertise and learn from one another.

Learn the uses of Glass's *Index of Registration Numbers†* and know where you can refer to one quickly. A knowledgeable comrade or a friend in the motor trade will show you how to establish the age of a vehicle by an examination of the trade mark on Triplex glass. Electrical equipment also has visible date codes. Learn them. This knowledge, used in conjunction

---

* Trade name for a commercial cleaning pad partly made of metal.
† British manual containing lists of licence plate numbers, from which the date of manufacture of vehicles can be determined.

with Glass's *Index*, will inevitably bring you arrests of real quality. The index mark should be one issued about the time the car was manufactured. Get to know the year, model and makes of all passenger motor vehicles, so that you can recognise them *instantly*.

Cultivate the acquaintance of garage proprietors and petrol station attendants. The old hands know all the tricks. They can, if you are liked and trusted as a discreet and reasonable man, indicate to you customers they consider suspicious or criminal. They are rarely wrong in their judgements, and certainly seem to recognise vehicle thieves at sight. Do not embarrass them by a too-prompt interrogation of those they suspect. If you do, it will be the last time they tell you anything.

Stolen motor-car accessories, such as high-quality spotlights and radios, seem to fascinate certain thieves, even those financially successful. There is no doubt that the theft of these and similar objects forms a heavy proportion of our reported crime. Therefore, when examining the contents of a suspect's car, never ignore a fitted radio or spotlight, and always ask the driver to account for his possession of these fittings. A thief may not habitually drive around in a stolen vehicle, but many are tempted to fit stolen accessories and fraudulent or stolen excise licences to their own cars. This is emphasised because it is so prevalent.

In the presence of the driver, look behind sun visors and underneath all seats. On many older Ford vans there is a 2 in (50 mm) ledge around the inner top of the windscreen and doors. Small articles, for example a stolen driving licence, may be conveniently hidden there. Under the rear seat is a favourite hiding place for housebreaking tools or car-stealing instruments. Small, high-value stolen articles may be in the pockets of clothing lying on the back seat, so of course can dangerous drugs. The boot is often a fruitful spot for a discerning policeman (Fig. 4.1). Look underneath the spare wheel and in the small areas forward of the rear wheel cowlings. Spare wheels are very frequently stolen. Is the spare wheel painted the same colour as the other wheels? In other than nearly new cars you should be suspicious if the spare tyre is brand new when road tyres are well worn.

If you have become motor-car minded you should be able to detect quickly housebreaking or car-theft tools among genuine car tools. Bolt cutters, even small ones, should make you instantly suspicious, as should tyre levers with sharpened lips, ignition keys on wire rings, unusually shaped pieces of wire—used to manipulate vent window catches—of about the same thickness as clothes-hanger wire (Fig. 4.2) and lengths of Bowden cable (similar to pedal-cycle brake cable), looped at one end, which are

35

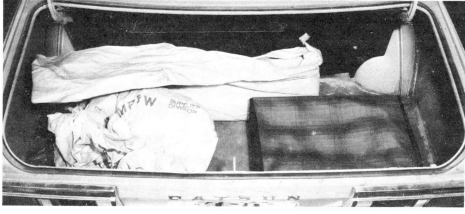

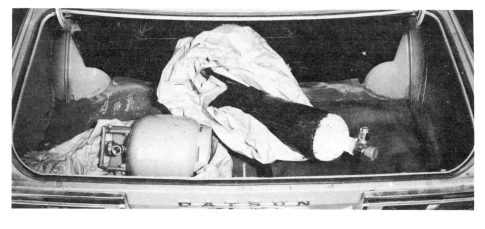

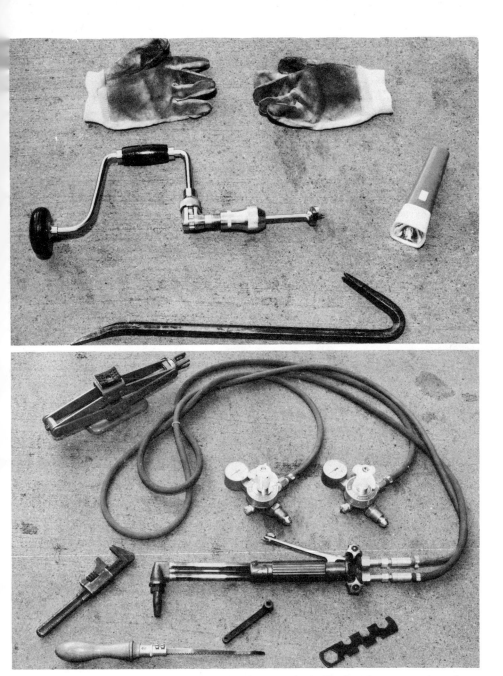

Fig. 4.1 (pages 36–38). A series of six photographs indicating the progression of searching and to indicate how easy it is, upon a *cursory* examination of the contents of the boot or trunk, to miss the incriminating material concealed, *all of which* was in the boot.

Fig. 4.1 (continued).

used to manipulate inner door levers. Hook-nosed beer-can openers are useful implements for the car thief.

Question in your mind the possession in a car of what are usually considered innocent articles, if they seem out of place. A knotted nylon stocking, a woollen Balaclava helmet, a comic false nose, a rubber 'monster' mask and plastic toy guns (especially if painted black or brown) can all have sinister uses. A scarf may be used as a mask. In summertime it may be a little unusual to carry one (or more than one) in a car. A large number of coins of one denomination, 5p* pieces, for example, may indicate theft from meters, gaming machines or juke-boxes. A rubber or plastic hose with a metal or plastic can may indicate petrol thefts.

* British coin about the size of a quarter.

38

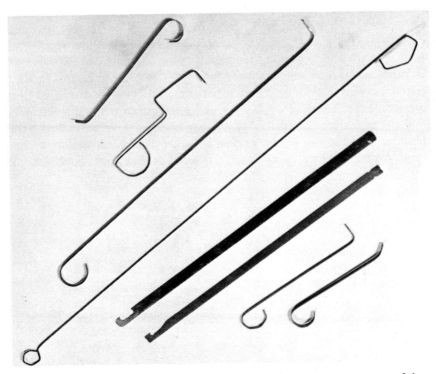

Fig. 4.2. *Vehicle entry tools.* Many motor-vehicle thieves use one or more of these rods, bars and wires to break into locked vehicles. You must be able to recognise these tools at once, even if they are mixed up with normal everyday tools. Remember, such tools kept in a bedroom drawer or concealed in a living room would be extremely incriminating. Consider photographing such finds in the place you found them; this can be most convincing evidence. (Courtesy Edward M. Davis, Chief of Police, Los Angeles Police Dept.)

Innocent motorists may well carry long lengths of wire, with the ends fitted with crocodile clips, for legitimate purposes, but you should be suspicious of short lengths of wire so fitted. A pick-axe helve in a car is always questionable—two are twice as questionable. An 8 in (20 cm) or longer screwdriver, with its bit deformed by sharpening to a point, is suspicious. Look in toolboxes with care (Fig. 4.3). Do you know the appearance of the special pliers used to crimp detonators? Make it your business to see and handle such implements so you can pick them out instantly.

It is a fact that explosives have been concealed in grease guns in vehicle toolboxes. It is difficult to describe the smells of commonly used explosives—often a sickly sweet 'headachey' or marzipan-like smell—but most are very different from the smell of grease. Explosive of the sort used by criminals to blow safes has been found concealed in hub caps. Political terrorists often have quite different home-made explosive, produced from nitrogen-based fertiliser—it is very bulky compared with commercial or military explosive. Commercial or military explosive may be used with this fertiliser-based explosive as a 'primer'; in other words, it is used to increase its shattering efficiency. Any form of welding gear or metal bottles should

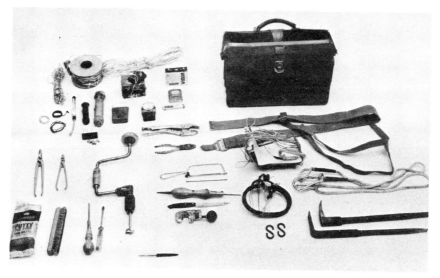

Fig. 4.3. All these safeblowers' tools can be carried in a briefcase. (All rights reserved.)

arouse immediate suspicion. Any empty sack, old pillow-case or large plastic bag (of the sort often sold in self-service launderettes) in a car boot should make you alert. It often indicates an intention by the driver to go shopbreaking and to use the sack or bag for stolen cigarettes or similar bulky property. Stainless metal beer barrels are very valuable and are rarely, if ever, privately disposed of by brewers or licensees. You should therefore be suspicious if you find them in the possession of persons not in the licensed trade* who may intend (a) to sell them to scrap-metal dealers

* The legitimate liquor trade.

if they are merely thieves, or (b) to use them as the casing of explosives if, in the much rarer circumstance, they are terrorists. The same applies to metal milk churns.

In relation to a suspected driver's documents, ask the man for his particulars before asking for his driving licence and insurance. When you have the licence, remember the tip—already mentioned—to ask again for particulars, but this time the address first. A suspect is more likely to give you his correct date of birth at the beginning of a street interrogation and before he realises you really suspect him. Know how to establish true dates of birth from documents.

Subsequently, he may produce driving documents inconsistent with the particulars he first gave you; this could be evidence justifying his arrest on suspicion of having committed an arrestable offence, or, where local enactments permit this course, for 'unlawful possession'. Watch everybody concerned closely and, if the men you are interviewing suddenly make a run for it, try to detain the driver. Your most direct evidence is against him.

Forging, altering, using, lending or allowing the use of a driving licence, certificate of insurance (or other document evidencing insurance in lieu of a certificate), a test certificate, a driving examiner's certificate of appointment (and certain other documents, etc.), with intent to deceive; or to make or have in one's possession any document so closely resembling such documents mentioned as to be calculated (i.e., likely) to deceive, are indictable offences (two years imprisonment upon indictment; summary conviction fine of £100 and/or four months imprisonment) by Section 169 and 4th Schedule of the Road Traffic Act 1972.

Forging, fraudulently (altering or) using, or fraudulently lending or allowing to be used, an index mark or a hackney carriage (in North America a 'cab') distinctive mark, or any trade plates, or any vehicle licence or vehicle registration document, are also indictable offences (two years imprisonment upon indictment; summary conviction fine of £200) by Section 26 of the Vehicles (Excise) Act 1971.

Therefore, should you find any person committing these offences in the night (i.e., after 9 p.m. and before 6 a.m.) you have power there and then to arrest, by virtue of the general power of arrest contained in Section 11 of the Prevention of Offences Act 1851.

Drugs are often concealed in motor vehicles, in the usual hiding places. The following list can be used as a check catalogue to ensure you miss nothing. Remember, gloves often contain small incriminating articles. Be suspicious of gloves in a glove compartment or elsewhere in any vehicle, particularly if your suspect is not the sort of fellow you would expect to wear them normally. A flashlight, a mirror and a metal extending tape-measure are extremely useful in searching vehicles. Search in this order. Let it become a drill, so that eventually you will not require the written list.

1. Inside all fabric linings.
2. Inside or under cushions and upholstery, particularly at the back.
3. In or behind the dashboard and its cavities.
4. Under floor mats.
5. Behind the mirror.
6. Behind sun visors.
7. Under the spare tyre in the boot.
8. Under the mat of the boot.
9. Under the battery or to its side.
10. Attached to the inner aspects of the front or rear bumper.
11. In the hub caps.
12. Under the ashtray lid.
13. Inside the radio loudspeaker.
14. Inside hollowed-out motoring books.
15. Behind headlamp reflectors.
16. Jammed in the ducts of the heater.
17. In door and other cavities.
18. Anything fastened by adhesive tape behind the brake, clutch or accelerator pedals (particularly to the large brake pedal on automatic transmissions).

Always look under the vehicle—your mirror can assist here. Look in the vicinity of the radiator for an additional box, bolted or welded on. Any sign of recent disturbance anywhere, e.g., new screws or fresh paint, should receive extra attention.

Remember that motor thieves, particularly youngsters, are often users of prohibited drugs; addicts in their turn are often motor-car joy-riders. Groups of these youngsters may well stand about the footway, near their own or borrowed vehicles, engaged in discussion about drugs or in the preliminary transactions concerning trafficking. So watch your suspects closely as you approach them; their bad consciences are operating on them the moment they see you. Their natural impulse will be to discard all drugs and paraphernalia before you arrive. This can be used to your advantage, as a crowd of youngsters with a 'pusher' present may, by their worried appearance and a 'pariah-dog' attitude towards the principal, reveal his identity as you approach and thus lead to a successful search. Confirmed drug takers are ingenious in personal concealment. A small heroin tablet is sometimes carried in the folds of skin between the fingers, for example, especially immediately after an illegal sale. The inside front pocket of jeans and overall trousers is a common point of concealment. The waistband of trousers, the seams of underwear, the knot of a tie, shoulder padding and a pouch suspended by string inside the trousers have all been used. Drugs can be secured by adhesive tape to the body. Between the shoulder blades, just below the rib cage and above the belly, the crutch and the inner aspects of the lower leg are all favourite positions. The potency of LSD breaks down in sunlight; thus, any pills wrapped in silver paper are suspicious.

The seller of hard drugs sometimes is accompanied by a young male homosexual or 'drop-out' female, who are the ones who actually carry the drugs either on or in their bodies. When a deal is made with a purchaser, he or she goes to a nearby public lavatory, enters a vehicle or goes into a common hallway, then removes the amount required and hands it to the dupe who has paid the principal. Try to get evidence to encompass all concerned in this sort of conspiracy.

Deals can still be made with the pusher or his companion(s) even when they have no drugs on them. Money is accepted and the purchaser is told where the drugs are—on a window-sill, in a drainpipe or inside a nearby vehicle, etc. Beware of the premature arrest!

Drugs and, for that matter, weapons have been concealed in the cases of cheap transistor radios, where the inner working parts have been removed. Pieces of cannabis resin may be carried in the mouth immediately after purchase (as may other drugs if protected against saliva). If you suspect this, follow until the purchaser removes them from his or her mouth. To endeavour forcibly to remove drugs from a suspect's mouth can be dangerous. The power in a adult male's jaw is considerable, and fingertips can be severed. I, myself, sustained severe injury to two fingers in such a situation. The best way of preventing swallowing is by a sharp slap on the suspect's back. Holding the nostrils closed makes swallowing difficult, but not impossible, especially if the chin is down towards his chest. Remember, the unfortunate with drugs in his mouth, intending to swallow them, can cause his own death, especially if he or she is in the physically exhausted and run-down state usually found with addicts. Your sworn duty is to protect all lives. Remember this truth if your slap on the back of an addict, in these circumstances, is challenged in court by a lawyer who might infer that what you did was a gross infringement of liberty.

A street seller of drugs often has the bulk of his supplies concealed in a refuse bin or a vehicle some distance from where he is standing. Dustbins (trash cans in North America) at the rear of restaurant and hotel premises, in city side streets, are not uncommon places for such transactions. If the trafficker has had previous convictions he may use a fresh-faced young person to fetch and hold the supplies while he negotiates separate sales. Keep this in mind and, whenever possible, ensure the arrest of the person really deserving prosecution. Places of sale will often be near the larger type of public lavatory, so that purchasers may quickly avail themselves of privacy.

The recurring presence of discarded drugs in police vans, area cars, charge rooms, clubroom floors and the like, in circumstances where no one can be prosecuted, is mute testimony to the drug users' skill in concealment and abandonment.

Watch for
▷ Small parcels which may be dangerous drugs (or stolen property, or the implements of crime) being taken to or from premises where there are 24-hour lockers or left-luggage offices, *often being transported by car or van*. Remember, not only railway and bus stations but, these days, some underground or urban railway stations, bowling alleys, air terminals and department shops have them. The behaviour of an addict, trafficker or thief, placing or taking such property from a locker, is subtly different from the actions of an honest person. There is the intent looking around, the delay, then the over-rapid actual insertion or retrieval.

Spend an hour watching the sameness of the behavioural patterns of honest travellers. This hour will not be wasted, for antisocial persons will now certainly stand out when you do see them.

Get to know locker and luggage attendants, cultivate them, give them your telephone number, be a patient, sympathetic listener to their trivia, encourage them to talk about their family circumstances and their aspirations, and one day they will tell you something that will make you jump! Such people will be pleased to help you again if, when thanking them, you say something like, 'That was shrewd of you to spot that—you've missed your vocation you know, you would have made a wonderful policeman'.

(Never say this sort of thing unless you honestly mean it, and even then only if they truly deserve such a compliment. But if they do, do not be shy about it—*say it*.)

Watch for
▷ Suspicious delivery of bulky articles from official railway carriers, and from other nationally known bulk carriers, to the common, unattended hallway entrances of the less fashionable, multi-premise business house or run-down office building. A not uncommon method of stealing by the dishonest delivery employees is to load on to their vehicles, at their depot, property they well know is not consigned to their delivery area. Then, when driving about and when they see a suitable out-of-the-way common business entrance, they dump it, return to their vehicle and drive away. Later (perhaps even at the time of dumping) they will telephone a confederate or receiver to pick it up. These parcels may contain bulk delivery of pharmaceuticals—including soft drugs.

If you see this sort of behaviour, note the appearance of the driver. (When you have to note rapidly a description get age, height and colouring. Then ask yourself: 'What was the most *striking* thing about his appearance?') Then note the index mark (licence plate) of his vehicle. Quietly and covertly cross to the common entrance and look at the delivery labels on the package(s). If the address is different, watch from a secure place and arrest the confederate or receiver when he comes to take possession of the property. Let him load it on his own vehicle before you take him, and do this a few yards from where he loaded it. You can legitimately ask him to explain his possession of it. If he does not realise you have seen him load it, he may there and then give you a lying and fanciful explanation which can confirm absolutely that you have caught a troublesome thief! If more than one thief or receiver turns up to take the property, this short delay makes it quite possible that they will *all* incriminate themselves.

5. Serious crime in progress

If you want to catch quality thieves—here are cardinal pointers.

Learn to identify immediately those fleetingly suspicious situations involving vehicles which may be over very quickly as far as your sight of them is concerned. They can be part of transactions leading up to or following the commission of serious crimes. Alternatively, they can be part of the life-style of persons engaged in crime. For example:

Watch for
▷ Two or more men in an unlighted vehicle at night, stationary or moving slowly and suspiciously; they are *always* worth inquiry. If possible, and certainly when alone, note the index mark in your pocket book (or even in ball-point pen on the back of your hand) before approaching a really suspicious vehicle. A car with its engine running while stationary should always be investigated. Men, or women for that matter, in motor cars can 'frequent or loiter with intent' just as they can on foot.* There may be evidence in the car justifying a subsequent prosecution for conspiracy to rob, conspiracy to enter premises burglariously or conspiracy to steal motor vehicles. To prevent a serious crime by such an arrest is more praiseworthy than subsequent costly detection.

Watch for
▷ The car at rest, with the bonnet open, the engine running and with a man examining the engine. Remember, this may be a lookout's trick. It enables thieves to park their vehicle near the crime without suspicion, to have the engine running again without suspicion and, if a getaway is required quickly, all that needs to be done is for the bonnet to be slammed shut and the vehicle driven away. Be particularly suspicious in these

---

* In Great Britain it is punishable by three months imprisonment to 'loiter with intent to commit an arrestable (i.e., serious) offence', and arrests of pickpockets and intending car thieves are often made under this provision.

circumstances if, in addition to the man apparently tinkering with the engine, there is another man sitting in either the driver's or passenger's seat. In similar situations consider 'Road closed' and 'Diversion' signs. Are they genuine? Thieves have falsely used them to divert vehicles, which they wish to rob, on more than rare occasions.

Watch for

▷ A parked car, with a man sitting in the front passenger seat; again this may be a lookout's trick. Whereas a man loitering in a motor car and sitting in the driver's seat usually arouses quick suspicion, a man sitting in the passenger seat seems to diminish suspicion. An observer agrees in his mind that a passenger *must* wait for the return of the driver. Thus, rightful suspicion is blunted by a simple ruse. Do not be taken in.

Watch for

▷ Damage showing on the front of a new-looking car or truck. As has been observed, most owners have repairs done promptly, whereas thieves (or dishonest hirers over-holding hire cars—types almost invariably up to no good) just do not have the necessary feelings of proprietorship to do this. As already said, a leaking radiator in a moving vehicle is particularly suspicious. Has it recently been involved in a 'hit-and-run' accident? If at night, perhaps the vehicle has been used as a power source, with an adapted baulk of timber or piece of tubular scaffolding held against the front to act as a ram so as to force in the door of a shop or store. When this is done, the radiator can easily be damaged if the timber or scaffolding pole slips while in use. Sometimes an old rug or blanket is placed between the adapted ram and the front of the vehicle—fibres may then be embedded in the grille. The presence of fibres of cloth in the metal or the grille, therefore, is always most suspicious and need not necessarily mean a hit-and-run accident. Always stop drivers who commit breaches of moving traffic law, even if you do not intend to report them for summons—they may be nervous thieves who have 'lost their cool' and who are taking foolish chances.

Watch for

▷ Any unusual actions observed while *en route* by car *to the scene of serious crime*, where you have been sent by radio. If the crime is reported as having apparently been committed by one or two men on foot, a girlfriend or a male accomplice may be driving the intended escape vehicle around the block formed by four streets, *intending to pick up the thieves when convenient*. This may well apply where there are severe parking problems in the streets near the scene of the crime. A woman seen driving in these general circumstances should always be watched narrowly in the hope of seeing the 'meet' with the thieves. When a vehicle is driven about like this, without a definite destination, it can be picked out easily from other traffic travelling normally. A woman driver alone in the front of a moving car and another woman or man in the rear of the car (so that the nearside front door and both rear doors can be opened quickly) is particularly suspicious. A car seen in the evening with a young male driver and one or two young males in the back of the vehicle (i.e., no one beside the driver) can be suspicious. It has been noted that such a disposition of young men in a car may indicate an intention to indulge in horseplay by grabbing young girls and boisterously pulling them into the vehicle, not intending any great harm. But such behaviour can easily escalate into tragedy, particularly if drink is present. It should be discouraged, and this can be done by stopping the vehicle and examining licences and the like. You will be unpopular but it is in *all* their interests, whether they realise it or not.

Watch for

▷ The driver who carries his driving licence casually in a shirt pocket, or in an upper jacket pocket. While most straightforward motorists look after their driving licences carefully, thieves using stolen licences tend to be casual. A driving licence freshly soiled by oily fingermarks may indicate, too, that it is stolen or at least owned by a thief. An honest driver hardly ever opens his driving licence himself, and only rarely produces it to a policeman. Therefore his licence will usually be clean and intact. Thieves, on the other hand, are frequently producing their licences to suspicious policemen. Consequently, a grubby, tattered or torn driving licence should always arouse thoughtful suspicion.

Watch for

▷ The dishonest or disqualified driver who has to search his pockets for a driving licence and, when he has found it, tries to read it before handing it to you. Why is he reading it ? Perhaps he has more than one irregular licence and is making sure he is giving you the right one for the circumstances in which you have found him. His true licence, if he has one, is probably still in an inner pocket or concealed somewhere in his vehicle.

Perhaps he is having a last minute 'learn' of the name and address shown on it.

Watch for

▷ The same type of suspect driver who, with a driving licence, pulls out assorted bank and credit cards. Try to get a sight of them, saying, 'May I help you, hold something for you, sir?' then take hold of them gently and firmly, as if you were concerned to help him in his fumbling. Experience has shown repeatedly that even the cleverest of thieves are foolhardy enough to carry such stolen and forged cards loose with other documents, and even to carry two or three driving licences in different names.

You have immediate grounds for arrest if the driver is unable adequately to explain possession of differently named licences or cards. Very few people have accounts at more than one of the 'big four' banks;* thus, the possession of two or more cards, even in the same name but from different banks, is in itself suspicious, unless the person is obviously of real wealth. Criminal manipulation of bank and credit cards is so much in the domain of the expert expatriate Australian shoplifting teams that I would add that an Australian accent, in these circumstances, is additionally suspicious. Try, then, to see if there is any brand-new, departmental shop gear or clothes in the boot. Remember that cheque fraudsmen rarely fill in the counterfoils when uttering forged cheques. Several bank cards have a white band lengthwise across them on one side, on which is written, in ink, the holder's signature. Thieves steal a card, mask either side of this band with ordinary adhesive tape, then spray (or paint) white quick-drying enamel over it, adding whatever signature they like. Be very suspicious indeed if you are shown or find a card with traces of white paint on this lengthwise band.

Watch for

▷ The driver who has two or three screwed-up or discarded HO/RT/1's (the small forms issued by uniformed policemen to drivers who are unable to produce driving documents at the time they are stopped, and to remind them to produce the documents at a police station within five days), either on the floor of his vehicle or in the parcel tray/pigeon hole. Does this mean that other policemen have found him in quasi-suspicious

* The four principal English banks are Lloyds, National Westminster, Barclays and Midland.

49

circumstances recently? It may indicate, too, an irresponsible attitude towards producing driving documents, so typical of a thief or disqualified person. Get a sight of these discarded forms. No shyness about it, say firmly, 'I must see those forms, sir, they are police property'. Be polite, but direct. The discarded forms may show that the same driver has recently given different names, has recently been in other vehicles and, lastly, may confirm suspicions justifying arrest there and then.

When you are speaking to a driver whom you really suspect has produced a false licence, hold it out of his view, then ask him for his address first. If the licence is false and the driver has committed the particulars to memory, he will be expecting to give the name first. To give false particulars out of anticipated order tends to disorientate a liar and makes it easier for you to get at the truth.

Watch for

▷ and make yourself familiar with the actual construction of the more popular motor cars. Visit car-breakers' yards and see the skeletons of these common cars. (These breakers' yards are delicate areas, so go with another officer and, if in plain clothes, record it in your diary.) Stand back and ask your companion, 'Where could stolen gear be hidden?' Incidentally, where would you hide property in your own car? Remember that sometimes valuable stolen car accessories—radios, spotlamps and the like—are roughly fitted in thieves' cars so they can be transported without the same suspicion that would be attached to carrying them loose in the boot or on the back seat. Therefore, if such fitted accessories are either inoperable or not electrically connected, be suspicious. When searching a car, look for and see what is inside torn upholstery. Such tears within reach of the driver's hands are likely places for weapons or false documents.

Watch for

▷ Medium-priced saloon cars (Cortinas, Escorts, and the like, even Anglias and Minis*) fitted with large balloon tyres and racing wheels, similar to the sort usually found on powerful 'beach buggies' and racing cars. Bear in mind that these cost about £200 a set and, if the car is a cheap or ageing one, driven by a youngster, it is not unfair to assume the possibility either that the wheels and tyres are stolen, or that they were purchased with stolen money. Bear in mind that truthfully declared

* British model names of cheaper automobiles.

particulars in such a case, on an insurance proposal, would result in insurance fees so large as to be nearly prohibitive for low-income group drivers, especially youngsters. Be suspicious generally about low-priced saloons being 'accessoried up' to look like racing cars; this is often the sign of the compulsive car stealer and joy-rider.

Watch for

▷ Cars in which people appear to be asleep, particularly in lonely places. Persons murdered, or unconscious, or dangerously injured have been ignored by constables anxious not to appear officious or interfering. Valuable time in an important inquiry has been wasted in this way. Lives, too, have been lost. You will not be thought a busy-body if you make your inquiry in a frank and open manner. Remember that alcohol, with barbiturates, is a common form of attempted suicide. If you cannot easily rouse a man or woman driver you find in such surroundings, beware of thinking that they are 'just drunk' merely because they smell of drink. With any such person you cannot rouse and keep roused, get them to hospital. If there are tablets in the car, take them with you and show them to the doctor. Now and again you will look a little foolish, in the eyes of some of your insensitive colleagues, by taking a well-known and troublesome drunk to hospital. What does that matter if you one day save a life in such circumstances ?

Deliberate carbon monoxide poisoning by connecting the exhaust pipe of a running engine with a hose to the interior of the car is not uncommon with would-be suicides, although because carbon monoxide is so rapidly effective it is unlikely that you will ever be able to save the life of such a driver. Always try, however, by switching off the engine, getting him into the open, giving artificial respiration and arranging rapid transfer to hospital. While dealing with suicide, I would like to suggest it is worth while to

Watch for

▷ Persons loitering at railway crossings, at the far ends of railway platforms or in the centre of railway or river bridges, or at cliff tops. They may be ordinary people interested in trains or admirers of landscapes. They may, too, be persons contemplating suicide. It is very much part of your duty as a peace officer, despite what some civil libertarians might say, to dissuade persons suffering from mental stress from harming themselves. This can be done by approaching them in a normal and open

51

way, and asking them if you can direct them or help them, as if you imagined they were lost. Their reaction will quickly show you whether they are persons under severe strain or just ordinary watchers of the passing scene. You can then act accordingly. The recent commission of crime, particularly violent crime, often unbalances a person to the degree that they actively contemplate suicide. When dealing with such situations, keep in mind this possibility; do not dismiss a person as a harmless 'nut' too easily.

Watch for

▷ A man or woman leaving a 'rest room' or lavatory with a wet sleeve or cuff. This may indicate that they have secreted, or retrieved, contraband, stolen property or a weapon from the cistern of a lavatory. This would apply particularly to stewards, male or female, at ports, railway stations or airports. Of course, it also applies in any premises you enter under a search warrant.

Watch for

▷ Reports of inordinately large sales of sugar or cheap grain to people outside this line of business, especially those whom you suspect of being concerned in the running of shebeens. You may reasonably suspect that spirit liquor is being distilled on their premises (or on waste land that is not overlooked). The sickly sweet and intense brewery-like odour of the mash being 'cooked' prior to distillation is unmistakable once experienced —so if there is ever an opportunity to visit a detected still, *do so* and 'arm' your sense of smell (Fig. 5.1).

Watch for

▷ Reports of letters or sums of money occasionally found by children in unusual or lonely places, often in empty food tins. It may not be stolen money, but could be a 'dead letter box' or 'drop' in blackmail or other most serious crimes. If you find or hear of such a thing, make certain your senior detective is told *promptly*, and do all you can to prevent the scene being disturbed pending his decision whether or not to keep observations. If the tin or cover has been moved, find out everyone who has touched it and try to preserve latent fingermarks.

Watch for

▷ An opportunity, when interrogating an unhelpful witness or indeed any hostile-minded person of bad character, to appeal to their nobler

52

(a)

Fig. 5.1(a). An illegal still.
Fig. 5.1(b). Set up in a kitchen.
(See overleaf for Figs 5.1(c) and (d).)

Fig. 5.1(c). Components and materials.
Fig. 5.1(d). Raw materials.
(Figs 5.1(a)–(d) reproduced by courtesy of HM Customs & Excise.)

(b)

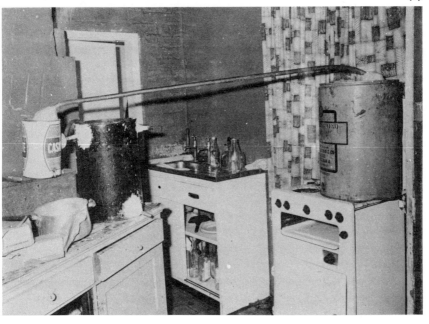

(c)

(d)

instincts. You think this would be a hopeless exercise? There is good inside even the apparently depraved. This may sound sloppy, but it remains true, and intelligent use of this truth can be an invaluable investigative tool.

For example, some 15 years ago, when endeavouring to get vital information from hard and corrupt men who had been trading successfully in juvenile prostitution, my bosses smiled indulgently at (what they considered) my innocent optimism when they heard me say to arrogantly silent men, 'This is a wicked business. Do you think your mother suffered and fed you for this sort of cowardly behaviour? What would she say about you not helping us to find this girl? She's someone's daughter, someone's sister'. Despite the patronising smiles of superior and worldly policemen, the plea hit home in the majority of cases in hand, *and produced the required information.*

Such appeals must be done with dignity and an intent sincerity, in as near a private situation as possible. Sincerity can never be counterfeited. The secret of getting through in these circumstances is truly to believe in what you are saying. It will then show in your eyes and in the ring of your voice, and so convince the man to whom you are speaking.

When appealing to the honourable side of an apparently hostile man, remember that should he have a daughter his reputation with her will probably be dear to him. He will care very much what she thinks of him. Use this knowledge when phrasing your questions to him.

Finally, *never make it difficult for a timid or reluctant witness to tell the truth.* With these people avoid the use of stark words such as 'murder', 'stab', 'rob', 'rape', 'steal', 'confess'. It is far better and in no way dishonest to use tamer words such as 'hurt', 'hit', 'take', 'punch', 'interfere with', 'tell the truth', and the like. It is not soft or unmanly to be humane, nor with gentle people to be gentle.

6. Other categories of motor-car criminal

More subtle street circumstances which plainly indicate criminal conduct, and some notes on the commercial fraudsman; he is a commoner sight in our streets than is generally thought.

'Many persons of bad character are disqualified* from driving' (Dr Terence Willett, in *The Criminal on the Road*). So, when interrogating a *suspected* driver regarding his possession of a vehicle or its contents, bear in mind the possibility that he may be a disqualified driver. Thus, he could be answering your questions suspiciously and acting strangely, not because he has stolen the vehicle or its contents, but because he is disqualified. If you suspect this, a straight question firmly asked, 'Are you disqualified?' can well bring forth a truthful answer. If your suspicion is very strong be even more confident and definite by asking, 'What was the exact date you were disqualified?'

Road traffic legislation enables a constable in uniform to arrest, without warrant, a person driving or attempting to drive a motor vehicle on a road if he has reasonable cause to suspect the person of being disqualified from holding or obtaining a licence. Note that the provision relates both to persons disqualified under the principal Act and to those disqualified on grounds of age.†

Constantly bear in mind that criminals who are *not* thieves also use motor cars. All readers can recall violent and treacherous sexual crimes against children and women where a motor car has been used by the degenerate responsible. Men that procure and protect prostitutes (see Chapter 11) are habitual users of motor cars. Both these categories of criminal could hardly be described as thieves yet they will, when questioned by a policeman, show discomfort and arouse suspicion in a way almost exactly similar to

---

* The British system of cancelling the validity of a driver's licence for a specified period as a penalty upon conviction for an offence, usually (but not exclusively) a traffic misdemeanour.

† Sections 96 and 100 of the Road Traffic Act 1972.

the behaviour of a thief. Try to differentiate between the various types; if you do become skilled in this, many otherwise inexplicable incidents you observe will become crystal clear.

In relation to these classes of vehicle criminals:

Watch for
▷ A male motorist loitering alone in his car near where children play or where housewives shop (and where male shoppers are rare), especially if the loiterer has a newspaper or coat over his lap. Classically suspicious behaviour by such men is the frequent manipulation of the rear-view mirror, so they can watch, but still avoid actual eye contact with, passing females, young or old. A newspaper or jacket over a lap may be covering the otherwise exposed penis of a man intending to exhibit himself to women or children.

Possession of confectionery of a type not normally eaten by adults (e.g., 'sherbet fountains', 'sticky chews', 'gob-stoppers') may be significant, especially if the suspect is plainly not a family man. Possession of obscene photographs, especially if easily accessible, say on the front bench seat beside him or in the glove locker, can be considered very suspicious. If the photographs are wholly or mainly male homosexual ones, involving boy subjects, the evil inference is obvious. The possession of any obscene photograph involving children as subjects should make you keenly suspicious. The unmistakable smell of semen is also very questionable in these circumstances, whether in the car or about the man's clothing. Obscene photographs on which the subjects' bodies are disfigured by needle holes or by crude ink additions, or have their eyes blacked out, may indicate a latent but dangerously violent pervert.

Watch for
▷ Men 'picking up' known or suspected prostitutes in the early hours of the morning in a matter-of-fact 'husband-and-wife' manner—easily recognisable and so different from the opening gambits of prostitute and client which are (as is mentioned in greater detail in Chapters 11 and 12) so tentative and awkward. You may be able to identify a 'ponce' and obtain the index mark of his car.

In most cases there may be no need to interfere at the time. In some circumstances, especially in the first category, all that may be necessary is to let the loiterer know he has been observed. This can be done by asking him whether his vehicle has broken down or by offering to direct him to his destination as though you imagined he had lost his way. If he is a guilty man, he will see through this charade and be warned. If you have mistaken the innocent behaviour of a respectable man, no harm has been done.

Watch for

▷ Van or lorry drivers with teenage girls in their driving cabins, especially if the youngsters look unwashed, unkempt or prematurely 'tartish'. They may be absconders from their homes or escapees from approved schools. It is absolutely right that you should question them and discover whether they are runaways. Remember, if you are accused of needlessly interfering, that runaway and friendless girls, hitch-hiking and leading the vagrant life of near-prostitutes, are vulnerable to being savagely attacked and even murdered, quite apart from the probability of becoming diseased in mind and body. This is ample justification for police inquiry. Such girls may have the smell of semen about their clothes in a similar way to the loiterer already described. Your duty to investigate is plain; do not be put off by insults from them or their male companions.* It is harder to spot, but travelling salesmen also occasionally pick up these girl absconders. Question without being offensive—start on a tack quite separate from your original suspicion, perhaps a traffic matter, and make your mind up as you go along. It may become clear that your suspicions are groundless. With a tactful approach no one has been offended.

In all these cases, privately note the index marks and brief circumstances in which the vehicles were observed. You may provide useful, and sometimes vital, evidence in a serious matter subsequently coming to light. I emphasise that the best place to record such details is in a pocket diary, where a note can be made conveniently of the time and place. Fuller particulars can be written into a notebook or register at the end of your tour of duty, but the contemporary note is the vital one. Your diary record is permanent, accurate and overwhelmingly convincing when produced in the witness box many weeks later.

The commercial fraudsman—catch him in the street

In certain circumstances some very sophisticated criminals are exposed and vulnerable to acute and worldly uniformed officers. For example, one

---

* There exist ample legal powers to arrest escapees or to take juvenile absconders to a place of safety.

of the strongest growth industries in Britain today is fraud, and well to the fore of this form of crime is the 'long firm fraud', or 'LFs' as their slang term goes. These are the conspiracies where fraudsmen induce manufacturers or wholesalers to supply large quantities of goods onc redit, with the intention that the account will never be paid. Counterfeit creditworthiness is built up both by false references from other fraudulent associates and by ordering smaller quantities of goods in the early stages from reputable concerns, and settling these accounts promptly. These reputable concerns are then used as references, but are themselves duped when extremely large orders follow promptly after the settled account, with no intention of payment for these subsequent orders. The goods are then rapidly sold by the fraudsmen at 'knock-down' prices to various outlets.

The type of goods involved can run through the whole spectrum of supply, including confectionery, general foodstuffs, plastic ware, both high- and low-value electrical goods, blankets, woollens, clothing, clocks, toiletries, etc., although one basic similarity is generally that the goods will be the sort in popular public demand at the time in question, and suitable for quick disposal either in cut-rate stores or street markets. An exception to this generality could be where the fraudsmen have themselves obtained control of a failing wholesale or retail outlet of good reputation, and then use it ruthlessly both to obtain and to dispose of goods of the kind the outlet previously handled legitimately. The conspiracies can be very widespread and cause losses to honest firms of hundreds of thousands of pounds. They can be truly international, and indeed have in the past adversely affected our country's trading reputation.

Very interesting, you may reflect, but surely these are specialised detective matters and of no practical interest to ordinary policemen patrolling, in motor cars and on foot, whether in plain clothes or uniform. This is 'fraud squad stuff' you say, and so—in the latter stages—it certainly is, but *as with all crimes of consequence* motor vehicles are used at nearly all stages of these crimes and are invariably used to transport goods to certain sorts of premises; in fact, vehicles are the linchpins and general carriers of these frauds. All that has been said previously about the real likelihood of disqualification, about the propensities thieves have to use or fit 'iffy' or 'dodgy' (doubtful or stolen) licences, insurances, MOT certificates, accessories, etc., applies even to these 'gentlemen' con men. Thus, in two general senses, these conspirators—without themselves even realising wholly their danger—are vulnerable to shrewd and wide-awake street

59

policemen *but, as far as their long firm frauds go, in a different way from the direct street arrest,* as I hope to show you.

All peace officers, of whatever grade or function, should be worldly wise and have a practical and even materialistic understanding of all criminal behaviour. So, with a view to frustrating these conspiracies and better to protect the public:

Watch for

▷ *Activity at the premises of job-lot buyers.* On the face of it these traders are in the market to buy up bankrupt stock or lines that are 'sticking', and which other traders wish to be rid of. Of course, there are honest job-lot men, but experience shows they are frequently a popular outlet for long firm fraudsmen's goods. If you have job-lot buyers' premises on your patch, watch the vehicles delivering goods there.

If you see premises you suspect may be LF outlets, remember a difficulty for senior detectives in eventual prosecution is to link the 'front man' with the principal in the background. So, from that point of view, the index marks of cars and vans seen at the premises, and particularly *the frequency they are seen there,* can be of great assistance later. Not all LF fraudsmen deliver goods and, in such a case, these index marks can help to trace the quasi-respectable buyers with a view to proving, at subsequent prosecution, the purchase of goods well below cost price.

Since the virtual end of retail price maintenance, selling below recommended prices is not now as strong an indicator of 'something wrong' as perhaps it once was, but if the majority of the goods are well below the sale price of similar gear *sold by reasonably similar traders in the same area,* it may still be a good pointer.

The sort of premises that might be suspicious—you must use both your own local knowledge and that of your respectable commercial informants here—are the permanently unsuccessful shop premises. Every area has them—those premises that have seen many changes of occupant and which suddenly blossom into intense activity. Perhaps a senior detective colleague can find out discreetly if the shopfittings, the business furniture and the shop or store itself are on very short hirings or leases. A combination of these factors can be very suspicious. The empty warehouse, long disused, that suddenly becomes a cash-and-carry emporium should similarly awaken your interest, especially where the 'warehousemen' seem never carefully to check with lorry drivers either the receipt or despatch of goods.

Watch for

▷ *The regular attendance of a private vehicle of some quality and style at any such suspect premises.* It may indicate the identity of the backer or one of his principal associates, and may be vital evidence later on to link all the conspirators. Remember, you are no longer looking primarily for suave and polished commercial fraudsmen, although of course these still exist. Long firm frauds have been so successful in the past few decades that they now attract every sort of thief, even those who in the past made their money by violent crime. There is good reason to believe that money made by trading in prostitution, and by pornography, is 'invested' in long firm frauds, so quite rough-looking 'minders' may visit the premises in their cars just to see that the backer is not himself being defrauded. If the outlet or premises are outside London, watch for the Greater London Council registration numbers, and run CRO checks on the registered owners. You may be surprised.

Watch for

▷ The commercial vehicle that has recently left a suspected LF fraudsman's premises, loaded with goods, presumably to deliver to an outlet. There are subtle, but none the less tangible, differences from the usual commercial pattern of delivery. For example, instead of the honest method, where the driver involved would have detailed delivery documents on printed forms individual to a limited company in order that the goods could properly be checked off at the point of delivery, quite often with LF transactions they will have either no documents or very scant documentation. Where there are documents, it seems, goods are often described in a vague and general manner. Quite a lot of LF operators make use of the cheap and mass-produced Challenge type of simple duplicate book, with the 'cover name' of the LF operation, e.g. 'A. N. Other's Cash and Carry', stamped by rubber stamp at the top of the page, instead of proper printed forms.

If you have to stop such a vehicle, however, and you become suspicious because of these factors, *never show your unease with the explanations supplied.* Play-act that you were checking for stolen goods or stolen vehicles and that, since you have seen the documents or heard the explanation, you are absolutely satisfied. Try and remember all the detail possible, and note it down as soon as the vehicle is out of sight.

It is vital that you regard your duties in this field as informative rather than investigatory, and these snippets of suspicion should be passed on to a middle-ranking detective officer, a man who values your information as worth while. The suspicions of LF fraudsmen are easily aroused, and once they are the fraudsmen will make subsequent inquiry difficult by carefully updating and improving the standard of their paperwork, or even by going to the extreme of absconding there and then. Consequently, if you have no alternative but to stop such a vehicle at, say, a road block or in some similar situation, I repeat, *play-act the part of the dense policeman,* easily satisfied by a brisk and fluent explanation, and thus blunt suspicion. You can change their poor opinion of your subtlety and intelligence subsequently, when you give evidence against them.

7. High-status shop and purse thieves

How to take them and—even more subtle—how to ensure the straightforward truth is laid before the court!

Keep a weather eye open for the appearance of skilled teams of shop thieves in the large departmental stores of your area, whether you are on or off duty. They can swamp the security defences of such a shop, geared only for ordinary thieves. Notice, no use of the term 'shoplifters'—this is a somewhat milky word too soft-sounding to describe the harsh reality and greed of organised thieves. While we should be ready, in appropriate cases, to deal with all offences brought to our notice, all peace officers have a wide discretion, and we are not discussing the child, or the disturbed woman, or deprived old people, all of whom steal from these stores. There is a lot to be said for leaving these unfortunates to be dealt with by store detectives and management, but of course making sure that no unfair advantage is taken of the detained person. We are dealing with insolent thieves, those of excellent intelligence, who steal with an eye to profit, and good profit at that; those that intend to steal a hundred pounds' worth of property each per day and who will never hesitate to be violent in a tight corner. They are worthy opponents for the shrewdest of young police officers.

Previously, it has been said that such teams are not infrequently expatriate Australians, that they also seem prone to using stolen credit cards and false cheques (with respect to these cheque books, the counterfoils are hardly ever filled in) and that they will have at least one vehicle parked near to hand, possibly in a multi-storey car park. This still seems to be the pattern. The driver is sometimes left with the vehicle in such situations, ready at a prearranged time to drive to a pick-up point. Therefore, whereas there are many reasons why honest people might choose to remain in their cars in one of the floors of a multi-storey car park, there is undoubtedly an element of minor suspicion about such a situation which should register with you. If the vehicle is a small van or estate car, with a rear 'tail-gate', perhaps misgiving is more justified. Do not be ashamed of being suspicious, it is a healthy police virtue; just sensibly control it and combine it with fluent good manners.

Watch for

▷ Signs of recognition between persons in the shop who otherwise would not be thought to be together. A fleeting expression of the eyes, or even the slight raising of an index finger or thumb, or a slow and deliberate touching of the nose are the signs to look for. Of course, you may have come across pickpockets and not merchandise thieves—their actions are similar in this respect. Alternatively, they might be store detectives or test purchasers about the proprietor's lawful business, so be careful of jumping to conclusions. Have patience and watch, and learn to watch from a distance. Recognition between shop assistant and customer, particularly if it has about it a clandestine air, may indicate joint thieving by the employee accepting fractional cash from the thief with or without actually changing price tickets. Marked friendliness, which has about it an over-rehearsed or counterfeit manner, by a customer to a shop assistant, might mean the customer is occupying the attention of the employee with a view to an accomplice stealing unobserved nearby. If the friendly one tries to occupy the attention of two shop assistants, her behaviour is doubly suspicious.

Watch for

▷ Those people that leave the shop but come back a few moments later, and those that enter a lift,* especially if it is going down, at the last moment, particularly if they have loitered and allowed other people to enter before them out of their turn. Look for those whose glances are sharp and intent as they look up and around while fingering goods upon a counter. These tell-tale glances are rapid fire, lasting perhaps only part of a second. They may be looking intently at customers, gauging whether a store detective is watching them. The closing up and leaving near the edge of a counter of, say, an expensive, folding, leather-covered travelling alarm clock is typically suspicious behaviour. Watch the clock, not the person who folded it up. Someone is going to steal it, or indeed more than one, and quite soon! Remember, both are guilty—the deliberate 'folder-up' and he or she who actually secured the property. Take both of them, well away from the shop, when they enter their vehicle. You may find it

---

* English term for elevator.

to be an Aladdin's cave on wheels! It is important to wait until this point because, if the car does contain stolen property, you will be able evidentially to connect them with it. There are hardly any circumstances when shop thieves should be arrested inside the shop. The best place is away from the store, near another shop doorway where sudden flight is difficult. *You* pick the best ground.

Watch for

▷ In winter, a man without an overcoat in the part of the shop where coats are sold. Valuable sheepskin coats are very much a target. If a cheap raincoat is left on a shop chair near the department, or in a washroom, you may be watching characteristic moves preparatory to the theft of a valuable coat or coats. The same applies to women's coats—again sheepskin is a target, as is astrakhan. I think these two are preferred because they are easier and somehow less suspicious to negotiate subsequent fraudulent sale to honest persons, whether in trade or privately. Valuable mink, sable and squirrel coats, wraps and capes are, of course, stolen by clever shop thieves, but they know that later disposal invites many more questions. Out-of-fashion clothes can be just as suspicious as out-of-season clothes. Very wide skirts or voluminous overcoats, when such look 'square', if worn by trendy or otherwise elegant women, may be intended as repositories or covers for stolen woollen goods. Elastic-legged pants are sometimes worn—with large slits in the sides of a skirt (or indeed trousers) much can be concealed!

Watch for

▷ A woman dressed in a feminine fashion but without a handbag, and in that part of the shop where real crocodile or expensive hide handbags are sold. She is worth surveillance, especially if accompanied by another woman. Remember, masculine women sometimes dislike carrying handbags, but of course may well be absolutely honest. Also, some female drop-outs shun ordinary handbags and carry beaded shoulder bags of canvas. The tip is only really significant with a woman who looks out of place without a handbag. However, if any shoppers examine fur hats, clothing or handbags below the level of the counter, you should be suspicious. Why? Because these are needless movements for honest shoppers. So is the unnecessary covering or secreting of the price ticket in the hand while trying on clothes or when placing a garment over an arm, or the handling of small objects rapidly.

65

Watch for

▷ Disdainful or contemptuous smiles. Yes, smiles! Really good thieves sometimes betray themselves by a joint glance together of silent, smiling amusement immediately after a successful theft. They think themselves clever and are amused with their tawdry triumph over the 'mugs' that work honestly. It is fair to say women in these circumstances are of two general classifications in appearance. Either smartly dressed, even elegant in the conventional sense, or smart but trendy dressers—slacks and inside-out embroidered Afghanistan sheepskin coats, with perhaps a medallion on a chain. The latter type of shop thief, the trendy drop-outs, are not easy to deal with as they have convinced themselves, in a Marxist sense, that '. . . all property is theft . . .' and can morally justify to themselves the rightness of stealing from large stores, the owners of which, in their eyes, are the oppressors. However mistaken some may consider their views, there is no doubt that they are themselves convinced they do no wrong, perhaps even that they are doing right. In any event, I have noticed they nearly always complain about police treatment, however innocuous or even friendly it is, so be circumspect.

Watch for

▷ The nervous strain associated with thieving; it manifests itself in not-so-obvious ways. There is, first, the repeated need for shop thieves to get 'away from the action'; so they will often loiter in lavatories or in empty parts of the shop floor, and at the landings of stairways. They want to get their 'breath back' in a place where they feel unobserved. Secondly, to give them time to think out some tactic of thieving or evasion, they will carry out false and unnecessary actions—for example, tying up a loose shoelace several times, using a make-up compact over-frequently, or picking up gloves or an umbrella dropped more than once. To a shrewd observer this behaviour, which is an endeavour to appear a casual and unconcerned shopper, is betrayed as very significant play-acting.

Watch for

▷ The direct and incisively searching glance of the thief, so intent, so concentrated and so revealing. I repeat and emphasise it because this is the master key to recognising people up to no good. It should be looked for particularly when it is associated with an outwardly innocent movement, for example, picking up a glove. When 'in action', thieves' glances are either flinty hard (and once seen, never forgotten) or at the other extreme are vacuous and dull. They wish principally to look casual and honest, so in their play-acting they overdo it and thus, as I say, look vacant and dull. If you see such alternate extremes of needle-sharpness and blankness, you are on to a good thing, but remember a policeman's glance is also often hard and intent (you do not think so ?—ask your wife), and if a thief's intent glance locks on to a plain clothes man's hard look, there will be recognition all right, but it will be mutual, and thus your 'cover will be blown'. These hard glances are transitory and last only a fraction of a second.

Watch for
▷ Valuable gramophone records or discs being stolen by being placed between the leaves of extra-large glossy magazines. It does not take long to steal a considerable number and they are easily disposed of. If you see an elastic band around a dozen or more silk scarves, ties or expensive tights, or any similar property, and done in such a way that it seems unlikely to have been put there by the manufacturer or the retailer, watch the items from a distance. You probably have come across property deliberately placed in a convenient position, waiting to be stolen. Try to notice such things without anyone else seeing that you *have* noticed. Such property may be continuously watched by the more nervous of thieves, while he or she is waiting to make the actual take. In most departmental shops of quality there is a well-furnished area, with carpets and diffused lighting, where expensive costume jewellery—simulated pearls and the like—is sold under a trade name differing from that of the main shop. Quite a bit of thieving can go on here. Women thieves try on more than one necklace and cleverly allow one to drop inside their dress as they fasten the catch at the back of their neck or when, in that typical movement of females, they pat the back of their hair. One of two small brooches, ostensibly being examined closely, can also be dropped down the front of a dress.

Watch for
▷ Smart-looking women coming into one shop, carrying the large brown paper or plastic carrier bags supplied by another shop. The second shop's property can be dropped clandestinely into such a bag and be hidden among that lawfully bought at the previous shop. It is not unknown for toddlers, accompanying thieves, to have valuable small articles thrust into their pockets. There is what thieves call 'outers'

67

here; in other words, a pat explanation if things go wrong. If the child is seen with the gear, he can be smacked, the property returned and everyone is happy—except the poor infant who was whacked without reason. A lot of dishonesty, too, takes place in the changing cubicles of departmental stores, but in my view these actions are outside both the responsibility of police officers and the scope of this book.

Watch for

▷ The fake disturbance that may be the cover for thieving. Adolescent thieves, black or white, can enter a shop—act very boisterously and attract all eyes—while confederates steal. This is a not uncommon behaviour in South London, to cover thefts from off-licences.* The 'fainting' woman or 'epileptic' can do the trick, too. A pair of proficient women shop thieves may be accompanied, but not obviously so, by a man who will provide 'muscle' if an attempt is made to detain the women. This may also be done in a subtle way. When the women break free and make a run for it he may physically detain the store detective, saying, 'What's the matter? Can I help? Are you all right?' at the same time making sure the employee cannot move quickly after the women. When all is quiet he, too, can fade away. Whereas allowances must be made for women store detectives to be so tricked, it should never happen to a police officer. Get such a man to the station, if necessary by acting a part and saying you want him to assist in identifying the escaping thieves by looking at photographs, etc. Then you can assess whether he is an accomplice or not.

Watch for

▷ Activity by shop thieves at closing time. When the bell rings at 5.30 p.m., the likelihood is that every member of the staff—*including the store's detectives*—is already mentally on the bus going home. Professional thieves know that vigilance is gone and opportunities will present themselves. This is the time when previously 'set-up' property is stolen.

Some shoplifters steal with the intention of bringing goods back to exchange for cash, saying they have changed their minds. Another variation is as follows. Thieves sometimes buy with cash—usually the exact or nearly exact amount—one expensive piece of merchandise (often first-class woollen 'twin sets' and the like) which are displayed in a manner where

---

* Liquor stores.

theft of similar articles is possible. Trying to attract as little attention as possible, they wait for their receipt and paper carrier bag, usually with the retailer's name printed on the side. They leave the shop normally, get rid of the merchandise to a confederate and return with the paper carrier bag and receipt. They steal as nearly an identical a piece of merchandise as possible and leave, and so on. One expert woman thief told me, and she was not a boastful girl, that she had effected this trick five times in an afternoon. It is called 'at the switch'.

When you arrest these 'hard-liners' with adequate evidence, those that steal from shops as a profitable way of life in teams of three or more—the sort that overwhelm the ordinary security precautions of a departmental store which is normally geared for ordinary shoplifters and dishonest employees—you may think it all over bar the formalities. You can be in for a surprise.

Experience shows that they will do what they can to mask the fact that they are greedy professionals who steal by co-ordinated and premeditated plans, because they know courts will deal severely with them if this becomes apparent. How, then, can they lessen responsibility for their actions? To begin with, they may see if they can bribe you, although it is unlikely they will speak openly and directly to you. However, as 'starters', they may say apparently innocently, 'Is there anything that can be done about this business?' just to see how you react. They want you to 'forget' details that plainly show greed or premeditation, or perhaps for you not to object to bail (so they can abscond). They will be anxious to conceal their previous convictions, too, if this is possible. If you ignore this loaded question and look hard at them, only the really bold will speak to you in the same vein again, although they may see if an outside confederate, skilfully posing as an informer, can approach another police officer to intercede for them with you, and perhaps offer both of you valuable-sounding information. This confederate may even go to the extent of first supplying that officer with really useful information. They are, you see, willing to sacrifice some peripheral associate, to be caught red-handed with valuable stolen property, if they think they can win your confidence with such ingratiating conduct. Sometimes a dishonest solicitor's clerk will make the approach, cloaking it by pretending to be seeking, quite properly, facts for the defence. If such determined efforts are made in an attempt to subvert you, the matter should be reported promptly. Do not try to deal with it entirely yourself and never endeavour to encourage a corrupt opening.

Remember that you are dealing with persons absolutely without scruple, and they may already have falsely complained about you to authority, saying you have demanded money. Your 'playing along with them', as you thought with the intention of incriminating them, can so easily backfire in such circumstances and sound incriminating all right, but against you.

There are two important points to remember. First, you can most effectively dress up, as distinct from dressing down, to achieve a certain disguise and so to merge into the background. [Figure 7.1 illustrates this and shows the author (right) with a colleague, now a Detective Superintendent in the Fraud Squad at New Scotland Yard, when they were in their early twenties and during their pickpocket-catching days in the West End of London.] Secondly, even today a conventionally well-dressed appearance tends to carry with it an air of authority, which in turn *tends to reduce the likelihood of either violent opposition or corrupt offers* when you have to tell thieves that they are to be arrested there and then. It will also be to your advantage if you have to ask for urgent assistance from the public. In a busy street, onlookers will not mistake you for the thief and the thief for the policeman, a not unusual occurrence.

Note that the innocent-sounding expressions 'Do you *drink?*' or 'There's a good *drink* in it for you and your mate', often used by corrupt persons in a 'friendly' manner, are really nice words for *money bribes*, and have nothing to do with any liquid except perhaps slime!

Lawfully and fairly to catch corrupt persons is a task where there must be careful thought and adequate preparation by experienced officers beforehand, with really senior officers acquainted with the proposed line of action.

The next ploy often used is to endeavour to cast the whole responsibility upon that member of the team of thieves who has no previous convictions, or at least has only minor ones. There may even be a genuine intention for that person to plead 'guilty', provided no evidence is offered against the others. Watch this, for if tacitly accepted or even just not resisted, the counterfeit plea made in mitigation for the thief would bring tears to the eyes of a Whale Island gunner's mate,* and the court will be misled. The police are thus outmanœuvred, and 'Old Bill'† will be considered a 'mug'. It will be *your* fault.

Lastly, they will falsely try to use those lines of defence frequently adopted by the ordinary 'amateur' shoplifter. For example, that the theft

---

* A senior naval NCO who, by repute anyway, has a severe and perhaps harsh attitude to offenders.
† London slang for the police.

Fig. 7.1. You can dress up to suit the background just as well as you can dress 'down'.

was mistaken forgetfulness or unbalanced behaviour brought on by great nervous or emotional strain, which they will specify and produce witnesses to 'corroborate'. If the worst comes to the worst and they are found guilty they will then, with some eloquence, indicate they are deprived and only stole because they were unemployed and hungry. Character witnesses, either genuine or confederates, will offer themselves as sureties for future good behaviour, and perhaps say they can obtain employment, 'If a certain course is taken by the court'. If they seem over-anxious to have the case dealt with summarily, they may be doing so because they know that if there is a remand in custody previous crimes, especially cheque frauds, may be traced to them. Regard with suspicion such 'hurry-up' requests by clever and intelligent thieves. They are shrewd, remember, and it is your sworn duty, without the least vindictiveness, to ensure the 'whole truth' is placed before the court.

Now to that interesting character, the skilled female purse thief, who mainly works the large departmental shops. Such thieves do, of course, work in street markets also, but the quality thieves are most often found in the stores where there are excellent pickings. Certainly in South London, and from what I hear of conduct in other cities, street-market purse stealing has degenerated these days into a rough-and-ready, potentially violent situation. Whereas the actual stealing is usually done by women, young hooligan males, black or white, do steal women's purses themselves, almost openly, with an implied threat of violence if there is quick reaction, or they hang about ready to assist a woman thief if she is observed stealing. They behave the same at bus stops and in underground stations. It can hardly be called 'picking pockets'; rather, theft with menaces and implied threats of violence.

Watch for

▷ The female purse and wallet thief in the better department stores. As I have said before, if the shop is mainly for women customers, the pick-pockets using the shop will mainly (but not invariably) be females, too. Their appearance will reflect a typical customer of the store. If it is an elegant store, they will be elegantly dressed. If it is a housewive's shop, they will be typically housewifely. Almost invariably, the male pick-pockets will be outside on the bus stops or in the vicinity of crowded underground stations, where they will themselves not look out of place and where they can be fleet of foot, if necessary.

Watch for

▷ The thief, not the theft. For several successive years, a plain clothes colleague (now a senior Fraud Squad detective) and I were posted to the Oxford Street stores at Christmas and the sales seasons. It soon became plain to us that it was fruitless to wait haphazardly for a purse theft to take place by a woman pickpocket within our field of vision. There is just no room for 'fire brigade policing' with pickpockets. You have to spot them before they start, and watch them until you have them actually in the course of a theft. You will then avoid long-drawn-out 'not guilty' pleas, as is frequently the case if you have to charge them with 'loitering' rather than an actual theft. However genuine you are, your credibility at court suffers if your pickpocket arrests are always 'loitering'. With women prisoners, too, it looks a little heavy-handed to unthinking people. While not against the Vagrancy Act charge, it certainly has real merit against housebreakers and car thieves (as is shown in Chapter 9), but it is of restricted value against pickpockets, who rarely have incriminating tools with them, are usually well dressed and can advance a convincing explanation as to why they were in the shop or market concerned. A useful spin-off with an arrest for the complete offence is that you have the thief's respect for your ability, and he will not have that resentment that 'loitering' charges so often bring.

Watch for

▷ The opportunity to have others spot for you. Store detectives are only marginally interested in pickpockets; their primary task is to detect merchandise thieves. Thus they can be induced to be a valuable source of immediate current information for you, as they can spot pickpockets as well as anybody, and better than most. You must cultivate them if you want them to help you. How? First, know their full names and whether they are 'Mrs' or 'Miss', then when you meet them in your police station with their prisoners be both courteous and helpful to them. They often meet with a frosty reception and are ready for a friendly word. Lastly, talk to them about things that interest them and not always about duty or what they can do for you! Invariably thank them for the least help, and occasionally give a trifling gift—flowers, for example. The head shop detective of a famous Oxford Street store, a most elegant lady, had previously been in HM Prison Service and knew, I suppose, every West End woman pickpocket who had served a sentence. Unlike so many of his casual colleagues, my 'buck' treated her always with an urbane deference

73

and admiring respect. We were always as helpful as possible to her at court. Nothing was too much trouble for us in respect of her attendances at our station (Marylebone Lane) and at court. Out of all the plain clothes policemen in the vicinity, guess who were the ones she went out of her way to warn when an expert pickpocket entered her store? No prizes for the correct answer.

Watch for

▷ The very real possibility, when you have no alternative but to arrest for 'loitering', that the thief has already stolen, but before you spotted her. Give careful thought to the words you use when arresting in such cases. Consider saying something like, 'We are from Marylebone Lane CID office. Police officers have been watching you closely for 20 minutes, and we know you are here to steal. I am arresting you for loitering for that purpose'. Caution deliberately, pause for any reply—then say, 'I must ask you now for all the property you have stolen, give it to me here and now, please'. It was my repeated experience in the 'fifties, and it is still the pattern now, that such a firm and confident request *will bring forth* previously stolen property, which might otherwise skilfully be abandoned *en route* to the station or which—when the thief has had time to think up a lying tale of explanation—may be thought to be her own property. You have the psychological advantage at the time of arrest; in the public interest, use this advantage in a determined but fair way. One of your duties is to do all you can to restore stolen money to the victims, who in most cases can ill afford to lose it, however affluent they may appear on the surface. There is plenty of proud and genteel poverty about, especially in West London.

Watch for

▷ The prisoner with concealed, really concealed, money. One aspect of these sort of cases is that, like most prostitutes, nearly all women pickpockets—if they are any good—have 'ponces', that is, men who live with them and take the lion's share of the money they steal, usually to be wasted on 'flash' cars, gaming and betting, and even on other women. This causes many women thieves, like their sisters in prostitution, to conceal money from their ponces and carry it hidden about their clothing. A really thorough search of the linings and sewn folds of clothing and handbags, by a woman officer, is justified in nearly all pickpocket cases. Money is often concealed in brassieres, but not usually pushed into the top of this garment. If placed in the brassiere from the bottom, folding money is less likely to be seen by the searching woman officer, unless the garment is completely removed.

Watch for
▷ The methods of the dishonest pickpocket prostitute who steals from the pockets of semi-drunken clients. A thorough search of body orifices, unpleasant as this is, may be necessary. If a mature and sensible woman officer or matron suspects deep interior concealment, have the divisional surgeon called (leaving the matron or woman officer with her until he arrives) for a proper examination, with consent of course. When such a prisoner sees your determination to get medical attendance she may see the inevitability of detection and cease her deceit, voluntarily producing the hidden money. Give her the opportunity then to do this without too much embarrassment, by leaving her for a reasonable period in the matron's office or similar private room with only mature women present, preferably only one such lady. Male prostitutes also conceal money in this way.

Watch for
▷ The real danger of being a prig and disdainfully unhelpful to prisoners. No matter how depraved you may choose to consider such women thieves, *never* show contempt or even disapproval in your face or eyes. You will make an enemy if you do, and no active policeman whether superintendent or constable can afford the luxury of even one unnecessary enemy. A disgruntled and unscrupulous woman has only to say or write from prison, '. . . he stole £5 off me', or worse, '. . . he touched me in a dirty way' and, however innocent and straightforward you are, you will at least be very much inconvenienced by such spiteful lies. If it happens twice in your service, you may well be quite dangerously embarrassed. Rigid or pettifogging observance of every rule, if combined with contempt, seems in some way to generate lying allegations from certain prisoners, '. . . it'll bring him down a peg or two', '. . . serve him right, the stuck-up pig' are perhaps the thoughts in their minds. An old station sergeant at Albany Street* used to philosophise about these female liars to indignant young officers, saying '. . . however bad you think they are, son, remember it was a worse man that made 'em that way'. Sentimental perhaps, but there is some truth in it. In any event,

* A famous London police station.

nobody ever complained about him and he was the last person to be considered weak or effete in his dealings with offenders. Understanding and not making moral judgements is one of the principal secrets of handling troublesome prisoners.

Watch for

▷ The other pests found in large and crowded shops, in fact anywhere where people are densely packed—the man who behaves unpleasantly to women in crowds by rubbing up against them. The practice must be old established, as its slang term remains 'bustle-punching'. It is easy, very easy, to mistake their movements and behaviour for that of a thief positioning himself to steal from women's handbags, and cases have occurred of their being mistakenly charged with '. . . being a suspected person loitering to steal'. Some male homosexuals behave in a similar fashion towards other males.

Some people might say such gross men have only themselves to blame for the danger they run of being arrested for and convicted of an offence of dishonesty. Nevertheless, it is absolutely wrong and no amount of hedging will alter this. The proper charge, if there is evidence to support it, namely indecent assault in a bad case, or in the right location 'insulting behaviour' in lesser matters, should always be preferred.

If the mistake only comes to light after he is charged with 'being a suspected person loitering', you are bound to see right done. If the evidence justifies it, a further charge of 'insulting behaviour' should be added and, when at court, the facts of your mistake should be stated plainly, without too much attempted justification, and no evidence offered in the 'suspect loitering' charge.

If there is insufficient evidence to support even the charge of 'insulting behaviour', the court may be willing to bind the prisoner over under their general powers.

If you follow the course of action I have suggested, your face will be red and some of your colleagues will consider you pedantic, but what they say will be as nothing compared with the reputation you will have at that court for being fearlessly truthful, even when you are made to look foolish by it. The magistrate and his clerk will think '. . . even to his disadvantage this officer can be relied on unconditionally for the truth'. The accused will admire your honesty, too. In the early stages of an active police career you may well be in the witness box daily. *Such a reputation is absolutely priceless.* Important cases are bound to occur where everything depends on your word, where you will be outnumbered by witnesses with contrary views. Your reputation will then, almost subconsciously, be weighed in the scales by the Bench.

The lesson to be learned, in this and every other set of criminal circumstances, is to get independent corroborative evidence from the public whenever possible. I repeat—get independent corroboration.

8. The three-card trick

Know all the ingenious deceits of this thieves' hoax—it is the commonest of street and racing crowd frauds, and is international.

Every capable officer should know the subtleties, feints and dishonest manoeuvres of the three-card trick,* which is really clever collusion by several tricksters (Fig. 8.1). The artifice is profitable, and travelling 'firms' of 6–10 cheats can expect to extract hundreds of pounds a week from those confident fools who imagine they can 'beat the system'. This will depend, of course, on whether these tricksters can avoid being caught too often by sharp-eyed police officers. Now, few officers and fewer lawyers know the fundamental mechanics of this trickery. You do not believe that? Well, many times I have asked officers on selection boards, those recommended as 'experienced and qualified in all respects', how it is done, and have never once received the right explanation, even from those who have themselves arrested these sharks. Contrary to popular belief at courts, there are no hinged cards, no movement in any way of cards into the

---

* Called 'three-card monte' by professionals. The phrases 'chase the king/queen/jack' (as the case may be) and 'find the lady' are occasionally used, too, but are considered old-fashioned by the younger tricksters.

Fig. 8.1(a). The three cards held by an expert operator, just before the 'throw'. It will be made to appear that a picture card is the first to descend on to the table but, with the speed of cine picture frames moving through a film projector, it will be the card above it that first descends. Note the slight bending down of each card—in its top left-hand position by the operator's right little finger, by his right ring finger in the case of the king, and by his index finger in his left hand. The use of this fold is described in the text. (b). The corrugated appearance of cards used in the three-card trick. This induces a 'springiness' and ensures the miniature corner fold will always fall (as far as the thrower is concerned) in the top right-hand corner of the cards. (c). The bending of one of the corners of each of the cards used in the three-card trick or, as the professionals call it, 'three-card monte'. *Note*: Fig. 8.1(a) shows a common idiosyncrasy of card cheats—wearing their wrist watches on the inner aspect of their wrists.

dealer's clothing, nor is the queen or other picture card palmed and another substituted. I know it has been stated otherwise, even at court, but nevertheless sleight of hand, not substitution, is the vital element. You can search a dealer to the buff (as I have seen done more than once) but you will only find three-card sets. Policemen are sometimes misled when they find no queen, but the trick is as often done with a king or knave, and sometimes just with numbered cards. There may be no real or criminal significance in this absence of a queen.

The method used by street cheats is as follows:

Watch for

▷ The principal who has three cards, one being a picture card, usually but not invariably a queen. After moving these about on a collapsible table, orange box, opened umbrella or a spread-out coat, so as to attract a crowd or 'hedge of mugs', as the sharks call them, he picks the cards up holding one in his left hand and two in his right. They are held lengthwise between fingers and thumb, i.e., the top or head of the card with the top of the finger, and the bottom of the card by the thumb. They are face out towards the crowd. The picture card or 'queen' (sometimes called the 'donnah') is one of the two cards in the right hand, the lower of the two, wholly visible, and facing outwards. By moving the hands about, still holding the cards, and then by putting them down and picking them up again, he will draw specific and repeated attention to this card. The operator himself nearly always holds the money, but with really expert firms, a 'banker' or 'cashier' stands beside him holding a large 'flash' bundle of bank notes, mainly £1 notes, although a few £10 or £20 notes will additionally be held between his fingers as an added 'come on'. When held by the principal, the notes will be folded lengthwise and in his left hand. The principal then throws the cards face down in a line in front of him and moves them about, stops and invites the 'mugs' to pick out the picture card, offering attractive sounding odds to them. (Naturally, with a left-handed dealer everything said should be reversed.)

Watch for

▷ The essence of the deceit, which is this: when the cards are thrown down, after having been shown to the crowd, it is made to appear that the bottom card (i.e., the picture card) in the right hand is the first to descend, whereas actually the upper card is the one that first hits the 'table'. (This is similar to the card sharks' trick, in other games, of occasionally dealing a card from the bottom of the pack, but is in this case, of course, reversed.) Thus, from the start, the watching dupes are mistaken as to the position of the queen. They then foolishly concentrate all their attention upon seeing where the card they imagine to be the queen is moved to by the principal, before bets are called for. The operator moves them about quickly, but not too quickly, so that the 'mug punters' will think this rapid moving of the cards about the table is the guts of the trick and the method used to confuse them, although of course the trap was sprung when the cards were 'thrown'. In gamesters' slang the principal of the firm is called 'the thrower'. He is the indispensable member and takes the lion's share of the profit.

Watch for
▷ The early stages when a confederate, pretending to be a punter, stakes and wins, stakes and loses, stakes and wins substantially. This is the final come on for the mug punters or 'greedy pigs' as they are otherwise called. (It is interesting that card sharks morally justify their conduct by alluding to the greed of their dupes in these unflattering, even abusive, terms—perhaps it helps them to live with themselves. You will have noticed that this is a common reaction with nearly all law breakers; they are super-critical of their victims.) When performed even by only lightly skilled sharps, it seems to the watching public easy, but not too easy, to spot the picture card. Therein lies the second key to the trick, the victims think to themselves '. . . you've got to be quick to see where he moves the queen but I am quick enough'; thus, a cunningly induced false confidence is built up. Often, all sorts of variations are performed simultaneously, to confuse the watcher mentally. The position of the cards before the sleight of hand 'drop' is constantly varied, fascinating chatter or 'spiel' is given out, with a distraction of some sort synchronized to take place actually at the time the cards are 'thrown'.

Watch for
▷ One variation where the principal acts the part of having his attention distracted and turns his head around, leaving the cards down in front of him. A confederate, play-acting the part of a punter, will quickly look at each card and bend the corner of the picture card, smiling conspiratorially to the public. The principal, having dealt with the counterfeit interruption, returns his attention to the cards, picks them up and, while handling them, unbends the corner and then bends another card's corner. Down they go again. The punters bet heavily and lose again. At this time the

punters may consider themselves defrauded; this ploy is frequently the last one before the firm break up to meet later at a café or public house.

Watch for

▷ The manœuvre in a really dishonest game, if the pace is fast and furious, when unscrupulous 'inside men' (as the confederates standing adjacent to the principal are called) will induce wagering, from reluctant punters, as follows. Holding a £5 note in their hand, they ask for change from a member of the public, so that they themselves can bet. When a dupe produces change, they will push his hand down, still holding his five £1 notes, on to a card, which of course loses. The principal rapidly takes this money. The £5 note offered for change will also have been staked on this losing card by the inside man. If the reluctant punter objects, two or three inside men will crowd him, calling out 'Welsher!' or 'Bad loser!' and thus silence him.

Watch for

▷ Another dishonest variation used by the tricksters. During the spiel the principal will indicate that, if the police arrive, everyone taking part stands the chance of being arrested (theoretically true, of course, but most unlikely). This is 'outers' for him or, in plain language, insurance against financial loss in the following circumstances. If a really knowing punter or perhaps a rival card sharp (pretending to be a member of the public) is wagering successfully because he understands the false throw of the cards, there will be several sudden cries of 'Police!' or 'Look out!' or 'Heads up!' or 'Up!' from confederates and, while confusion reigns, off will go the team with the money, if necessary snatched from the hand of the winning punter. When the team just want to finish, after a financially successful episode, they may falsely use this ploy just to get rid of the crowd. In some firms a simple verbal code lets the inside men know the position of the picture card, although this is not absolutely necessary.

Watch for

▷ The chance carefully to examine the cards used, even in cases where you are not personally concerned. Note that, to ensure that all the cards are sufficiently springy to be flipped or thrown in the manner described, one side, longitudinally, is slightly folded in a rounded, corrugated fashion. This is almost invariably the case, except with brand-new cards, which for a short time have sufficient inherent springiness. Additionally, each card will have one corner slightly and very neatly creased, so that it would be an easy thing to turn up, or quickly to turn back, this one corner of the card. The corrugated nature of the cards ensures that this tiny fold will always fall in the top right-hand corner. Young officers have one great advantage. Without the least loss of dignity they can say '. . . I don't know. Show me how it's done', and, before they are bailed, most arrested gamesters, if they have been treated with the no-nonsense fairness rightly expected of practical policemen, will be flattered and only too willing to show how the cards are manipulated. Never be too proud to ask—you only appear naïve once, after that you are on the road to expertness!

Charges to consider are 'taking part in gaming' (Section 5 of the Gaming Act 1968), and for the lookouts, called 'outside men', who warn of your approach, 'obstructing police in the execution of duty' (Section 51 of the Police Act 1964). Additionally, 'obstructing free passage of the highway' (Section 121 of the Highways Act 1959) may prove useful. Like Section 5 of the Gaming Act it has a *statutory* power of arrest, which 'obstructing police' lacks. A railway carriage is a public place as far as gaming is concerned (Langrish *v* Archer 10 QBD 44).

Arresting the principal, or one of the inside men, those that are actually part of the gaming, is not easy, even in plain clothes. To get past the lookouts, not to be noticed, having the ability to blend with the background in a crowded street, is in some ways a state of mind. We all know the officer who can remove his helmet, slip on a civilian raincoat and instantly be indistinguishable from one of the crowd. On the other hand there is the officer who, even in complete plain clothes, will always be recognisable as a policeman. If you wish to pass the lookouts you must play, or rather live, the part of the inoffensive and disinterested civilian. You must not feel in any way self-conscious, excited or conspiratorial and—at all costs—you must avoid the hard, intent glance of the police officer 'on duty'. If you do any of these things, it will show plainly in your face and make it obvious to a lookout who you are. As they say in the East End of London, you must have 'chutzpah'.* Do not walk faster than the average pace of the crowd you are in, and never dart diagonally. A successful policeman needs to use a lot of this chutzpah, for example to be able to fall in step with an elderly

* Yiddish word meaning brazen confidence or presumption, especially when playing a part. It is pronounced 'hootspah'.

lady shopper as if you were her son, and walk and talk with her right up to the tricksters' position—that will fool them.

The Section 5 offence carries a maximum fine of £50, with no power to imprison. These tricksters can only be deterred by imprisonment or really substantial loss of money. They can be brought into this frame in two ways only. First, if your Justices exercise their powers of binding over offenders not to repeat the offence in really substantial sums, then they will be restrained. Not all courts are willing to do this, and it is absolutely a matter for their discretion. The second way is to find some criminal charge suitable for the circumstances. This is not so easy as it may appear.

If the inside men snatch money from dupes and run or put it on losing cards without the loser's consent (as described above), that is plainly theft or, in a joint action, perhaps a conspiracy to steal. If the trick of turning up one corner of the picture card, which the principal pretends he has not seen, and who then turns that corner down again, clandestinely turning another card's corner up, so to induce wagering on a card bound to lose (also described above), there is authority (R *v* Moore (1914) 10 Cr App. Rep. 54) that this is an 'ill practice' within the meaning of Section 17 of the Gaming Act 1845, and therefore punishable criminally as fraud. Incidentally, in the same case it was considered that evidence showing immediately after the prosecutor complained that he had been defrauded a stranger gave him money, was admissible as part of the *res gestae* (facts of the case). Such a partial return of money to an outraged and loudly complaining dupe is a not infrequent occurrence, even today. It is usually done by the 'cashier' or 'banker'.

The fact remains that, by itself, the three-card trick, simply performed, with no attendant pressures and refinements, is probably not criminal but is merely sleight of hand. In the leading case (R *v* Brixton Prison (Governor) Ex parte Sjoland and Metzier (1912) 3 KB 568 : 77 JP 23), commonly called the 'Governor of Brixton Prison's Case', it was established that the fact that two confederates pretended to a prosecutor that they were strangers to each other and thus induced him to play the three-card trick with them, and to lose substantially, was not *part of the game* and not therefore a false pretence in playing with cards, and not within Section 17 of the Gaming Act 1845. *The cheating must be in the play itself*, and not in any preliminary proceedings. Of course, the whole of the transaction may be a common law conspiracy to cheat. In the same case, Lord Alverstone said : ' . . . the three-card trick as I understand, is a game in which one person backs his ability to spot a particular card. In this case it was a card with figures on. It might have been the Queen of Spades or any particular card and the man backs his ability to spot the position of a particular card but by *sleight of hand* or quickness of movement or by manipulating the cards in some way which deceives the eye, the other player is able to induce the player, backing his ability, to put his finger on the wrong card. That in my opinion does not amount to any fraud.'

The Lord Chief Justice, who had a sporting reputation, certainly knew his 'three-card monte', for what he said in 1912 is as true now as it was then, namely that the 'trick' can be a game of skill, and difficult strictly to prove otherwise.

9. Loiterers

Every serious crime is prefaced by some form of consideration, reconnaissance and familiarisation, however short in time. Take a thief at this stage, if you can. It is in his interest as well as that of the public.

The proper use of Sections 4 and 6 of the Vagrancy Act 1824* to arrest and charge suspected persons found loitering with intent to commit serious crime (particularly housebreakers and car thieves) should never be regarded as reactionary or harsh, as is so often alleged, because it helps us positively to prevent the actual commission of serious crime and enables the intending criminals to be taken before they have committed themselves to the full responsibilities and penalties of the major or violent crime they had in mind. Who can say this is not as much in their interests as that of the public? This point is well worth remembering in cross-examination, where you may be asked why you intervened at the stage you did. Whereas there are special considerations with professional pickpockets (as has been explained in Chapter 7) remember that in your General Declaration, when you joined, you promised you would 'cause the peace to be kept and preserved and prevent all offences against the persons and properties of Her Majesty's subjects . . .'. Section 4 is a preventive piece of legislation with major crime and should be regarded always in this light.

Imagine an inexperienced advocate saying to you in cross-examination, 'If you were so certain my client intended to steal from these cars surely you should have waited until he had taken something rather than prematurely interfering and relying on this flimsy evidence as you allege, of touching door handles'. Your reply should be something after the style of, 'No sir, it was and is my duty to prevent crime occurring if I possibly can.

---

* This is a criminal provision in England and Wales which prohibits, under a penalty of 90 days imprisonment, persons loitering in public places with the intention of committing a serious offence. The section is particularly used against persons known to be professional criminals.

I am glad I arrested the accused before he stole anything. It is certainly a less serious matter for him'.

The Metropolitan Police Instruction Book (Chapter 13, para. 21 *et seq*.) and several well-known manuals (Reginald Morrish, *Criminal Law and Police Investigation*, Keech's *Notes*, Moriarty's *Police Law*, and *Notes on Criminal Law and Procedure* by the staff of the West Yorkshire Metropolitan Detective Training School) deal with suspected persons. All that is required to be known of the law on the subject is contained there, and all practical officers should be familiar with the provisions explained. *But there is more to suspects and loiterers than mere knowledge of the law, as I intend to show in this Chapter.*

In the beginning of this book, attention was drawn to the need to be persistent in street interrogation and to avoid the fatal feeling that it is luck that rules success. A similar state of mind is necessary with regard to the proper use of powers concerning 'suspected persons loitering'. Some officers voice the opinion that loiterers rarely can be observed and caught prior to their intended crime, or even by officers in uniform at all. This is arrant nonsense, the counsel of despair and a convenient excuse for idleness. Think of it this way—there may have been 30 burglaries in a year on a particular beat, so who can deny that, just prior to the actual commission of these crimes, there were 30 or more 'suspected persons frequenting or loitering with intent to enter premises and steal'. If they had been taken at this stage we would have had 30 fewer burglaries on the debit side of our crime returns and, more important, possibly 30 or more young men would not have committed a major crime with all the heartbreak this eventually brings them and their families.

Let no defeatist talk from tired men deflect you from a determination to keep the area assigned to you clear of street criminals. It may sound trite and obvious, but again it needs to be said that intending thieves are in our streets every day, waiting in fact to be taken or deterred by active and vigilant police officers.

Young officers often ask how intending thieves do loiter. The subject is vast but the discriminating officer will soon see them idling in all classes of residential district, walking slowly without apparent purpose, looking for houses to break into. Sometimes they call from door to door pretending to be looking for the address of a friend, or offering to carry out repairs or gardening, or to clean windows. In this connection, when suspicious of window cleaners, see what they have in their buckets—full or empty!

Very often, and lately with a greatly increasing frequency, thieves use motor vehicles when loitering. Dishonest men and women can loiter in a motor car just as they can on foot, and convictions have been obtained in the past many times in these circumstances (Bridge v Campbell (1947), 63 T.L.R. 470). Thieves follow delivery vans in their vehicles, waiting for the honest roundsmen to leave their vans unattended. Similarly, they follow bread and milk roundsmen, waiting for an opportunity to snatch their takings in a lonely street. If you have a large housing estate in your area, get to know the rent collectors and, if you see any men watching or following them, make sure you thoroughly interrogate them. If the watchers or followers are in cars and have bad intentions, experience shows there will be something in or about the vehicle that will justify their detention or prosecution. Serious crimes can be prevented by the sensible activity of wide-awake officers.

Try to recognise the principal traits of the solitary and opportunist car thief (see 'How to recognise a car prowler', page 38 et seq. of Nelson and Smith's Car Clouting, Thomas, Springfield, Illinois, 1958). Conduct similar to British thieves has been observed with American car thieves operating in the cities on their west coast. The thief will walk along lines of cars, occasionally looking towards the vehicles. To a watching policeman, he may be a thief or an honest man merely interested in cars. The 'crunch' comes when a thief sees something he intends to steal in a car. The change in his manner is unmistakable. He is no longer interested in other cars, as an honest man would be. His commonest course is to proceed to the building line or a recess, to consider what he has seen. He may continue on a few yards, then come back and stand near or even against the chosen vehicle. Cleverer ones may return to their own car or van to obtain an implement or merely to consider the matter and the opportunity. Nervous thieves may walk around the square formed by four streets, 'whistling in the dark' as it were, but all will return to the vehicle where the unmistakable change of mannerism took place. This trait is the commonest one I know, and is of the greatest value to the watching policeman in sorting the wheat from the chaff.

If you see a man leaning with his back against the front of a car, watch for one of the commonest methods that thieves use to break the glass of the quarter-light, i.e., by drawing back the bent elbow and returning it sharply against the glass. This movement can take place in a busy thoroughfare without suspicion being aroused. The commonest way, of course, is to break the quarter-light with a spring-loaded centre punch, a screwdriver or a large stone, as mentioned in Chapter 3.

Watch for

▷ The street loiterer whose distant head bobs down behind a line of cars, or who suddenly moves into a side turning. Never stop and look intently in that direction. Go on with the natural rhythm of walking at a normal pace in that general direction, as if you had seen nothing. Further suspicious acts will occur (important points of evidence if you have eventually to make a 'suspected person loitering' arrest) if the man watching you thinks you have not seen him. *He will at least watch you more boldly.*

Never break into a sprint towards a suspicious character you intend to interrogate, until you are about 20 yd (18 m) from him. He is probably younger than you, less encumbered with clothing and, if he runs at the moment you do, it will be exhausting to make up the intervening distance and overtake him. If you are more out of breath than he when you do catch him, he has the advantage if he intends violently to resist arrest.

Watch for

▷ Dishonest, wandering car cleaners. They are often old alcoholics and common lodging-house men, who take a bucket (often a stolen fire bucket) and, in pairs, clean cars without instructions hoping for a substantial tip upon the return of the owner. While they themselves only occasionally steal (probably because they have no permanent contact with a good receiver), experience shows that they are often car thieves' informants. In other words, they will note any car containing valuable property which they see in their wanderings and then tell or telephone the details to a thief, who will drive to the scene and do the stealing. Remember, they could become your informants as well, especially if they consider the thief has not tipped them sufficiently generously.

Watch for

▷ The fascination that multi-storey car parks seem to have for ill-disposed loiterers and thieves. There is perhaps an anonymity about these buildings, an echoing loneliness, a feeling of being unobserved, which is attractive to a thief, and of course attractive to any disturbed person who may intend to harm himself or others, or perhaps to assault children. In a recent Kensington bank robbery, the final escape vehicle, owned and taxed by the man killed in the armed fracas, was parked in a multi-storey car park, *only a few score yards from the bank.*

It pays to know as many people as possible likely to act as extra eyes for you. So cultivate the permanent attendants at these car parks; give them your telephone number and explain to them how they can ask for you to ring them back promptly if you are patrolling in a radio car at the moment they ring. Tell them you are interested in anything that seems in any way out of place or unusual, whether it is a vehicle itself, or the people that left it, or its number plate, or its excise licence, or even the visible contents. Any person left in the car apparently ill, drunk or asleep is also worth gentle inquiry. Remember to thank your informants, even when nothing results from their call.

Now, a note of warning. If you are keeping a specific observation on such a car park from some distance away, it is best not to have these attendants in your confidence over the actual observation in hand. There is always the outside chance that, however friendly and informative they have proved to be, they may still have a liaison with (or perhaps merely a corrupt tolerance of) certain select vehicle thieves. Informants are often selective; they will give you genuine and helpful information about certain crimes and still 'run with the hare' over other crimes. That is the way of the world. We will never change it, and I suppose it has advantages because informers need to 'keep their hand in' to be knowledgeable and thus useful. It is no good having informers who know no thieves and know nothing of the ethos of thieving!

Watch for
▷ The loiterers who steal vehicles, and from them, in car park yards and multi-storey buildings. Their behavioural patterns and those of honest men entering to get their own cars are so different.

When an honest man approaches a car park his attention is towards his own vehicle. He may show passing interest in unusual or powerful cars, but principally he is looking to see if his own is still where he left it. He then directly enters and goes straight to it, enters it and, after manœuvring it with the confidence of long use, drives out and away with no intent glances to see if he has been observed by other persons. He, you see, just does not care.

The thief approaches the yard or multi-storey park looking about him to see if he has been 'clocked' by an alert policeman outside the park. No glances yet into the car park. When he does enter he does one of two things; he either glances about and walks around seeking a car that is a worthwhile 'mark', or obviously orientates himself in relation to the position of a car worth stealing which he has been told about—probably by phone—by dishonest attendants, who not infrequently are thieves' informants. You will not usually be able to get near enough to see the thief actually break into the car of his choice, but he will not drive it with the same ease as an owner. The patterns are so different that you should quickly detect them by observation away from and above the park. A cheap pair of Japanese or South Korean binoculars, costing £15* or so of 7×50 specification (so they can be used at dusk), are a good investment.

Do not absolve people from suspicion solely because they have what appears to be a ticket in their hand. It may be blank paper or, if a genuine ticket, for a decoy vehicle of their own, previously placed in the park either to provide an alibi or for transporting stolen gear. This is very much the pattern with multi-storey car park thieves.

Criminals loiter near banks, post offices and business premises, watching the pattern of cash deliveries and almost always with a vehicle near at hand. Small fry wander through residential districts looking for unoccupied houses, where they can steal lead and copper fittings, including garden ornaments. Before they enter any of these premises they will loiter nearby with their vehicle, awaiting a period when they feel unobserved. They may pretend to be honest 'rag and bone' men to disguise their deceitful intentions. If bicycles are left outside a public library or technical school, suspects will loiter in the vicinity, awaiting an opportunity to steal them. These days, cycle thieves use a van quickly after the actual thefts, as they do when stealing small motor cycles. There is an increasing and profitable market for stolen motor cycles, large or small.

To a practised eye such men and women will stand out for what they are, and skill in picking out these loiterers can be attained by any young officer determined to acquire it. Make a real effort to have a look at all thieves arrested in your area. When you attend court, look at the list of charges. Perhaps a skilled or persistent thief is appearing that morning. Make it your business to look at him and listen to him speak. Your knowledge of him may be invaluable to the public later in your service. Has this thief a novel way of stealing cars, or using vehicles in the commission of other crimes? Has he been breaking into houses in a novel way? Find out from the officer in charge of the case the new method, and watch for it being repeated.

* About $30.

Watch for

▷ Two or more males at a telephone kiosk. This is generally suspicious and worth inquiry or observation. For example, two inside and one outside, if they seem to be together, is certainly suspicious as it is the classic behaviour of persons stealing from the prepayment boxes. If one has a newspaper open or propped up inside the kiosk so as to obscure his hands this is an extra sign. Experience shows that such men will have with them some tool to force the money-box, so in most cases you can interfere quickly and arrest them for 'going equipped to steal' and not wait for the full crime to happen. The same applies to the thieves who steal from parking meters. Some obtain a key but many of the younger ones carry a small-hafted but heavy hammer and simply knock the head off the meter, stealing the contents at their convenience.

Watch for

▷ Unaccompanied men loitering in cars in the evening, near telephone exchanges,* teacher training colleges or nurses' homes. They may be respectable young men waiting for their sweethearts. On the other hand, they may be men intending to snatch handbags, or to expose themselves, or violently to assault one of the young women entering or leaving. You must decide whether to watch them or let yourself be seen, but never endanger a possible victim, child or female, by observation at too long a range. The same applies if a woman officer has volunteered to act as a decoy.

Watch for

▷ The possession of 'These are your rights' cards or pamphlets by loiterers generally. While this may be slightly suspicious, there is real reservation. Obviously, they will be carried by persons who consider it at least possible that they will break the law and be interrogated by police. Thus they are carried by male homosexuals, by industrial and other agitators, by 'Angry Brigade'† inadequates and similar amateur criminals, *but rarely by shrewd and hardheaded professional thieves.* The latter have no need for academic discussion of legal niceties; they know from bitter experience how to behave in custody. Anyway, possession of such written matter often means subsequent false complaint against you. Be circumspect with intellectual malcontents; they can be bitchy and smallminded in these complaints.

* May also be 'phone freaks'.
† British urban guerrillas.

Watch for

▷ Those suspicious circumstances, generally, where the loiterers you interrogate live in the immediate area. Unfortunately, because of television thrillers and novels, our minds expect crimes to be committed by a 'mysterious stranger'. This is completely at variance with the truth, for there is plain statistical evidence available to show that the great majority of violent sexual crimes, and indeed burglaries, are committed by persons who are either acquainted with, or in some way related to, the victim, or at least are familiar with the area in which they are operating. Of course, there are cases where strangers enter an area and commit vile crimes. News reports show this but, because of its importance to a flexible police attitude, I emphasise that the majority of such crimes are committed by local people or persons that were once local people. Consequently, never absolve people from suspicion solely because 'they live in the next street'. A subtle old detective sergeant once rather dogmatically said that well over half of all housebreakings are committed by those thieves, usually juveniles, who live less than three miles away from the break-ins. Nothing in my experience over the past 28 years has altered, in my mind, the basic truth of this observation.

Watch for

▷ In a general sense, the clothing of loiterers. There are subtle differences. At night, a suspicious character may have clothing seemingly darker than normal. Bear in mind his class of life, his age and his style of dressing. There is perhaps a subconscious desire by offenders to dress in such a way that they merge into the dusk at night time. They may not realise they are doing it, but they are attempting camouflage. This can be a pointer which, with other suspicions, may cause you promptly to interfere and interrogate. Once-white, rubber-soled tennis shoes that have been blacked over with shoe polish or black dye are suspicious.

Bear in mind that a similar ruse is not uncommon with car thieves—although the clothing here is usually a boiler suit, white or navy blue. Really good car thieves seem to prefer white. They can drive to the scene of their crimes, dressed in plain, respectable clothes. They put their boiler suits on inside their cars or vans and look for all the world like honest workmen. They commit the crime where they may or must be seen by witnesses. They then return to their vehicle, remove the boiler suits and drive away. Quite apart from a totally different appearance, they can now act confidently with a policeman speaking to them, posing as respectable middle-class men, backed by neat clothes.

Watch for

▷ The condition both of a loiterer's hands and his general appearance. The not-so-obvious differences between an honest working man and a lazy thief are often there for a discerning officer. For example, an honest working bricklayer's finger-ends are worn almost smooth through handling bricks. An agricultural worker has a hardness over most of the inner and outer surfaces of his hands; additionally, the back of his hands will have numerous scratch marks, particularly in summer. There will almost certainly be a 'livestock' smell about his clothing, and if he has daily dealings with poultry or swine the odour will be more intense than with a cowman. An urban local authority labourer has hardness and callouses, usually only on the inner aspects of his hands, as does a scaffolding erector. Their clothing will not have any distinctive smell. The odour of tarmacadam may be detected in the clothing of road-mending labourers. A clerk's right middle finger often has a callous on the inner aspect of the upper phalange, through years of pen-holding. Often, too, there will be ball-point ink stains on his cuffs and fingers. There is, too, an air about clerks difficult to define, a sort of docility and, in general, smiling agreement. Their clothing often has about it a certain faded gentility and 'establishment' look, especially with middle-aged (and older) clerks. A housepainter will have callouses across his shins, due to his frequent standing on one rung of a ladder, supporting himself against the next rung up—he may well have paint or distemper drops on his eyelashes, too, and possibly in his hair. White paint, frequently used by housepainters, will be in the corners of his nails, particularly on his working hand, probably his right. His hands will have the smell of paint and putty. A window cleaner's hands often have a 'washerwoman' look. A baker (not the roundsman) will have traces of flour in his nails, ears and hair and have the unmistakable smell of warm dough about him. Bakers also have a very distinctive paleness about their complexion. They are often about the streets in the very early hours. Schoolmasters will have chalk dust on their hands and clothes, and in facial hair, particularly their eyelashes. Electricians will have tiny half-healed pinpoint holes on the bulbs of their thumbs and forefingers due to frequently rolling and smoothing over of the sharp-ended strands of multicore wire when connecting them to plugs. Nurses, male and female, hospital porters and physicians will have a hospital smell about them.*

The hands of a confirmed car thief are often both oil-stained and ingrained with hardened, greasy dirt! Why? Because he often tinkers with the electrical contacts inside the bonnets of cars. Similarly, his hands may have rust stains on them, through tampering with used index plates and spare wheels. Be sensibly suspicious of these signs, as an honest car mechanic's hands may seem much the same, although with honest men *ingrained oily dirt will probably be absent.* There is a general tendency for thieves not to be over-fastidious with cleanliness, whereas an honest mechanic, so often a family man, will purchase and use chemical cleansers, for he has to be clean at family meals. The oil stains on his hands will therefore tend to be fresher.

Try to determine these differences between the industrial marks of an honest man and the general appearance of a thief. The significance of these signs to patrolling policemen is that it assists in coming to a conclusion when a man up to no good claims an honest trade or profession. There will be additional similar signs about those working men exclusive to your particular district; make an effort to recognise these as well; it is so worth while and occasionally you will have the pleasure of being thought very shrewd indeed when you accurately recognise trade or employment without questioning.

Watch for

▷ The 'athlete' dressed in a tracksuit, running about residential streets, either at dusk or in the early morning. While one must not become morbidly suspicious, experience does indicate that there seems to be a correlation between such persons and homosexual nuisances. I know of a man, respectably dressed in middle-class clothes, who was recently driving to residential areas, with a tracksuit over his clothes, and then running around looking for youngsters to molest. He then took off his tracksuit, put it in the boot of his car and, totally different now from any description remembered or circulated, left the scene safe from interrogation.

---

* Doctors and dentists, quite apart from this antiseptic odour, have a certain confident arrogance (I do not mean this offensively) about them, particularly when dealing with any matter even remotely connected with medicine. It is an easily recognisable trait once the observer has identified in his mind what to look for.

Wigs, Balaclava helmets and nylon stocking masks have obvious practical value as disguises for violent, professional thieves, but additionally these disguises seem to be associated with unbalanced males who intend some passive sexual parading or exhibitionism. Remember, if you catch a loiterer in possession of such bizarre gear you may not have a violent thief but only some pathetic unbalanced fellow who dreams of being a 'master criminal' or has sexual delusions. This reservation applies particularly if the arrest is at night, and in a poorer quality residential area where the pickings for professionals would be somewhat thin.

Watch for

▷ and think carefully about the 'lost person'. This is a not uncommon excuse of those found in incriminating circumstances. Is it really likely they are lost? When considering their explanation, find out how long they have lived in neighbouring areas; this could show their story to be unreasonable. Watch, too, for an unusual persistency—an individual who keeps coming back to a certain location is worth gentle inquiry.

Watch for

▷ The loiterer who has aroused your suspicions when you both are some distance from public transport. Remember, he may have a car parked nearby, which could contain incriminating articles. It is more sensible and productive to say firmly, 'Where is that vehicle of yours parked?' rather than, 'Do you have a car?' (do not say 'car' anyway; if it is a van* or motor cycle he will know you are bluffing).

Suspicious behaviour by any loiterer is, of course, of great interest to patrolling police but remember not all loiterers intend to commit offences of dishonesty. The behaviour of the more usual prowlers, intent mainly on thieving, has been discussed. Now the less usual come under consideration. For example, there are 'peeping toms', who prowl about parks and open spaces to spy on courting couples, and who trespass in housing estates and private property generally, hoping to see intimate acts through the windows of living rooms and bedrooms.

These days they use the lifts in high-rise buildings, searching at night to find a landing or roof where they can look down into the bedrooms of flats, often with binoculars. In such buildings the inhabitants are less fastidious about curtains, as they imagine they are too high up to be

* English word for truck.

observed. This attitude, of course, attracts these pests. If you are working in plain clothes bear in mind, before you rush to the scene, the possibility and the danger to your reputation, and that of your force, of being mistaken for such a man by outraged householders themselves searching for an offender. My advice is to keep in pairs in such circumstances, and before you go into or on private property, make sure you have told somebody, preferably a tenant or local householder, what you are doing.

Anybody seen or spoken of as frequenting the very top floor of a tower block of flats should receive attention. The roof is only rarely visited. Experience has shown that absconders from remand homes and detention centres, even prison escapees, hide and sleep there, sometimes in the room housing the lift machinery. It is also a not unlikely place for sexual offences against young children in the day and early evening time. Do not forget that boiler room warmth attracts homeless thieves 'on the run', as well as harmless vagrants. In winter, visit the boiler rooms of the big hospitals and large factories on your patch at least once in the' early hours. Ask the stoker about callers seeking warmth; you may hit on a badly wanted man.

Unattended and unlocked church and chapel stokeholds, usually under the tower if there is one, often house vagrants even though for most of the week there is no heat. Is there a badly wanted man or prison escapee who is local to your area? Cycle around to these places about four or five in the morning, especially in bitter weather, you may make quite a capture!

Wherever prostitutes congregate with their clients, or 'jockeys' as they contemptuously* call them, there will be other loiterers—the 'jims' who watch the transaction and purchased intimacies in a morbid and unhealthy silence. A small percentage of these men are dishonest, and will steal a courting girl's hangbag left beside a couple on the ground if they can. Prostitutes are too worldly wise to let their handbags out of their possession even for a moment. To take the liberal view, I suppose it can be said that mere watching, passive as it seems to be, is pretty harmless and not worthy of intensive police attention. This may be a superficial view, for many extremely violent crimes, the infamous A6 murder†, for example, have been triggered off—either against the peeper by an outraged man whose sexual privacy has been invaded—or by the peeper himself when his lustful

---

* This considerable contempt shown by prostitutes should be recognised and allowed for by police; it can sometimes be a motive for violent crime in itself.
† A notorious English 'lovers' lane' murder.

feelings have been stimulated beyond endurance. The line between violence and sexual behaviour generally, is a narrow one. A man who imagines he is being mocked over his virility or sexual capacity may become unreasoning and violent. This facet of life is one of the concealed reasons behind the murders of street prostitutes, and certainly is often behind the violence that can occur between man and wife. Other signs in this line of country which should alert you are as follows:

Watch for

▷ Any destructive act against property which, by a generous stretch of the imagination, can be thought to be in some way sexually motivated or symbolic. For example, placing or throwing ink or filth over the clean clothing of women or children, the cutting off of young girls' hair or the cutting with a razor blade of women's clothing, which can occur, unknown to the victim, in crowds or in bus queues. Women's underclothing is often stolen from laundry baskets and clothes lines, to be taken home by somewhat pathetic and passive sexual inadequates. This is always very much a nuisance, but when such stolen clothing is found ripped or cut, or fouled with excrement, blood or semen, especially near the scene of the theft, a different and possibly dangerous situation is hatching. Police officers should do all they can in these alarming circumstances to get the man responsible into custody as soon as possible, and available for proper medical care, before some tragedy occurs.

In your endeavours to catch this latter type of man, bear in mind the likelihood that he may be a local fellow of most respectable background. He may also be known to his intended victim, but whether he is or not, you can take it as a real probability that he will know her, or at least will have watched her at her work or in her home. He may be a most inoffensive-looking juvenile. Such statistics as are available overwhelmingly indicate these likelihoods. The stealing of female clothing tends to occur in estates of semi-detached or terraced houses, usually in the lower or middle socio-economic districts, at night. Patrolling such roads in pairs, in plain clothes, will probably be counter-productive as the culprit is likely to know the area very well and, as strangers, you will be too obvious. The best method seems to be static observation from a van parked in a rear entry or alley between gardens.

Simple mechanical or electric battery alarms can be rigged up across the private paths in gardens, and the use of chemical dye on clothes lines and on the tops of walls may be useful. The best system, however, is quietness by your colleague and yourself, and careful listening from your place of observation. Beware of idle chatter between you and your colleague when on long-drawn-out observations at night. The noise can carry many hundreds of yards. Be careful of smoking, too. Tests show a cigarette's glow can be seen for 300 yd (275 m) at night, a struck match no less than 900 yd (823 m). The aromatic smell of a pipe seems to carry farther on the night air, too. If you intend to eat sandwiches while on observation, have them wrapped in cloth not paper. Make arrangements for urination and take care to do this quietly. Take a wide-necked screwtop glass jar (the typical instant coffee jar is ideal) for this purpose. The use of cotton and pins to use as 'marks' to see whether a door has been opened, or a path along a back entry used in your absence, is now a little old fashioned. Transparent adhesive tape (Sellotape or Scotchtape) has many adaptations in this area of use, particularly with house or garage doors. A very small piece of this tape, placed at the bottom of a car door, overlapping the frame, will quickly tell you if a vehicle has been opened in your absence. A properly conducted and silent observation, the sort that succeeds, is a great test of self-discipline and beyond the abilities of slack and idle men. Take pride in carrying out these difficult tasks with professional skill.

Watch for

▷ Any lonely part of the police area for which you have responsibility becoming a well-known meeting place for homosexuals. Bear in mind that nearly everything already said about abnormalities in relation to male and female contacts occurs with homosexual relationships. Violence here is again very near the surface, with the added possibility of frenzied robbery of the passive party in the pairing or attempted pairing. All open areas frequented by homosexuals should receive attention by patrolling uniformed police, preferably in pairs, not with a view to harassing them, but to ensure peace keeping, and reasonable behaviour, and as a presence to discourage violence by certain unbalanced 'men' who deliberately prey on such unfortunates. Remember how prevalent in male-to-male robbery cases is the counterfeit 'Pompey defence'.*

* The 'Pompey (or Portsmouth) defence', so called because of its currency at one time in this large naval port, is as follows. Explanation by man arrested for robbery, 'Rob him, of course I didn't. But I admit hitting him because he made vile homosexual suggestions to me. It was more than a respectable man could stand. I don't know where his money went—somebody must have stolen it after I left him lying there.' The unmanly humbug and hypocrisy of this is obvious, but not easy to disprove.

Watch for

▷ Any close-knit group of three or more young men, especially if not of homosexual appearance (or rather what popularly passes as homosexual appearance), who are noticed repeatedly frequenting these areas at night—parks, towpaths and commons. They may have in mind evil and violent robbery, which they refer to euphemistically as 'queer rolling' or 'queer bashing'. One suspicious form of behaviour in such situations is an over-boisterous, over-loud, joint humour and horseplay which may be just high spirits, of course. On the other hand, it can be a joint working up of sufficient courage, if that is the right word, to 'haze'* a homosexual, especially one who has the appearance of affluence combined with meekness.

These young men should be approached and questioned. Do not fall into the trap of being terse and jumping to conclusions. Never use rough phrases or slang terms that may later be mistaken as bullying and certainly sound bad when repeated in court. Ask them politely where they have been drinking, get their names, ask about their vehicles. Never refer directly to your suspicions, just let them realise you have your eye on them, but in the nicest possible way. A group of young bullies, who rationalise their greed by pretending to themselves that homosexuals need to be 'punished', are unlikely to carry out their cowardly tricks if they have just had their names and the index marks of their vehicles (often motor cycles) taken by a couple of hard-eyed—but perfectly well-mannered—police officers. Unfortunately, some servicemen prey on homosexuals. They, too, can be dissuaded by the method described above.

Prevention of these crimes is particularly important as so many go unreported, are very damaging mentally to both the perpetrators (who may, after several 'successes', become either male prostitutes themselves, or go in for even more violent forms of robbery) and to the victims, who may be driven even as far as suicide over such evil bullying. Of course, this sort of violence to homosexuals has in the past led to deaths at or near the scene of the bullying.

When you are driving through the typically lonely places frequented by homosexuals, and your lights pick out a motor car with apparently only one occupant and then, as you get nearer, another head suddenly appears, oral masturbation may be going on. Whatever your views are over such

---

* Slang term for violent bullying of a homosexual, combined with insulting banter and ridicule.

100

behaviour, remember that such public intimacies can be the trigger of violent crime by others, and should be discouraged in the long-term interests both of the public and those of the persons indulging. Do not make moral judgements, just endeavour to reduce the likelihood of violent crime by getting them out of it.

Just to digress for a moment, circumstances will inevitably arise when you have to arrest homosexuals for 'importuning for immoral purposes' or 'gross indecency'. Public lavatories are often the scene of this sad behaviour and, perhaps because of this, a frequent and often false defence is that the person arrested has a weak bladder and, out of necessity, had constantly but quite innocently to frequent the urinal in question. This defence is occasionally corroborated, when the accused is wealthy, by imposing medical evidence.

My advice in these matters, and with 'indecent exposure' cases where this same defence is often advanced, is invariably to note in your official pocket book the number of times the accused man, after arrest and when at the police station, used the lavatory. It is difficult for such a counterfeit defence to ring true if in cross-examination you are able personally, or by the police advocate, to introduce the fact that in the (say) two hours, from the time of his arrest until his bail, he did not once (if such is the case) make use of the urinal facilities at the police station.

Watch for

▷ Heroin addicts in relation to crimes against homosexuals. As I have said in *Thieves on Wheels*, addicts are almost invariably thieves and sometimes violent thieves. It is noticeable that they seem to prey on male and female homosexuals, but particularly on the males. They may even pretend to be homosexuals themselves, so as to batten on to them. If you visit a chain restaurant or transport café and see a young person, especially if unkempt or haggard-looking, possibly with patchy face acne, taking inordinately large helpings of sugar in his tea or coffee, this may indicate an addict. They seem to have a huge appetite for sugar. Such young people who fold their arms across their chests and scratch their upper arms, and the sides of their chests, are going through the classic behaviour of the beginning of withdrawal symptoms of the heroin addict. Frequent yawning is also a sign. Because of circulation difficulties they may wear more than one pullover or cardigan, or a tattered sheep-skin coat in summery weather. If these signs are combined with a runny nose and red eyes, you are almost certainly looking at an addict and, by natural inference, a thief. Remember, too, that addicts are liars, even when there is no apparent point in lying. There is a marked similarity between the onset of the withdrawal symptoms of confirmed heroin addicts and the superficial appearance of the symptoms of the common cold developing into influenza and—in serious cases—into pneumonia. Be humane but careful with them. If they bite or scratch you when you arrest them, remember that a high proportion suffer from the venereal diseases; their teeth and nails are often left unclean for weeks, and a significant number have infective hepatitis, contracted from the use of a filthy or improvised syringe. Get medical attention promptly if you are bitten or scratched and, even if you have only touched them when searching, thoroughly scrub your hands. Try to do this out of their presence, so as not to offend them unnecessarily.

To return to the ways of prowlers. A significant number of night-time loiterers and wanderers are perfectly honest persons, trying to 'walk off' emotional, marital or delusional problems. Husbands and wives, following violent argument, not infrequently rush out into the street and walk for hours. Adolescent sons and daughters behave similarly after disagreement with parents. They may be so emotionally upset as to appear very suspicious indeed. Occasionally running for short distances, for example, or glancing back repeatedly, or looking intently into vehicles, trying to find a place to sleep—not to steal. They will frequently be heard talking to themselves. If they have gone out without tobacco, males may walk with their heads down looking for cigarette ends. If they are beside a line of cars this can, from a distance, seem exactly to duplicate the behaviour of a car thief.

These emotionally charged people, in an endeavour to cool their family resentments, drive their own vehicles heedlessly to the very limits of safety. This can appear very suspicious when they disregard or are impatient with automatic signs and the like. It is difficult advice, but try to discriminate between youthful motor thieves and such cases; remember, a police chase can escalate the situation into tragedy.

Both men and women in this emotionally induced wandering condition, and craving tobacco, may stop other late-night walkers to ask for a cigarette. This can appear very suspicious, both to the person stopped and to a watching policeman, it being mistaken for the opening gambits of street 'muggers' or prostitutes. Middle-aged women, under the stress of the menopausal condition, also wander in an emotionally disturbed manner.

If you have pride in yourself as a worldly man and good policeman, as you should have of course, learn to recognise these signs and act understandingly and humanely with the people concerned. Never treat them as if they were law breakers. Young people should be driven home promptly (if they will go—otherwise to the police station), as they are plainly in moral and sometimes physical danger. Mature people may be so disturbed as to be near to harming themselves; so even with adults there is a case, almost unchallengeable and in the public interest, that they should be taken home in a vehicle.

Wanderers at night who seem really ill, in a nervous, mental or alcoholic (not drunken) sense, need firm and brotherly handling by police. They may be 'hearing voices', 'know they are being followed by secret agents', 'are being gassed', 'are having their inner strength sucked out by radio waves', or 'must see the Queen'. They may be so ill as to be visibly shaking. Never try logically to challenge the foolishness of what they say. It will not work. Neither will telling them to 'snap out of it!' Be informal and friendly; never humour them with lies, because when they eventually realise they have been lied to, their sense of betrayal and persecution will be heightened by the plain evidence of your falsehood. It is unmanly to cheat in this way merely for short-term convenience or a 'laugh'. Of course, it is also inefficient and unprofessional. Try to get them willingly to a place of safety—the usual place being the station. If you are wearing a helmet or cap, take it off. Smile in a genuine way and say something like, 'How about coming and having a cup of tea with me? You look as if you need a sit down and a chat. You have an interesting story and we would like to hear it. You may think you are all right, but you cannot do yourself any good out here in the open, and you certainly look tired out. Slip in the car with me and my colleague (mate). I tell you plainly that if you were my own brother (sister) I would say exactly the same. Come now, into the car and put the matter in our hands.'

This sort of humane police action can avoid unneccessary violence and help positively in bringing them round. These people, when alone and wandering, can be near to harming themselves and are so vulnerable (particularly females) to being taken advantage of by unscrupulous people they meet at night.

The greatest single attribute in successful police duty, whether it be thief taking or dealing with straightforward people, is an ease and fluent charm of manner. An ease of manner with thieves need not lack firmness and is based on the absence of judging them. All criminals—thieves, ponces,

103

pimps, fraudsmen, sexual and violent offenders—are as quick as any other human to detect priggish censure of their conduct, even if done silently with only an intent and disapproving glance. This presumption to judge people *must be avoided*. You can never know the inner reasons why these people are what they are. Try constantly to think in terms of 'There, but for the grace of God, go I'. This attitude of mind leads naturally and genuinely to an open-handed manner, which invites frankness and which scores and scores again—even with experienced, hard-nosed thieves. The next most important attribute is to try to think like the opportunist thief. In the street, look around you and consider, 'What is there here worthy of stealing? How?' Think like this (with the best of intentions, of course!) and eventually you will be on the scene, or at least near it, when direct crime is being committed. What more can a young policeman, anxious to prove himself, want? If you wish to detect and expose crime, *understand criminals*, and remember Lincoln's phrase, 'You catch more flies with honey than you do with vinegar'.

Never be disappointed because your 'stops' are not always recorded as arrests. Who is to say that an apparently unsuccessful stop is not a crime prevented? Real effort will give your police area a reputation that it is a hot place for criminal loiterers and persons foolishly risking the conveyance of stolen property or contraband across it. Arrests and captures are important, of course, but activity by uniformed officers in speaking to loiterers and suspicious persons is what is required *to reduce the incidence of serious crime*. Do what you can to confine and restrict the mobility of criminals in their vehicles, and so diminish their chances of effecting tactical surprise at the scenes of their intended crimes.

10. Handling stolen property

How to be sharper than those who transport and traffic in stolen property.

In relation to 'stopping' suspect motor cars in busy streets, a few detailed words about valuable property seen or found inside such vehicles in suspicious circumstances. In London and many other large built-up areas, because of their vast size and because of the great mobility of thieves and receivers using motor vehicles within their borders, it will repeatedly occur that a driver will be found in possession of property of substantial value in his car, quite obviously stolen, but whose owner, it seems, is unlikely to be discovered. Thus the original theft probably cannot be proved. You will often have to make up your mind very quickly whether to detain the driver, often in difficult circumstances, perhaps with a great deal of traffic building up behind you and with the pressure of constant honking of horns.

Try to keep calm and bear in mind that the charge of dishonestly receiving (under Section 22(1) of the Theft Act 1968) does not necessarily depend on there being direct evidence of the original theft. This emphasises how profitable careful questioning (with questions previously listed in a notebook and with the replies accurately recorded in the same book) can be in convincing the court that the charge of 'dishonestly receiving' that you have brought against the driver is both fair and absolutely correct. The 'universal' questions I suggest you should have written down follow later in this chapter, but first I emphasise you must try to obtain some other evidence (i.e., additional to the absence of evidence of true ownership) upon which the court can hold ' . . . that *the circumstances in which the accused was found in possession of property* would lead any reasonable person to draw the inference that it has been stolen. . . .' (Noon *v* Smith, 1929 J.P. 48: [1964] 3 All E.R. 895). Actual proof of the ownership of the goods may be dispensed with (R. *v* Fuschillo, [1940] 2 All E.R. 489).

In the overwhelming majority of cases, the essence of what you have to prove is 'guilty knowledge' or, more plainly, belief that the goods were stolen *at the time* the property came into the hands or control of the man you are speaking to (R. *v* Johnson (1911), 75 J.P. 464, and R. *v* Tennet, [1939] 1 All E.R. 86); that the circumstances of such receipt plainly indicate of themselves that the property itself must be stolen; and that he knew it when he (dishonestly) received it (R. *v* Sbarra (1918), 82 J.P. 171; R. *v* Fuschillo, above). Remember, innocent receipt of stolen goods, and subsequent disposal with *guilty knowledge*, may be a criminal offence. Also remember that reckless and careless receipt of goods is not necessarily the same as receiving goods knowing them to be stolen (R. *v* Havard (1914), 11 Cr. App. R.2).

Although not absolute by any means, it is more than valuable to be able to show that the doubtful goods were purchased (or said to have been purchased) at an absurdly low price; or that they were secretly or covertly put into the car at an unusual time, at night or in the very early morning, for example; or that delicate and valuable gear (tape recorders, radios and the like) were found in a rough sack or hidden under the sort of valueless lumber often found in the boot of a car; also that perhaps the suspect has supplied you with an untruthful explanation of how the property came to be in the car, which other evidence successfully can challenge. A denial of possessing property subsequently found, in his presence, to be in the car, under circumstances where *he must have known it was there*, is certainly useful evidence. The fact that it was knowingly concealed in the car, and perhaps *that marks of identity on the property were intentionally altered or obliterated* without good explanation, can be very convincing prosecution evidence indeed.

As I said before, it is advisable to have numbered and standard questions you can ask in strict order. Until you are practised and flexible in putting these questions it is more helpful to have them written out on a piece of card in your pocket book. An additional advantage is that you have only to write down replies received, if you invariably ask the numbered questions in strict order.

Where there is more than one suspect, separate them and question independently. If you have a colleague with you, arrange for him to keep all the suspects under close watch while you question them separately one at a time. This will enable you to compare the answers of all concerned. If you are posted consistently with the same officer, alternate the system and jointly become more expert in the matter. *It is certain to bring results.* Remember this, too—when suspects are separated it is very difficult for them to co-ordinate either an assault on you or an attempt at escape.

Independent questioning can quickly frustrate a lying tale of explanation. The questions are:

1. Where did you get it?
2. How long have you had it?
3. How much did you pay for it?
4. How did you pay for it?
5. How much do you think it is worth?
6. Did you get a receipt for it?
7. What is the name and address of the seller?
8. Did the seller have other similar articles with him when you bought it?
9. Where did the sale take place?
10. What time of day was it when the sale took place?
11. Was there anyone else there whose name and address you know?
12. Did you pay the price asked, or was there bargaining?
13. Did you think it odd at the time you bought it that it was so cheap?

And, depending on the replies given, your last question before caution could well be:

14. Don't you think it odd that a person you have never seen before suddenly approaches you and asks you to buy property of this value in a public house/in the street/in a club?

The offence of 'receiving' is as much an offence under the Theft Act as it was under the old Larceny Act, and the authorities quoted are still valid. Nevertheless, it should be borne in mind that offences in this area of dishonesty have been widened considerably in their scope and there is available now (in the latter part of Section 22) a *finer meshed net* designed to catch a class of dishonest persons who were outside the provisions of the older statute. *Dishonestly undertaking the retention, removal, disposal or realisation of stolen goods* (by or for the benefit of another) *are now clearly crimes.*

The exact wording of Section 22(1) is as follows:

A person handles stolen goods if (otherwise than in the course of the stealing) knowing or believing them to be stolen good he dishonestly receives the goods, or dishonestly undertakes or assists in their retention, removal, disposal or realisation by or for the benefit of another person, or if he arranges to do so.

Remember the latter points of this section when you are following up inquiries or find evidence *that others were involved previously* with the stolen goods.

107

11. Men trafficking in prostitution (I)

Five straightforward and proven steps which will secure overwhelming evidence.

Trading in prostitution, certainly when it involves libertines living well on the degradation of frailer human beings, has always aroused revulsion. With policemen this feeling is intensified, perhaps because they see at close quarters the sordid exploitation that it is, and know there is no motive involved other than rapacious greed.

A few years ago there was current a trendy view among social scientists that these gross offences were 'victimless crimes', and never worth for a moment the police effort necessary for effective prosecution. 'Would it really matter if you never again arrested a ponce?' they would quack with quite profound unworldliness, inferring that the man-hours necessary would better be spent in '. . . catching real criminals . . .' and leaving these 'fancy men' alone.

The superficiality of this view has recently become plain enough, but then it seemed to be quite overlooked that, if financially successful ponces were not subject to a continuing and rigorous enforcement of the criminal law, huge amounts of untaxed money would regularly accrue to persons of basically criminal character. In turn, this idle money would be used secretly to finance other crimes, particularly major fraud, to corner the filthy trade of hard pornography where profits are enormous, then to corrupt public servants, and eventually to entrench the criminals in a counterfeit but well-heeled respectability, making prosecution a costly and major police effort. 'Gelt gait zu gelt' (Yiddish for money makes money) applies in organised prostitution no less than in any honest commerce. One of the sternest tasks facing the reorganised Metropolitan Police Force in 1972, a chore now happily almost completed, was to put these matters right. So much for the theory of 'victimless crimes' when applied to ponces.

In England and Wales the offence was created by the now defunct

Vagrancy Act 1898. It now forms Section 30 of the Sexual Offences Act 1956, and reads:

30. (1) It is an offence for a man knowingly to live wholly or in part on the earnings of prostitution.

(2) For the purposes of ths section a man who lives with or is habitually in the company of a prostitute, or who exercises control, direction or influence over a prostitute's movement in a way which shows he is aiding, abetting or compelling her prostitution with others, shall be presumed to be knowingly living on the earnings of prostitution, unless he proves the contrary.

The offence is punishable on indictment or summarily. On indictment, imprisonment for seven years can be inflicted; summarily, six months. The accused cannot claim to be tried on indictment. The mode of trial is the absolute prerogative of the prosecution (R. *v* Dickinson, ex parte Grandolini (1917) 2 K.B. 393). Summarily, a fine of £100 may be imposed (Section 27(3) of the Magistrates' Courts Act 1952, as amended).

The provision of the shift of onus of proof, shown in the second subsection, was designed to bring into the frame of prosecution those ponces* or *souteneurs* who, although living parasitically on prostitutes, had either employment or means of their own, and were thus in a position to pose to a court as outside the criminal provisions. The burden of proof so placed on a man in these circumstances is not so heavy as that placed on the prosecution generally in criminal cases. An accused can discharge it by satisfying a jury upon the basis of 'balance of probability' rather than 'beyond reasonable doubt' (R. *v* Carr-Briant (1943) 2 All E.R. 156), and a jury should be directed upon this point. Nevertheless, the provision is invaluable in its ability to cast a finer meshed net, and evidence to bring a ponce within its provisions should be sought for relentlessly.

Bear in mind that police experience has shown repeatedly (disregarding the occasional lesbianistic relationship) that where there is a prostitute, there will be a ponce. No matter what is said by the woman, no matter if superficial inquiry confirms her denial of his existence, do not be deflected, he is there. One of his attributes is that he gives the prostitute, often shunned and lonely in her private life, a husband-like companionship. It seems immaterial that he is probably violent to her, that he takes most of her money and squanders it, the prostitute wants someone to care for in a womanly way on a permanent basis, and is willing, even anxious, to pay the

* London slang for pimps—see Glossary, however, for the differences in definition.

price. Thus, one of the rarer ways of police coming to know about a ponce is by way of complaint by the prostitute. But if she does complain, there is no absolute rule of law that her evidence must be corroborated. She may or may not be an accomplice, but juries are invariably warned to be cautious with her evidence (R. *v* King (1914) 111 LT 80 and see R. *v* Pickford (1914) 10 Cr. App. R.269). In practice, of course, corroboration should be sought, either by a short period of police observation or by inquiry. Remember, the woman is reporting a serious crime, punishable on indictment with seven years' imprisonment. Whether or not full corroboration can be obtained, the best course is to take a full statement from her, reduce it to the form of an information, and take her before a Justice of the Peace, so he can consider whether to issue a warrant for the accused's arrest under Section 1 of the Magistrates' Courts Act 1952, or a search and arrest warrant (to be discussed later) under Section 42 of the Sexual Offences Act 1956. If the complaining prostitute is the wife of the accused man, she is a competent but not compellable witness (R. *v* Leach (1912) AC 305; 7 Cr. App. R.157, H.L., and Section 39 Sexual Offences Act 1956).

Police usually get to know about a ponce by using their eyes and seeing him together fleetingly with his prostitute(s), so

Watch for

▷ The mannerisms these people have with each other in the street, which are quite unlike the prostitute and client relationship. The latter is a stilted and formal negotiation; with a customer the prostitute has a strangely distant manner, a sort of sly and smiling contempt. The customer is usually hesitant and embarrassed, whereas the ponce has the familiar husband-to-wife assurance, which is unmistakable. If you see a prostitute in the early hours of the morning, with a much older and more conservatively dressed woman, each of them perhaps carrying a small zip bag and apparently waiting to be picked up by car, you may be witnessing a prostitute and her maid about to be given a lift home by the ponce. If they take a cab, it is likely the ponce will meet the taxi in his car, after the maid has been dropped off. You can then 'clock and house'* them.

Watch for

▷ An excellent time to see ponces and prostitutes together. It occurs during the popular Sunday lunch-time drinking, in the better class

* Slang terms meaning to see and remember their faces, and then to follow them to their home.

110

'drive-in' public house. For some reason they do not seem to suspect they may be watched on this day, and are careless and indiscreet. The ownership of the vehicles they use, and the location of their joint homes, are easily discovered then, whereas infinite care is taken to conceal these facts on a working day.

Although they must be tested independently (beware of false spite), anonymous letters and telephone calls are often a source of valuable information.

In any event, establish and substantiate your case over a four- or five-day observation (make Sunday the second day of the observation for the reasons given above) and then,

STEP ONE

PROVE THE WOMAN WAS A PROSTITUTE AT THE MATERIAL TIME

Watch for
▷ Direct evidence of the woman at her trade, actually soliciting motorists or passers-by in the street. Evidence of her entering motor cars frequently, usually after a short conversation with the driver, who is almost invariably the sole occupant, and then to return half an hour or so later, to the same place, by the same car, is the classical conduct. So is her friendly acceptance by smiles, greetings and gossip with other women acting in a similar fashion nearby.

Watch for
▷ Activity at the actual premises where the woman takes her customers, or where she is operating as a 'call girl'. In the latter case this can be supplemented by test telephone calls in answer to the Post-card-type advertisements exhibited in certain newsagents' windows. (These newsagents may be committing the offence of 'living in part on the earnings', as will be discussed later.)

Watch for
▷ Activity by these women on waste ground, in public parks and on commons, or inside derelict property. Prostitutes who have no inside room for their business, especially those who solicit motorists, frequently

have favourite open areas where they direct their clients to take them by car, time after time. These particular prostitutes, often of no fixed abode or runaway youngsters,* are very much at risk. It is upon this class of street girl that so many violently depraved men vent themselves.

The presence of two uniformed officers, regularly and opening patrolling these out-of-the-way, derelict and lonely spaces, in a marked and lighted police vehicle, not to harass or embarrass, but rather to 'show the flag', can do much to prevent these violent crimes. Quite apart from the tragedy it obviously is to the victim and her parents, it is less apparently so but still a disaster for police. Bear in mind the major concentration of police resources, scores of officers, clerks, typists and vehicles, that rightly are mustered when the murder of such a street girl takes place, very much to the detriment of the standard of policing generally in that police area. Some would say quite unavoidably so, but perhaps it was for the want of assertive and discerning patrolling.

Formal proof of recent cautions or convictions for soliciting prostitution is valuable evidence, but it is not necessary to prove the woman is a convicted prostitute. 'Prostitution' means the habitual offering for reward by a female of her body commonly for purposes of lewdness; it is not necessary to prove that the offer was for the purpose of natural sexual connection; it can include active acts of indecency performed by the woman herself, for example masturbating a male client or permitting (mock) masturbation of herself, but it would not (in my opinion) include a female stage performer no matter how lewdly she acted, who had no physical contact with her audience. Actual proof of the payment of money does not appear necessary (R. *v* de Munck (1918) 1 K.B. 635; 82 J.P. 160, see also R. *v* Webb (1963) 3 All E.R. 177; Winter *v* Woolfe (1931) 1 K.B. 549).

It is sometimes overlooked that the woman herself can, if she is willing, and some are, be persuaded to give evidence admitting that she is a prostitute or—as good and less embarrassing for her—that she was during the period of time that the charge against the ponce alleges. Remember, in certain classes of case, the prostitute's maid can, if she is willing, and many are, either prove or corroborate these facts, if it means the conviction of an unpopular ponce. So can another prostitute who knows the woman in question, particularly if this woman is strongminded and independent, as some are.

* The near-vagrant girls of this type are often referred to as 'mysteries' by ponces.

Watch for

▷ The chance to cultivate certain informers. Remember maids, as a class, seem intensely antagonistic to ponces, and are often the originators of anonymous letters concerning them. In nearly every case where an established prostitute has premises for her trade, away from where she lives with her ponce, she will employ a 'maid'. This is often an old prostitute or thief, whose duties are to answer the telephone,* to describe the type of service offered, to open the door to callers, to prevent queueing or any other suspicious behaviour outside and to keep nervous clients occupied with either salacious reading matter or pert conversation until they can be seen, in turn, by the prostitute. Apart from a daily wage, the maids receive tips, occasionally substantial ones, and are expert in extracting them from clients. Some may work for one prostitute in the afternoon and for another in the evening. They are, of course, frequently the prostitute's intimate confidante and thus their accumulated knowledge of prostitution, and ponces, is encyclopaedic. In many cases they tend to become a mother substitute to the prostitute (some maids are in their late sixties or early seventies) and it is this kin-like relationship that may give them their extreme aversion to ponces, whom they consider are stealing the lion's share of the money that 'their' girl earns. The older maids may come to the attention of the police when arrested for shop-lifting.

My advice to all officers engaged in this class of duty is to go out of your way to cultivate them as informers, but one word of caution—beware of the maid placed at the premises by a ruthless ponce or by his agent; when maids are 'minders' they will be interested only in the ponce's interests. These women seem often of a Mediterranean or North African background, and of course are untrustworthy.

STEP TWO
PROVE THE ACCUSED MAN WELL KNEW THE WOMAN WAS A PROSTITUTE

Watch for

▷ The accused himself soliciting or importuning men as customers for the prostitute or prostitutes concerned. This is undoubtedly the best

* The fact that they control the telephone indicates how easy it is for them, if so inclined, to give you immediately current information without danger to themselves.

113

evidence of guilty knowledge, and is itself an offence, if done persistently, with power of arrest. Some will carry the prostitute's business card and pass it to likely-looking clients in bars, clubs and licensed houses. Possession of a number of such cards is totally incriminating.

Watch for

▷ The accused man visiting the premises where the prostitute takes her clients, when she is actually there with a customer, under circumstances where the accused must know of the woman's activities. Some ponces will covertly watch their prostitutes on their 'pitches' for a variety of reasons, and if this is seen it is valuable evidence. It is occasionally possible to prove he was present in the premises, even in the room concerned, during a substantial period of the prostitute's workday. Nearly all prostitutes are nervous of 'kinky' (unbalanced) clients, some are quite unreasonably so, and wish their ponce to be near at hand. With the even lower grade of man who battens on to a poorer class of street girl who, not having suitable accommodation, takes clients to open spaces or derelict property, he may be seen to follow the girl and customer for the same protective reason (or, of course, to make sure no money goes to another ponce or is kept by the girl herself!). Evidence of such conduct, certainly if regularly undertaken, is good testimony indeed.

Watch for

▷ The presence of ponces in the public gallery or precincts of a court when their prostitutes appear on soliciting or other charges (brothel keeping, indecency, etc.). Some are arrogant enough to put themselves forward as sureties for the bail of such women; the more discreet will make arrangements with confederates or other prostitutes in nearby cafés and licensed houses. Similarly, they may arrange for fines to be paid through intermediaries. This behaviour can be translated into vital evidence of guilty knowledge. Court staff, especially the gaoler and matron, will be quick to notice such conduct.

Watch for

▷ or rather listen for, incriminating conversation by men of this class. It takes place between the prostitute and the man in public houses, cafés, clubs and even in the street. It seems that discretion is ignored if there is an argument, especially if over money or infidelity. Some of the men cannot resist boasting to similarly minded men of either their dominance over, or the financial success of, a particular prostitute under their control, and this sort of chatter is not uncommon in betting shops, in gaming establishments and in the type of café where these fellows congregate. It sounds a tall order to get such evidence, but the fact remains it can be done. The observation officer concerned needs to have a brazen, confident, play-acting skill—the chutzpah previously mentioned—combined with an ability to merge into whatever background exists at the time. Remember, too, this sort of evidence need not necessarily be entirely police evidence. Inquiries, subsequent to arrest, can produce persons willing to repeat on oath what they heard the accused say. Cab drivers, garage men, porters in flats, for example, do hear such incriminating words.

STEP THREE
PROVE THE ACCUSED LIVED WHOLLY OR IN PART ON THE EARNINGS OF PROSTITUTION

Watch for
▷ Money payments in public places, by the prostitute to the man concerned. Old-fashioned? So foolishly indiscreet as to strain belief? Maybe so, but it still happens, time and time again. Quite apart from a voracious eagerness for money which ponces seem to have as a class, their way of life involving betting heavily, gaming substantially, entertaining in clubs, arranging expensive leases, being required as a matter of reputation occasionally to lend large sums to confederates, brings about situations where, suddenly and urgently, they need immediate cash money. Discretion is then thrown to the winds and the prostitute or her maid will be there and then visited with an insistent or violent demand. If the prostitute is on her pitch or in a club at the time, she will be contacted there, without a second thought as to the incriminating danger involved. These demands are usually met, but such circumstances tend to arouse resentment, particularly with maids. After the arrest of the accused man, a shrewd officer may be able to use this resentment to obtain independent corroborative evidence of a most telling nature.

Watch for
▷ Direct evidence which plainly shows that the ponce (a) has no lawful occupation or other means, or (b) by reason of an extravagant standard of

115

living, such lawful means that he does possess are hopelessly inadequate, and he therefore must be living on the earnings of prostitution. Accurate details of his scale of drinking, of his betting, gaming, scale of rent, expenses on food and clothing, mode of transport, hire purchase repayments, etc., are valuable in this context.

It has been held that a payment by a prostitute (to a man) for goods or services supplied for the purposes of prostitution and which would not have been supplied except to one who was a prostitute, is within the terms of section 30 of the Sexual Offences Act 1956 (Shaw *v* D.P.P. (1961) 2 All E.R. 446; 125 J.P. 437 H.L.: R. *v* Silver and R. *v* Thomas (see later) considered). Further, in the case of Calvert *v* Mayes (1954) 1 All E.R. 41: (1954) 118 J.P. 76, it was established that living on the earnings of prostitution may be indirect, as where a male person receives payment from men who resort to his house, or use his motor car, with women with whom he associates and whom he knows to be prostitutes. There is authority that the offence may be committed as regards one day only (see an interesting old Portsmouth case R. *v* Hill and Churchman (1914) 2 K.B. 386; 78 J.P. 303; 10 Cr. App. R. 56), but even if one day only is specified in the indictment, evidence is still admissible to show what the relationship between them was, both before and after the day in question (ibid.).

In nearly every set of circumstances, with single-minded inquiry the burden of proof can be shifted to the accused man, and, if this can be achieved, the prosecution's case is strengthened. Therefore, if possible:

STEP FOUR

PROVE THE ACCUSED LIVED WITH THE PROSTITUTE, or PROVE THAT HE WAS HABITUALLY IN HER COMPANY

Both these points are easily capable of proof in the ordinary case where the prostitute and the accused have a husband-and-wife relationship. However, it is not essential that a man must live with a prostitute, or even habitually be in her company, for the burden of proof to be passed to him. When a man imposes on several prostitutes (still not common in this country), and takes care not to live with any one of them, it is still possible to bring him within the scope of the provision which shifts the burden of proof, if evidence is available to

STEP FIVE

PROVE THAT HE EXERCISED CONTROL, DIRECTION OR INFLUENCE OVER THE MOVEMENTS OF A PROSTITUTE IN SUCH A WAY AS TO SHOW HE WAS AIDING, ABETTING OR COMPELLING HER PROSTITUTION

Watch for

▷ The man conveying the prostitute to and from her pitch in his car, or accompanying her in a taxi cab. Watch for signs that he knowingly arranged for the rental of premises for immoral purposes and installed the woman there; that he followed her about when she was soliciting and generally supervised her; that he warned her of the approach of uniformed police when she was soliciting or behaving indecently.

Watch for

▷ The ponce intimidating or ejecting troublesome clients, or assaulting or coercing the prostitute by threats for failure to earn enough money. It is possible for an observation officer, or for that matter any witness, a cab driver for example, to overhear instructions as to prices to be charged, the class of client to be entertained, even the streets to frequent. These, together or even singly, may be enough to shift the burden of proof, whether or not he lived with the prostitute and whether or not he was habitually in her company.

Watch for

▷ The possibility, with foreign-born prostitutes, of securing evidence showing that the ponce, or one of his agents, arranged for a clandestine marriage* between the prostitute and some worthless drop-out of British nationality, or that perhaps he paid her fare into the UK through a bank account or travel agency. Has he ever acted as an interpreter for her in any business transaction? If he made arrangements when the lease of a flat was negotiated or when domestic gas and electricity supply were connected, then these are all proceedings where thorough inquiry can produce incriminating evidence from witnesses (the officials concerned) of excellent character. It can be called either directly or, alternatively, to form useful 'back-up' questions for counsel, in a contested case, for use in cross-examination.

The best tactics of arrest in these cases, the powers of search and the prosecution of smaller fry are discussed in the next chapter.

---

* To ensure, if convicted of soliciting or for that matter any criminal offence, that she is not deported.

12. Men trafficking in prostitution (II)

Ten tested ways of obtaining best results just before, during and after arrest.

A little forethought concerning tactics to be employed in the actual arrest of ponces is worth while, for there are in nearly all cases opportunities to secure, at this stage, overwhelmingly incriminating evidence. It should never be the unplanned 'Get your coat on, Sarge—we'll nip round and get him before lunch!' A worldly knowledge of the patterns of life these people follow is the key to taking a ponce at his most incriminating time, with all the psychological and evidential advantages this brings. For example, in those cases where a ponce is also a pimp, in other words where he helps personally to secure customers for prostitutes, and particularly when he does *not* live as man and wife with any of the prostitutes in your case,

Watch for (1)

▷ The chance to take him while he is actually soliciting or importuning for the prostitute or prostitutes concerned, especially if the actual arrest can be delayed until there is an arranged confrontation between him, the prostitute and the police officer or other witness who was last importuned. It can be imagined that, provided there is already evidence of prior persistent solicitation by this sort of ponce, even if over only the previous half-hour, your case has almost proved itself. The flood of ludicrous explanations and patent admissions that are made at this moment, even after a full and soberly stated caution, must be experienced to be appreciated. They often include an acceptance that he is living on the earnings of prostitution, as well as importuning for immoral purposes, for which he has been arrested. At this moment of confrontation, the words he uses to the prostitute are invariably deadly in their self-incriminatory terms. In the circumstances described, charge the ponce with both offences and, after fairly stating a full caution, tell him that he can put his admissions in writing. While it is unmanly and unworthy for a policeman to use the least pressure to obtain such a statement, it is right and fair, and in the public interest, to let an accused know that he can make such a written statement, and for you to be ready to facilitate it.

While cases continue to occur where a ponce is also a pimp, it is more usual for him to act the complete parasite and take no active part in assisting a prostitute in her day-to-day trade, but merely take the money which is the fruit of it. Most established prostitutes have the two establishments I have already mentioned: the flat or room where they carry on their trade, which our grandfathers would call a 'house of assignation', and the house or apartment where they live, possibly with their ponces. If these are the general facts of the case you have under observation, it is still possible that the moment of arrest can be in the most incriminating of circumstances, so

Watch for (2)
▷ The opportunity to arrest the ponce when he is visiting the premises where the prostitute is working, especially if this can take place while there is a customer or customers present. This tactic is particularly valuable where the ponce and prostitute do not live together, as it may be the only concrete evidence available to shift the onus of proof on to the accused man. In any event it is incriminatory and prevents him subsequently pretending, in court, that he did not know what was going on.

You must always bear in mind the dishonest prostitute and ponce team, whether their method of working is the simple luring of a drunken man to an alley, by the woman, so he can be robbed with the assistance of the ponce, or the more subtle sneak theft by the ponce inside premises, so

Watch for (3)
▷ The rarer situation where a ponce is frequently, regularly and for long periods at the work premises in the late evening. He may be engaged in stealing from clients' clothing while they are intimately concerned with the prostitute. Cases have occurred where such men conceal themselves behind dressing tables and in cupboards in the dimly lit room used, and repeatedly steal about half of the 'jockey's'* money. When they leave such premises the victims are usually unaware that their money has

---

* Prostitutes' contemptuous slang ('gonk' is another word used) for a customer. The term 'john' is also used to describe a client, and it is no accident that the same word is used as a euphemism for the cheapest type of sheath contraceptive.

been stolen; by the time they do discover it, they probably do not know the location of the premises anyway. Here the cunning of the ponce in not taking all the money shows itself. If the victim has enough cash to get home, he is likely to take a philosophical view of his loss and not report the crime to the police.

Whether my experience is statistically significant or not, you must decide for yourselves, but of all the really skilled inside sneak-thief ponces I have known, every one was homosexual. This amounts to about a dozen or so men. Ponces are not invariably heterosexual; regular companionship seems just as important (in my observations of the scene over the years) to a prostitute as male sexual attractiveness. Homosexuals, themselves often lonely, can certainly give companionship, and may have fewer moral reservations about stealing from men in intimate situations with whom they have little sympathy. Additionally, they are unlikely to patronise a prostitute in their conversation and attitudes. This is very attractive to prostitutes, who are usually very sensitive to the way clients, social workers and others treat them as a somewhat distinct class of human being.

In 1964, I took an expert ponce who was stealing in this way and, while doing so, dressed himself in a red pullover with the sleeves over his hands, a pulled down red woollen ski hat and women's red slacks. Over some weeks he stole several great sums of money. The room was illuminated only by one red electric light bulb, which had a red shade. Tests later showed that a man dressed thus was practically invisible. Outside rooms were brightly lit, by contrast, to add to the effect

Watch for (4)

▷ A prostitute who seems overly to favour semi-drunken clients or those who are obviously tourists and visitors. In these circumstances you should be particularly suspicious of the likelihood of such thefts taking place; with expensive prostitutes the thieving will be at premises, but with near-vagrant street girls it will be in open spaces, alleys or mews. Cab drivers are good sources of information about these dishonest but 'better class' prostitutes, and their equally dishonest ponces, both classes being universally detested, even by persons who would never think of inform-ing on an honest prostitute or even to speak to police about her ponce. Cab drivers, you see, are often used in conveying clients and prostitutes to such premises, most particularly if the client (or rather victim) is befuddled with drink. They see little wrong with this, it is to them just another fare, but if they (the cab drivers) realise they are being made 'patsies' by thieves, or even feel they might be suspected of being concerned in the thefts themselves, they will take a very different view indeed! But do not expect them to tell you on their own initiative; you must ask around and question them closely, but in a straightforward way, then they will tell you one or two suspect addresses. Properly thought through and discussed with an experienced colleague, you should be able to arrest, redhanded, a particularly evil team. Charge them with being concerned in stealing or a conspiracy to steal, if you can, but—if the evidence is there as it should be—do not forget to charge the man with poncing as well.

Watch for (5)

▷ The subtle signs which will identify what appears to be a street robbery of a drunken pedestrian late at night for what it really is, namely a ponce and prostitute theft that went wrong. With the systems of thieving by ponces, described above, there is always present the real likelihood of violence, sometimes dangerous violence, flaring up if a client suddenly becomes aware of such a theft taking place. The victim can be quite badly knocked about and abandoned in a nearby lonely street. When seen by police at hospital he may well report a robbery, but say it was an attack in the street by several men. He will not be ashamed of that, but he will be ashamed of explaining how he was robbed in a whore's bedroom. The victim's family can accept a street robbery as a negative experience of life, but would not take kindly to the other situation. Naturally, he realises this.

It is your duty, in the public interest, to get the address out of the victim. Do not use harsh or embarrassing phrases; say, 'Did you offer to take a girl home and were then suddenly set about?' If he concedes that point it will not be long before he tells you the whole truth. Be sympathetic and discreet—you need the address. It is good crime prevention promptly to squash such tawdry and treacherous conspiracies. Not only grave injuries, but even deaths, have resulted from such situations in the past. Remember that dishonest prostitutes and homosexual ponces may conceal stolen money in body orifices, and you may require medical opinion and advice in such a situation.

But to return to more normal cases, and my experience is that most prostitutes are honest. If she does live with the ponce at her accommodation, apartment or house,

Watch for (6)

▷ The possibility of taking the ponce, with his prostitute, in a husband-and-wife situation, preferably in bed and in the early morning. This has material advantages: first it is just about the most disconcerting moment possible and will disorientate the shrewdest and most hard-nosed of commercial ponces, making the incidence of incriminating admissions, even after caution, very likely indeed; secondly, search can there and then be made, in their presence, for incriminatory articles.

Watch for (7)

▷ The chance of violent resistance. Some ponces, especially those from minority groups, when faced with the imminence of arrest, can resist you with some ferocity. To lower the temperature, to prevent unnecessary injuries and an unnatural escalation, surprise is all important. Perhaps a helpful prostitute's maid or other trusted resident can obtain a duplicate key. You may decide to use bluff to obtain an entry; if you do, have an alternative method of entry planned and rehearsed in case your bluffing goes wrong. It often does! When you are inside, and in control of the situation,

Search for (8)

▷ and seize, in the presence of the accused man and the woman, any documents indicating a joint financial interest or undertaking, e.g., cheque and bank books; bank statements and bank manager's letters; rent books, especially the one concerning the premises where the woman carries on her trade—if you find it concealed among his papers, could anything be more incriminating?

Search for (9)

▷ and seize photographs of the prostitute and ponce taken together and, of course, any other articles that indicate plainly their use in commercial prostitution, e.g., large quantities of obscene pictures, especially if mounted in albums—the sort that are found in the anterooms of prostitutes' rooms for waiting customers to read—bulk quantities of cheap sheath contraceptives, electric massage machines or miniature electric tooth-brushes with adapted fixtures for masturbation and, of course, whips, chains, canes, handcuffs and the like. You might think that the latter type of article would be kept exclusively at the 'work premises', but experience repeatedly shows that carelessness after purchase of these articles causes some to be left at, or forgotten in, the joint accommodation address. You may well find ampoules of amyl nitrate in a small tin or cardboard box roughly the size of a flat packet of twenty cigarettes. In their legitimate medical use these ampoules are broken and inhaled to alleviate heart attacks. They also have the alleged quality of prolonging sensation in sexual orgasm, and are not infrequently made available to clients by really expensive prostitutes.

Watch for (10)
▷ The opportunity, after arrest and in a disputed case, to trace to the ponce himself his purchase or acquisition of those articles used solely for prostitution, and which, because of what intrinsically they are (or the quantity in which they are acquired), would obviously only be of use to a prostitute. If it can be shown he did this for some form of reward, it will bring him within the framework of the decision of Shaw *v* The Director of Public Prosecutions (already mentioned). It may also show he is influencing, controlling or aiding her in her prostitution, thus shifting the onus of proof to him (see Chapter 11).

In such an arrest, in the joint home as described above, be confident of your powers to both search for and seize articles and documents of evidential value. As I have said before (*Thieves on Wheels*, page 65), you have quite extensive common law powers to secure evidence in such a situation. I suppose Elias *v* Pasmore [(1934) All E.R. 380; (1934) 98 J.P. 92], remains a basic authority, where Mr Justice Horridge upheld, first, the right to search a prisoner (see also Bessell *v* Wilson, 1853), and secondly upheld the right to take and detain property in possession of a prisoner, likely to be useful in evidence against him (Dillon *v* O'Brien, 1887), or anyone else. Thirdly he gave his view that the interests of the State (i.e., that material evidence must be preserved, if at all possible) will excuse the unlawful seizure of articles or documents in the possession, or under the control, of a person arrested, if subsequently it should appear that they are evidence of a crime, committed by anyone. It was also confirmed that police are entitled to retain articles or documents seized until the conclusion of the case in which they are material (R. *v* Lushington ex parte Otto 1894). The wholesome robustness of this judgment has been somewhat diluted by Ghani and Others *v* Jones [(1969) Crim. L.R. 605, and *The Times*, 29 August 1969] and, in minor cases especially, particular caution must be exercised when considering the seizure of articles or documents where they belong to, or are under the control of, persons not shown to be concerned directly with the suspected crime.

Section 41 of the Sexual Offences Act 1956 originally stated: 'Anyone may arrest without warrant a male found committing the offence of knowingly living wholly or in part on the earnings of prostitution.' This is the same section giving the power of arrest of a man found persistently importuning for immoral purposes (and of women controlling female prostitutes), but by Schedule 3 of the Criminal Law Act 1967, this power to arrest male ponces (and women controlling prostitutes) was repealed. But, since Section 4 of the Street Offences Act 1959 increased the maximum penalty for ponces (and women controllers) from two years to seven years' imprisonment—while leaving the importuners' maximum at two years—poncing has plainly become an 'arrestable offence', and by Section 2 of the Criminal Law Act 1967 the power of arrest has been enlarged beyond recognition. Now, a police officer may arrest without warrant any person reasonably suspect of being about to commit, or of having committed, or of committing, the offence of living on the earnings of prostitution and may enter (by force if necessary) and search any place where that person is or with reasonable cause the police officer suspects him to be.

By Section 3(1) of the same Statute, a person may use such force as is reasonable in the circumstances in effecting or assisting in the lawful arrest of persons living on the earnings of prostitution, or even of being suspected of living on the earnings of prostitution.

This extensive widening of the powers to arrest and search in relation to 'arrestable offences' has removed the desirability of obtaining a warrant (under Section 1 of the Magistrates' Courts Act 1952) to arrest a ponce, as was almost invariably the practice prior to 1967. The only situation where a warrant would be of practical use these days is in the circumstances where you are acting almost solely on the evidence of a prostitute who is complaining that a ponce has been criminally imposing on her.

Section 42 of the Sexual Offences Act 1956 provides that, 'where it is made to appear by information on oath before a justice of the peace that there is reasonable cause to suspect that any house or part of a house is used by a woman for the purposes of prostitution and that a man residing in or frequenting the house is living wholly or in part on her earnings, the justice may issue a warrant authorizing a constable to enter and search the house and to arrest the man'.

As I have previously written, this section must be read with great caution. It only applies to those occasional circumstances where the ponce resides in or frequents* the house where the woman carries on her trade as a prostitute. In London, it is rare these days for a ponce to reside in the house or flat where the prostitute carries on her trade. He may visit it, but remember that occasional visiting may not be the same as 'frequents'. This word is defined by *Webster's Dictionary* 'to resort to often or habitually', and even in the case where there is evidence to show the ponce visited the prostitute, it is submitted that unless he is there habitually, almost on a day-to-day basis, he cannot be said to be within this section. So, in the majority of modern-day circumstances, in London anyway, the provisions of Section 42 are nearly useless.

Landlords who knowingly let premises to prostitutes, or knowingly to their agents or ponces, at high rents and realising the premises will be used for habitual prostitution, are now firmly within the provisions of 'living wholly or in part on the earnings of prostitution'. This was not always so. In the case of R. *v* Silver (1956) 1 All E.R. 716; 120 J.P. 233, it was held that a landlord letting premises, knowing they were to be used for prostitution, was not, to that extent, committing the offence of 'immoral earnings', whatever other offence he might have committed. This somewhat singular decision was (fortunately) not followed a year later, when in R. *v* Thomas (1957) 2 All E.R. 181 [affirmed (1957) 2 All E.R. 342; (1958) 121 J.P. 338], a landlord who let premises at a highly inflated rent to a prostitute so that she could carry on her trade, was stated plainly to be within the provisions of Section 30. Many successful prosecutions have occurred since that year. Indeed, following Shaw *v* DPP, a landlord who knowingly lets accommodation to a prostitute for her professional purposes would be living in part on her earnings, even if he only charged her a normal rental.

They are far from easy cases, however, because the landlords rarely have a man-and-wife relationship with the prostitute, and may genuinely never have seen her. The shift of the onus of proof is usually quite impossible. So, if you want to bring these elite ponces before a court,

Watch for
▷ The disillusioned, dissatisfied or financially badly used prostitute who may be willing to give evidence and, more importantly, to persuade her

---

* An exception is the occasional case where a ponce is also a sneak thief, mentioned previously.

125

friends to do the same. If you can interview them promptly after they have been assaulted or degraded by persons enforcing the payment of high rent, or the recovery of unpaid back-rent, you may well be on to a good thing. Sometimes the rent collectors themselves are ill-used and assaulted. Be on the alert for such a person's evidence. The maids I have already mentioned may have physically taken rent to a landlord or his agent, or have overheard the demands made. They are quite likely to be game enough (it does take nerve) to give evidence. Can the deflated falseness of the entries in the rent books be proved? Does a genuine register, where true amounts of cash are entered, exist? Perhaps it is in a bank's safe deposit.

Prove the landlord knew of the use of his premises and the inordinately high rent paid, and you will bring down a bad man, one who may well be financing other crimes with the large amounts of untaxed money he is accruing. Greed grows on greed, and in their arrogant confidence they will have made some mistake, or badly used some person, during their criminal commerce in the world of prostitution. This key is there for a shrewd officer to find, and it is not necessarily a sterile exercise to appeal to the latent nobler motives of persons, whatever their background, who may be in a position to assist you. However morally depraved some people may choose to consider prostitutes and their maids, they will have a sense of 'fair is fair'. This can be tapped by the genuine approach of a man of good reputation.

To deal with some small fry. Newsagents that display for payment post-cards advertising prostitutes' services, may be committing an offence against Section 30. First, they must of course be males, for a female newsagent would not be within the frame of this Section.* Secondly, they must know they are providing a service to prostitutes for the purpose of prostitution and which would not have been supplied except to one who was a prostitute (Shaw v D.P.P. (1961) 2 All E.R. 446; 125 J.P. 437 H.L., previously mentioned). You must all have seen the cards I mean, some of particularly elephantine humour, e.g. (actual cases): 'For sale—beautiful butterfly—needs mounting' (telephone number); 'Young lady seeks superior position' (telephone number); 'Consult Miss Stern for expert tuition in deportment and discipline' (telephone number). Some shops may have as many as a hundred such cards; a very profitable sideline.

* If some of the advertisements are by male prostitutes and a female newsagent knew this, she might well be committing an offence of 'man or woman living in part on male prostitution' (Section 5 of the Sexual Offences Act 1967).

Watch for

▷ The chance directly to prove that the women offering tuition, butterflies and the like, really are female prostitutes. Test telephone calls can be made, but a few must be interviewed. When they are interviewed, experience shows that some will make statements agreeing the advertisements were theirs, what it is they were really offering, that they are prostitutes and how much they were charged by the newsagent. A selection of the advertisements can then be seized, the boards photographed and, if a prosecution is considered, a 'Notice to Produce' can be served with the summons or warrant for all the cards.

Useful evidence is often obtained by sending officers in plain clothes into the newsagent to insert both a 'straight' advertisement and a typically worded prostitutes' advertisement to note any significant difference in cost.

Force practice must guide you, but these newsagents are best dealt with by a caution, or perhaps even two cautions by senior officers under formal conditions, before a warrant or summons is considered. The nature of the offence does not (in my view) justify summary arrest and a summons should be obtained only after a determined disregard of warnings.

13. How to succeed in searching premises

There is more to 'spinning drums'* than swearing out search warrants.

Now to offer some detailed words about searching and raiding premises. I trust I am not suspected of speaking academic or speculative nonsense. Over the years I have searched many hundreds of premises and know from bitter and foolish failure the mistakes that can easily be made. This is written so you may avoid these, and positively succeed where it is at all possible.

It is just not feasible for a man leading a search warrant team always to cover every contingency at his briefing. Younger officers should respond sensibly without being told, understudying and even anticipating what is wanted by their inspectors and superintendents. The circumstances affecting the arrest of quality criminals inside premises can change like quicksilver, as can situations in West Indian shebeens, other disorderly houses or with deranged persons barricaded in rooms. True discipline and obedience involve being flexible and adaptable to changing situations. It is unmanly to excuse a lack of necessary and expected initiative by hiding behind blind and doctrinaire obedience to orders previously received, which have obviously become obsolete in the changing situation. A true sign of a potential leader is his willingness, when in subordinate capacities, to take decisions affecting the achievement of the goal, but involving radical change. It takes grit to do so, especially when you have a hard 'guv'nor', but in the long term he will admire and recommend you for it, whatever he may say about it at the time.

Whatever was said at the briefing, at the scene make sure the back and sides of the property are covered. Ensure you do not all arrive together, bunched up and excited. If you are driving one of the vehicles to the scene, stop it well away from the house or premises in question. *Never* slam doors, and *never* use the gong or klaxon horn *en route*. The quietest way to shut

---

* London slang term for searching premises.

car doors is slightly to open windows so the closing door does not compress air inside the vehicle. Door catches can then be engaged quietly. As with every driver engaged in taking teams to the scene, you should *always* have a prior reconnaissance of the address and know the most direct route there. Do this by cycling, or riding a scooter or bus, past it in daylight, some time before the raid. Twice in my service, when taking part in raiding parties, secrecy had been so overdone by those in charge, that the drivers did not know where the premises were and, in following the lead car containing the senior officer, became hopelessly 'snarled-up' in traffic and naturally did not turn up in time for a successful 'turnover' of the premises. As a direct result of this foolishness, two wanted men escaped and a chief inspector sustained injury. Only have men you can trust, then be frank with them. They will respond with loyalty; but be explicit, tell them what is secret and what may be openly discussed.

In London, on a small scooter, you can make yourself look exactly like a probationary taxi driver learning 'the knowledge' (of London streets) for the Public Carriage Office written examination—a quite common and accepted sight. All that is required is to have a clip-board fixed to the handlebars and 'L' plates front and rear—put the 'L' plates on whether you are required by law to display them or not, they are an essential part of the charade. This is a simple and effective disguise suitable for any reconnaissance or moving surveillance in London from, at one end of the scale, riding right up beside street cheats at 'three-card monte', to the 'tailing and housing' of high-status thieves. Wear a badly fitting, awkward-looking crash helmet, together with a pair of National Health glasses and cycle clips; you will be able to follow them unrecognised right into their front yard! Have no false pride in your appearance when following quality offenders—success, lawfully and fairly obtained, is what counts!

Try to lower the temperature if the men in your team start getting excited before they arrive at the premises in question. Sensible behaviour near the front door is vital. Excitement, the first step towards losing your grit and grip, is terribly contagious. It communicates itself to accused or suspected persons and can be the cause of escalation to unnecessary violence. Any emotional involvement, or anger or disgust, even too much of the 'crusader' attitude, clouds clear judgement in police situations. Do not offend brother officers who have these attributes, but leave behind all excitable men, including those who previously have been violently involved with any of the men you intend to arrest (unless they are essential for identification purposes). Find them useful work to do at the station but, I

129

repeat, do not take them on any duty involving strain, or you endanger success. Develop the reputation of being ice cold in contentious street situations. Let your colleagues joke about you, but go after that reputation for relentless, unswerving—even frigid—pursuit of duty in stress situations. It requires conscious effort and practice, but is infinitely worth while, especially if you have the seed of sensible ambition inside you. Is there a need either to block vehicles parked outside the premises or to immobilise them by, for example, removing the distributor head or breaking the low-tension circuit? You should know how to do this quickly with the minimum of fuss. Always take the ignition keys of the police vehicle with you and, when you leave it, lock it. Never leave a hand radio in the vehicle.

If the door has glass panels, stand in such a way that the full outline of your figure is not seen. At some doors it is sensible to knock and look through the letterbox at the same time. Keep your eyes skinned for the movement of curtains. If the visit is at night, to a multi-tenanted and converted dwelling, with the intention of arresting a wanted man, knock lightly to begin with. If there are young children or babes in the house you can anticipate being able to awaken a young mother with very little noise and thus not rouse the entire building. These young women are light sleepers because of the need to nurse and feed their babies frequently during the night. They may come to the door themselves or send their man, sometimes following him down the passage. Your personality is tested here. If you are fluent, open-handed, polite and have the ability to *come quickly to the point*, they will let you in covertly, giving you and your team an immense advantage, especially if you are after a violent man. Have a woman officer with you, they always lower temperatures in any confrontation. Of course, be careful not to expose her to any deadly force by the thieves. Say something after this style: 'We are all local police officers from Notting Hill. This lady is a police officer, too. We have a warrant to search for and arrest a man on a serious matter. Please read the warrant and let us in quietly, because we know he is inside. If you help us we can get the matter over with fair play and no violence. That is in his interests. No liberties are going to be taken. Of course, you know it is your bounden duty to help the court' (do not say '. . . help the police'). Adapt this appeal to suit the circumstances where it is necessary lawfully to enter premises but without a warrant. These phrases may sound pompous and long-winded *but they work*, and they work best if the man chosen to speak has a pleasant, educated voice. Sergeant-major or 'tough cop' attitudes are just inefficient in the situations described, but if you suspect you are being deliberately delayed by lying accomplices of the wanted man, so that the order of the court is in danger of being frustrated, be ready—in serious cases—to enter at once without ceremony. Choose carefully someone in conventional clothes to speak for you. Young policemen and women these days dress in 'trendy' clothes. Who can quarrel with the march of modern fashion? Nevertheless, the officer doing the talking should be in the conventional 'hard white collar, dark suit' popular conception of the appearance of senior policemen in plain clothes. It is reassuring to nervous people, suddenly awakened in the early hours. A fatherly, well-dressed, pipe-smoking appearance, by at least one of the officers, has real value in lowering temperatures where hysteria by women associates of the wanted man is so near the surface, and can easily escalate the situation to violence.

Concealed observation of the premises before the arrival of the search or raiding team is important. Ensure that there is some form of easy communication by visual signal or VHF radio with the team watching. They may want to cancel the whole raid because of what they have seen just before you arrive. If they are in a nondescript observation vehicle, you should have prearranged signals—radio can go wrong. You could knock the side of the van twice. A similar reply may be for 'Go ahead', and three knocks, repeated after a short interval, for 'Cancel'. Make sure the team see you before you covertly knock these signals on the side of the van. Make certain all watches are synchronised. Take a powerful torch or better still a 'seek-and-search' lamp, even in daylight. All these points should be explained and emphasised at your briefing.

Always take your baton. There should be at least two pairs of handcuffs with the team. In an emergency, two pairs of cuffs can be used to handcuff four persons (Fig. 13.1). Lay one pair of cuffs lengthwise along the top of the lower arm of one prisoner so that the chain between the cuffs is above the prisoner's wrist. With another pair of cuffs, handcuff this wrist over the chain. You then have three vacant cuffs—one for each of the other three prisoners. With a violent man intending to harm others or attempting to destroy himself, handcuff him behind his back, palms outward. But never use handcuffs on a mentally deranged man. He will be insensitive to pain and even if you succeed in putting the handcuffs on without injuring him, he will tear and throw himself about until they have badly cut and injured his wrists. A broad crepe bandage, turned several times about his wrists, is far better if you have to restrain him from self-injury.

Only handcuff prisoners in those circumstances where you would be prepared to swear in a court that it was absolutely necessary in order to

Fig. 13.1. In an emergency, four violent men can be secured with two pairs of handcuffs. Remember, 10 out of 12 men are right-handed, so secure the right wrist. (All rights reserved.)

prevent escape or to forestall unacceptable violence. Remember, hand-cuffing is degrading and not to be undertaken lightly. Never let a man be photographed by the press when he is handcuffed. If absolutely unavoid-able, for example, when arriving at an airport or at a busy railway station, a raincoat can be thrown over the cuffs to conceal the unpleasant truth. Think on this—an offender is usually a fellow-countryman and, in any event, probably unconvicted at that stage. It is no part of a peace officer's duty to humiliate or shame anyone in their charge, or even to allow or facilitate others to do so. You have undertaken to protect your prisoner and his property; *his reputation is also in your charge.* Property can be replaced, physical injuries can heal, but unnecessary loss of reputation is difficult to put right. When putting a handcuffed man into a car, particularly if he is struggling, try to protect his head from the rain gutter on the side of the roof of the car. A nasty wound can easily be avoided by one officer cupping a hand and ensuring the prisoner's head is guided down and into the car.

But enough of handcuffing; if the premises are in a block of high-quality flats or apartments, get the common door open by ringing another tenant's bell or by some form of subterfuge—a well-dressed policewoman should be able to get any good-quality common door opened for her without arousing suspicion or alarm. Preferably face to face, but via the door telephone if unavoidable, use the same form of explanation to the occupier whom you hope will help you as those mentioned above, suitably adapted to the changing social scene. Unless specifically detailed for other important tasks, make sure yourself that lavatories (there are usually at least two in a quality apartment) are entered immediately on entry. The flushing cistern is a favourite point of concealment for small contraband or weapons, waterproofed in plastic bags. If the occupants are guilty persons, and have obtained even the least warning of your entry, they will endeavour to flush away drugs or other incriminatory matter. I repeat, always be suspicious of persons with wet cuffs to their sleeves—has a hand been in the lavatory's cistern, or has that hand concealed a small object around the S-bend? If you see or sense anything suspicious in this area, do not hesitate physically to prevent flushing or further flushing and, if worth while, get a plumber to the scene. In some drug situations it may be worth considering secretly turning the water supply off in the premises concerned an hour before you intend to enter. Think about it—it is only justified in really serious cases, but it can make more difficult the disposal of drugs or dangerous chemicals into the sewage system.

In well-appointed kitchens, the rubbish grinder in the sink unit should also receive immediate attention. Is there anything suspended down the shaft of the 'dumb waiter' lift device, often found in good-quality apartments? When old apartments are modernised the dumb waiter shaft is sometimes boarded in and perhaps tiled or papered over. So look carefully in kitchens or breakfast rooms above ground level. Perhaps some receptacle has been fixed or bolted on the side of the shaft. The powerful beam of your seek-and-search lamp should show up anything unusual here, but endeavour to look up the shaft as well, with the lamp, from the ground floor or basement. The same applies to rubbish and laundry chutes. A fugitive can hide in some of these shafts and chutes.

Drugs are sometimes suspended out of windows: one refinement to this can be that the cord is only retained by the weight of the closed window and will drop the contraband to the ground if the window is opened carelessly. Always look down, around and up when you open a window. Check the ground level surround before leaving. Incriminating property has been attached underneath lifts (elevators) by adhesive tape. It is not easy to examine the base of a lift, this is why it has been so used.

133

Whenever possible, have the principal suspect with you when searching different rooms. *Spontaneous incriminatory admissions are more likely to be made if he or she is present when the find is made*, rather than if shown it a short while later. Additionally, it is some protection against false allegations of 'planting'. In the case of young persons living with parents, have an adult relative of the suspect with you.

Look particularly for concealed keys (Fig. 13.2a–c) and concealed left-luggage tickets. Guilty persons present are unlikely to admit they have

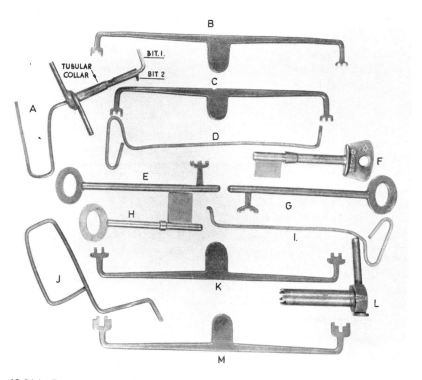

Fig. 13.2(a). Learn to recognise the general appearance of the various picks used in lever locks. A is a rudimentary but very efficient, independently acting, double-bitted skeleton key. Triple and quadruple examples (not shown) have also been made. B, C, K and M are blacksmith-made double-ended skeleton keys of Victorian vintage, but still found in the possession of thieves (rarely made nowadays). E and G are modern skeleton keys commercially available or easily made from blanks. D, I and J are suitable only for the simplest locks. H and F are blanks purchased for filing. L is a parking-meter key made from mild steel tubing. These implements may be found mixed with ordinary keys or generally with similar honest tools. You must know what to look for. (All rights reserved.)

MATCH BOX CONTAINING JIGGLERS.

Fig. 13.2(b). Jigglers: with these implements almost any simple pin-tumbler lock in a house, hotel room or car could be opened with the aid of a simple turning tension tool. Anyone, other than a genuine commercial locksmith, in possession of such tools should be regarded as very suspect indeed. (All rights reserved.)

vehicles parked nearby. In shebeen raids (Fig. 13.3), remember that the hard liquor (as opposed to the cans of beer) is often kept locked in the boot of a nearby car to be fetched when wanted. This is done to frustrate the seizure of these valuable assets by the authority of the Licensing Act search warrant. The 'drinker' operators can afford the loss, by lawful seizure, of the beer but not the whisky and rum! Try by all lawful means to connect this liquor with the sales inside the shebeen. Prior and alert observation may provide this evidence. Remember, too, that this style of liquor may be stolen or uncustomed (smuggled), and charges of 'dishonestly handling' or 'possession of uncustomed goods' may be justified.

Careful search in the vicinity and prior observation, together with testing car keys you find, may trace property in nearby vehicles, which can be connected with the persons who had the keys. Get to know what safe-deposit keys look like (simplest way—ask your bank manager to arrange

135

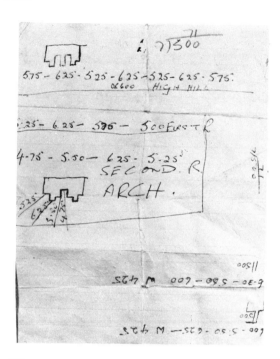

Fig. 13.2(c). When searching, look for incriminating papers. The illustration shows jotted down measurements for keys. Difficult honestly to explain away; in fact, totally incriminating for a non-locksmith. (All rights reserved.)

that you be shown some; tell him why you want to know, usually he will be pleased to help). If you find such a key when searching premises, bring it to the attention of your senior at once. He will certainly regard you as sharp-eyed and sensible. These keys are often concealed in unusual places, but again if possible try to *connect evidentially such a find with a person present*. Search every pocket of every article of clothing in wardrobes. Look in shoes and especially in ladies' boots. Property is often hung by string from a clothes hanger and is concealed by the folds of dresses. Contraband, stolen money and incriminating documents are sometimes placed at, or taped to, the back of wooden drawers. All drawers should be taken out, then the sides, top and bottom of the aperture left should be carefully examined. All lofts should be entered and illuminated. Look along horizontal beams. Breakfast food packets and food tins often contain unexpected articles. Is there anything taped under the table? Electric table-lamps frequently are used to conceal small articles—examine these lamps closely.

Fig. 13.3. Discreet observation before obtaining the warrant is always worth while. There is often good evidence to be found in the back yards of unlicensed drinking premises or 'drinkers' (less commonly but still referred to as 'shebeens' or 'blues'). The beer cans shown here clearly rebut the frequently heard defence that 'police smashed up a "birth night" party'. The principal(s) should be shown the evidence, cautioned, then asked if he/they care(s) to explain or comment upon it. Never try to extract comment, but there is the remote chance of innocent explanation which is just as much your duty to report to the court as any incriminating words. (All rights reserved.)

Look in garages with a discerning eye. Regard electrical repairs to ignition switch complexes with suspicion. Are there any spare ignition switch cylinders (Fig. 13.4)? Very suspicious! What work has been done on the bench? Have any tools been constructed, the use of which you cannot make out (Figs 13.5–13.7)? Are there any alarm-clock parts or minute hands of alarms, watches (these have to be broken off clocks and watches if the mechanism is to be used as a timing device for an electrically detonated bomb). If wristlet watches have been so used, the leather straps will be

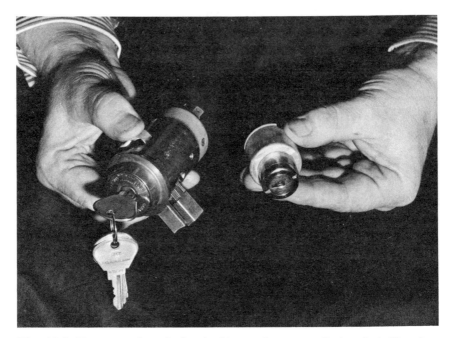

Fig. 13.4. Two examples of what ignition and starter cylinders look like. Any person who has more than one of these in his workshop or garage, or even one in his bedroom, should be regarded with great suspicion. He is probably a thief of some skill.

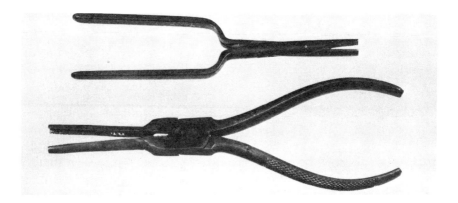

Fig. 13.5. Sharpened pliers, adapted to turn (from the outside) keys left in back doors of houses and old-fashioned hotel bedrooms.

discarded. Any of these straps on the floor of the garage? More than one cardboard box for an alarm clock or watch can be suspicious. Here are the boxes, where are the clocks? These boxes may be in the dustbin. Wooden spring-loaded clothes pegs, the commonest type, can be used as electrical 'pull' switches. Look for such pegs having wire wound around each of the jaws. If a shotgun has been shortened by sawing, you may find around the vice, in the teeth of a saw or on a file, metal dust which subsequently can be forensically identified as gun barrel steel filings. There are roughly two sorts of person who unlawfully have firearms in this country. First, the usually harmless 'gun buff' or 'gun nut' who is fascinated by weapons and collects them, even illegally. Then there is the criminal or criminal supplier. One pointer to indicate the latter is their powerful fear of leaving fingerprints. They often tape, with thick black electrical insulating tape, the butts of pistols and shotguns. Sometimes they tape the barrels as well. They imagine this precludes the leaving of finger impressions. Remember, fingermarks are often left on cartridges. For some reason the same care is not taken to keep these free of latent marks. Carefully preserve the exact condition of any cartridges found. In other words, do not leave your own finger impressions on them or smudge any latent marks. Criminals sometimes endeavour to remove serial numbers on weapons by drilling or polishing, something a gun nut would never do; nor would he disfigure a weapon with the tape I mentioned. Almost invariably, a taped gun is a criminal's gun. Is there a portable electrical water pump in the garage or workshop? It is difficult to imagine an honest use by ordinary persons for such a piece of equipment that is essential for the manufacture of LSD.

A subtle point about a motor thief's way of living is sometimes revealed by the condition of his 'work garage'. They often have premises, perhaps in low-class mews or under railway arches, where minimal honest work may be done as a blind. To a discerning eye there will be an intriguing difference between these premises and those of the motor repairer in a small way of business. The thief's premises will be very much more untidy. This sign will leap to your eyes, provided you are experienced in visiting most sorts of small-time motor premises. In the ringer's or receiver's garage there will be far more spare parts of some considerable size and weight, in direct contrast to a straight man's work place. A combination of greed and laziness is the fundamental reason; like all criminals, motor thieves are in an impatient hurry to make their fortunes. They cannot wait to attend to the lesser chores of life, the mundane tasks of tidiness and order, as 'honest mugs' have to. Thus, let me emphasise it by repetition, when you see valuable parts of car engines and motor cycles, carelessly disassembled and haphazardly lying about premises—apparently forgotten and certainly uncared for—your senses should sharpen to needle point—you are on to a good thing. Watch, too, for paper ashes consistent with the burning of the sort of books, guides and maps one often finds in motor cars. If a car is stolen and its appearance changed these books and maps must be disposed of; dustbins are too dangerous for this purpose. So burning, either at the premises or on nearby waste land, is often the way out. Thus, such ashes found on waste land indicates a thief's garage nearby.

However unpleasant the task, always physically search the dustbin, and the rubbish bins in the kitchen. Broken or damaged locks found in a dustbin, especially if in new condition, may indicate some person near at hand who has been experimenting in ways to force these locks in preparation for a series of house, shop or factory breakings where similar locks protect valuable property. Abandoned or burned company accounts, minute books, petty cash or postage ledgers, etc. may indicate a nearby safe-breaker who has removed a safe bodily to force it at his leisure, and has then had to get rid of incriminating matter. It may also indicate an absconding long firm fraud operator (see Chapter 6). Broken alarm clocks, broken cheap wristwatches or several empty small packaging boxes for goods of this type, in a dustbin, may indicate the presence nearby of either political

---

Fig. 13.6. Thieves' implements.

(a) A geared device, commercially available abroad. When the blade is inserted into the keyway of a Yale-type lock (in a house or car door) and the trigger pulled, the blade oscillates rapidly in the keyway. In so doing, it clears the keyway and enables the cylinder to be turned by a simple tension tool as in (b). Such devices, found in the possession of anyone other than an established locksmith of good reputation, are extremely suspicious. Should this style of tool be held by a non-locksmith in a street situation, or in premises other than the man's home address or a legitimate workshop (in a corridor of a block of apartments or hotel, for example), the circumstances would probably justify the seizure of the implement, and the detention of the man, certainly until his bona fides are established.

(b), (c) A tension tool and a spare blade (to turn the lock cylinder at the same time as it is picked either by the geared device shown in (a) or by an ordinary lock-pick.

(d) Device used to pierce rubber surround of quarter-light window and to lever up interior door-locking buttons.

(e) Simple wire devices to manipulate the interior hand winders of car door windows. There are many variations.

(f) Another device used to manipulate interior car door window winder, after quarter-light rubber is penetrated by some form of cutting instrument. Again there are many variations.

(g) Beer-can opener—a common and efficient thief's general-duty tool.

(h) Sharpened stainless-steel spoon, used to cut through the rubber surround of a car door quarter-light window, preparatory to inserting a wire device as in (d) and (e).

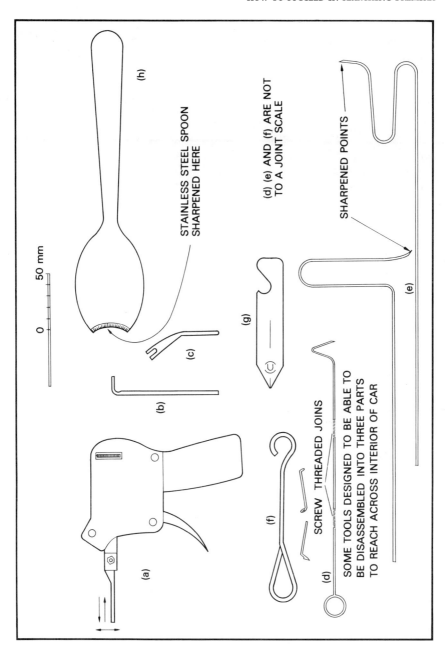

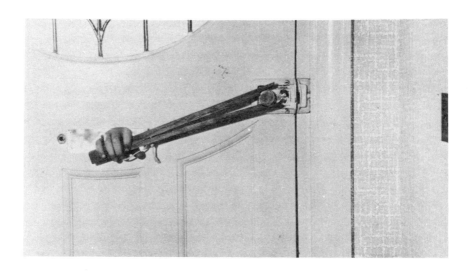

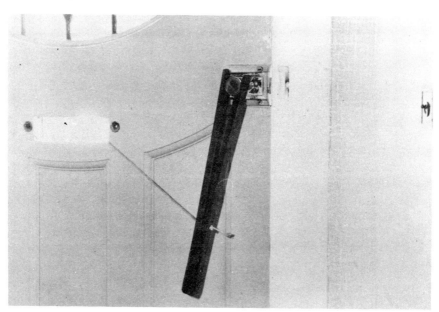

Fig. 13.7. A wooden, self-gripping tool, typical of those made by thieves to open the simpler type of door lock found in some districts. (Courtesy Surrey Constabulary. All rights reserved.)

dissidents or shop thieves. Remember that the actual owner of the dustbin may be quite innocent, and that 'nearby' is the descriptive word for the actual disposer of this sort of incriminating material. Cases such as these should be reported to the senior CID officer of the station area.

While almost unacceptably distasteful, this examination of dustbins is important in brothel and 'using premises for habitual prostitution' cases. In a disputed case, prosecution evidence that parcel(s) of soiled condoms and old contraceptive cartons were in the dustbin is difficult to explain away.

An important point when searching premises is not to become harassed, hurried or too involved in conversation. Do not respond to insults. 'Nothing personal in this, we are just doing the job we're paid for', is a useful phrase to take the bite out of proceedings. Stop, think and move about the premises systematically. Many policemen (it has happened to me) have been made to look abject fools by being locked in a bedroom or other room by escaping offenders, when foolishly concentrating too much on the actual searching. If you go into a room, make sure the key is on the inside of the door or remove it completely. Have a brother officer deputed to do nothing else but watch the suspect. One officer to one suspect.

This officer can also point out places you have missed: 'The spectator sees more of the game than the player.' Generally speaking, when searching more than one floor, work downwards. Always leave at least one officer at the front door. Some experienced men suggest he should be in uniform. However, you must bear in mind that persons delivering drugs, contraband or stolen property may arrive unknowingly in the early stages of a search. A 'buyer' may attend with a large amount of cash to purchase the stuff. Both sorts will be frightened off by the sight of a man in uniform. They may still follow through if the man you post to the front door is in plain clothes and has the real police sense to be aware of these factors and to stand back just inside the passage. Be flexible about this, some 'raids' and searches demand the presence of uniform, especially those in minority areas; some are better dealt with by all the participants being in civilian clothes. The important thing is to consider all the factors and make a decision at the briefing. Always tell the detailed man that his job is detaining suspects *arriving* as well as preventing offenders *leaving*.

In both occupied and semi-derelict property, when looking for a wanted man who may be hiding from you, take police dog teams to assist you if you possibly can. In a 'hurry-up' situation, if you cannot, there may in some circumstances be use for 'four-legged bluff'.

Give commands to an imaginary dog handler, implying in these commands that the dog is quite a savage example of his species. Use a name like 'Viceroy' or 'Khan'. It may bring about the surrender of nervous thieves. Not only can dogs smell the location of hidden intruders, but can hear minute sounds like breathing or the squeaking of leather clothing, belts, braces or shoes—even the opening and closing of an intruder's mouth makes a slight smacking noise within the audible range of a good dog. Do not be prejudiced against the use of dogs. Of course, they have failures and make mistakes and can embarrass you in good-quality premises, but on a profit-and-loss accounting they are infinitely worth while.

Remember, introducers or fugitives may stretch prone along a girder or a wooden beam, or on top of a display case (in a shop). Look upwards as well as around you. They may get in packing cases, under rubbish, old clothes, a tarpaulin, even under a pile of coke. In summer have you checked disused chimneys and boilers ? A quick-thinking thief once stripped a carpet from the floor of an unused bedroom and hid in it, rolled up against the wall of a box room. When Victorian high-ceilinged rooms are refurbished, a plastic lower ceiling is sometimes fitted. Stolen gear or contraband—even a wanted man or deserter—can be concealed here, the man lying parallel with the side of the wall between the ceilings. The four-legged bluff has been mentioned—do not reject the 'long-goodbye' deception. This is allowing the unsuccessful search team to leave the building and not too quietly to drive off. You remain concealed. The team come back in exactly 15 minutes. You may have heard enough in the interim to pinpoint the hidden man or men.

Now, some more pointers. Top-class thieves and criminals may have very valuable small articles or banknotes (their escape 'stake' perhaps, or a year's profit) concealed in what appears to be a tin of a popular brand of soup or beans. Remember, if you are doubtful in this area, that paper labels from genuine tins of branded goods can be placed around a tin, filled with incriminating items, closed up and 'lidded' by a domestic tinning machine ordinarily used for canning home-grown fruit. If so, the tin will look genuine and unopened. Do not be morbidly and foolishly suspicious in ordinary cases and unnecessarily open cans of food, but in a serious case consider weighing suspect tins, on domestic scales, with a similar branded tin you have had sent out for from a nearby shop. In really serious cases you may find something quite revealing.* Remember, fingerprint evidence

---

* Small cubes wrapped in silver paper in the tray of a refrigerator are very probably LSD-impregnated sugar. Do not remove or even undo the wrapping as LSD evaporates rapidly. Try to get such exhibits to the laboratory quickly and hermetically sealed.

in such a case may be important. The typically oval (or square) tins of scented or baby's talcum powder can be opened at the shoulder of the can, cash or contraband concealed inside and the powder and top replaced. Cash can be taped behind a picture. A pistol or sawn-off shotgun may be in a duffel bag or wickerwork basket both packed with dirty, even filthy, clothes to put you off. Weapons have been suspended on cord in the cavities between brick walls. A rifle or full-length shotgun is almost instinctively placed, even by honest householders, among the brooms in a cupboard. Full-length weapons may be laid along girders or beams. Incriminating articles may be hidden by female criminals in boxes of menstrual napkins or among female contraceptive paraphernalia, in the femininely shrewd hope that embarrassed young male officers will not search these thoroughly. This is another reason to take a woman officer with you in the team—her eye will see if the cartons are disturbed and worth thorough examination.

When you enter premises with a search warrant, you have (usually) authority to search all the people you find inside the named premises. Do this first. This is another practical reason, if one is needed, always to take with you at least one woman officer.

Getting into the room or apartment from a common hallway often presents difficulty. Consider the use of deception and bluff, but have another plan of entry ready and rehearsed if the charade goes wrong. My experience is that it often does. A male officer may give a convincing and suitably accented bluff at the briefing, but have stage fright when outside the door in question, merely alerting the man inside by his plainly un-convincing attempt.

Has the wanted man a car of his own outside? If it is of reasonable appearance and particularly if he has been seen previously to wash it, the 'bad accident' bluff can work well. Get a plain clothes woman officer first to note the make, colour and index mark of the car and then, through the door of the apartment, to say she has just collided with it. She can add that the landlady (whom she names) told her the car was his. Ideally, the woman officer should have a well-to-do voice to be the most effective, for she then says she would like to settle at once without her husband or the insurance company knowing. A combination of curiosity, annoyance and greed (the chance to take the woman driver's money in settlement) will bring most criminals to the door and, if the woman officer is elegant, as so many are, he will come out into the hallway where he can be secured. The justification for this play-acting, if you are called to account for it by an unfriendly

145

advocate, is that it prevented violence and was therefore in everyone's interests, including that of his client.

If you are patient and the case is not a rush one, waiting until one of the inmates goes to buy food, liquor or tobacco is one way to get in, as he or she comes out. The messenger is likely to be the least wanted of the persons concerned, and probably the female. Sometimes it is best to pass up the opportunity offered when she leaves the room and to wait until she returns with her purchases. Then the room can more conveniently be rushed.

You may be able to get hold of the key, or a copy of it, from the landlady or a treacherous associate of the wanted man. Before you attempt to use it, inquire whether it is possible to bolt or secure the door independently of the lock. If so, the key may not be of great use, but if the arrest is to be made in the early hours when the subject will probably be asleep, it is certainly worth testing it, but with great care and silently. After the key is turned, lift the door (so that hinges do not squeak) before you gently push inwards.

Consider the likely contingencies arising if you are successful in gaining silent entry and are able to arrest a man in bed, in the early hours. He will usually be with a female companion. The sudden switching on of electric light or a torch will probably disorientate them long enough for the man to be secured. Once this is done, attend to the niceties. Never embarrass the woman, who is likely to be nearly naked and in a shocked state. Always allow the woman officer to supervise her dressing out of view of any male officer. Modesty is a strange quality—apparently depraved people can feel quite heated and intense about it. Who are we to judge anyway? Attention to modesty is important as it lowers the chances of violence by the man, who must feel protective towards the woman. Make sure she is referred to as 'Mrs' (followed by his or her name, whichever is appropriate), however abusive she may be, and do not allow young male officers, smarting under the sort of obscene insults such women can spit out, to return like for like. The same general advice applies if you find the wanted man in bed in a possibly unnatural situation with a male companion. Make no degrading reference to what you see in such circumstances—your business is solely to detain the wanted man safely and without violence, not to make comments or judgements of a moral nature. Keep other officers quiet about it, too. If these contingencies are likely ones, have them mentioned at the briefing, together with strictures that no ribald comments will be permitted. Point out the reason why they are forbidden, namely that they are unprofessional, unmanly and often provoke unnecessary violence.

Having secured the man, he must get dressed. Do not allow him to go to his pile of clothes and dress. Ask him where his clothes are, search them carefully and then hand them to him, one garment at a time—shoes last or, with a man with a reputation for severe violence, perhaps not at all.

With a deranged man, locked and perhaps barricaded in a room, much the same applies—but here be ready for real violence. Wall weaknesses should be considered. A plasterboard wall is often easier to penetrate than a stout door. In a hotel room there are likely to be old and quite frail dividing walls, constructed when double rooms were made into single ones. Does this apply to the room in question? Old-established staff will probably know if this is the case. Perhaps the hinges of the door can be uncovered and unscrewed. Always try to 'talk down' a deranged man in such a situation. It is important to get him talking to you. Try to convince him there will be no loss of face on his part if he opens the door and speaks face to face with you. Do not use emotive phrases like 'surrender' or 'smash down'. Be optimistic, assure him that help—not punishment—is obtainable through you. You understand. You understand. That is the message you must get over to him. Of course, you will have failures when dealing with absolutely intractable men, but then even one success out of ten is infinitely worth while. It is a great test of personality, fluency and policemanship. Appeals to the nobler side of the man's nature, even flattery, are sometimes very effective. Remember that, with a barricaded deranged man alone in a room or house, time is *not* of the essence. You have all the time in the world—but he will get hungry, thirsty and emotionally exhausted. Do not risk injury to other policemen or to police dogs in such a situation, when perhaps all that is needed is patience and understanding.

In getting into a disorderly club or dishonest gaming premises to execute warrants, much of what has been said applies in a general sense. You should have tools available to ensure access if lawful entry is refused. Do not display these—out of sight in the van is the best place for them. Is it necessary to devise some form of visible identification for each member of a large plain clothes raiding party? This is worth considering if there are numerous frequenters of the premises in question—a dance hall, for example. Is it a good idea that officers of the raiding party be supplied with a list of written questions according to their function, so they may quickly 'process' frequenters by merely writing down the answers they receive? Would it be advantageous to the smooth running of the operation to have 'release passes' prepared on scrap paper, stamped with the police station's date stamp? Perhaps a dozen or so could be issued to each member of the raiding party before you start. This way, otherwise innocent frequenters, after satisfactorily answering the required questions, can quickly be routed out of the premises past your colleagues guarding the doors, without needlessly rechecking identity, and so avoiding those bottlenecks that so easily occur at exits when crowded premises are 'raided'.

Bear in mind the problem of the doorman, who may have an electric bell alarm to operate if police suddenly appear in strength at the entrance. These bell-pushes are often on the floor, to be operated by the doorman's foot. With 'flash' premises, which may have a top-hatted, uniformed linkman outside, consider the possibility that he, too, may have quick access either to such an alarm or to a telephone. The hat-check girl in the cloakroom may have a bell or a house phone. Detail someone to keep an eye on them and prevent them obstructing the execution of duty.

Embarrassing failure has hit me more than once because of inadequate prior consideration—in other words, I was made to look an officious fool at the head of a thwarted raiding party, with all evidence of dishonest activity removed because I was not shrewd enough to think through the likelihood of such alarms. A woman co-proprietor in a plush and dishonest gaming club said to us in such circumstances, 'All dressed up and nowhere to go! We almost feel sorry for you, off you go back to bed'. In such circumstances—it is difficult—keep your temper, never make any remark that could be interpreted as a petulant threat and never—having been baulked of the execution of the court's warrant—turn to deal with really trifling breaches of the licensing, lighting or public health laws. Just leave in as dignified a manner as possible. Try smiling, there will be other times. A reputation as a good loser is not to be despised.

To successfully 'spin' any 'drum', the fundamental rules are the same. First, obtain all available information about the premises and the people in it, however disreputable the source of your information. Test this information if you can. Examine thoroughly the criminal record of every convicted person living in or frequenting the premises. Read all registered correspondence you can trace about the premises and these people themselves, however unlikely and inappropriate the subject title may sound. Look through collators' records with care. These chores are important, as you may learn something overlooked that may help you to prevent violence and so contribute to the sweet running of the main task. You may find that one of the persons concerned is already wanted for other crimes; this can forewarn you of the possibility of forcible and violent attempts at escape. Go yourself and look at the premises, not forgetting the sides and rear. These days with Polaroid-style cameras easily available, a photograph or two of the premises in question can be obtained easily and secretly. Certainly, in difficult cases, these photographs will be valuable at your briefing of the raiding party, and subsequently useful to refresh the memory after the passage of time and before court hearings. Know the route to the premises from the place of your briefing. Look at a copy of a local authority's large-scale Ordnance map. Then quietly and in private think through a plan. Write down your plan; it concentrates the mind. It also makes less likely foolish omissions and oversights. Even an imperfect plan is better than no plan.

If licensing hours are material to your entering certain buildings and to subsequent prosecution, *never rely on station records alone* for these details of hours and conditions. Check and compare original records at the offices of the Licensing Sessions, or other authority, as to the certified times and provisos of the particular premises. When doing this, to preserve confidentiality and to avoid possible leaks—even those innocently brought about— examine the particulars of several premises, inferring that your visit is merely a routine clerical exercise to bring police records up to date. You may dismiss this advice as over-pedantic thoroughness, but it will both give you confidence and may save you embarrassment. Fortunately for our reputations, we do not hear too often of licensed premises being 'raided by police' when no offences were actually taking place, but it does occur, particularly in areas of alleged drinking after permitted hours. Save yourself the possibility of a red face by invariably checking the conditions of the licence against *original records*. I must say I learned this lesson in a very hard school!

In dealing with non-criminal or 'technical' offences regarding clubs and licensed premises, i.e., those where actual dishonesty or the commercially motivated degradation of women and juveniles (with or without their consent, remember) is not the norm, beware of being too heavy-handed, of having too much of the clumsy crusader about your behaviour. For example, do not use too many officers in the visit or raid, or allow preliminary expenses to creep too high. While these expenses may seem sensible beforehand, later they can sound quite unreasonable. If frequent false membership is a link in the prosecution's case, do not allow officers to pretend membership in order to get in. In the class of case I have in mind, it rightly sounds vaguely deceitful when aired in open court. What may be justifiable in securing a violent thief or an evil ponce, may not be viewed so understandingly by juries and magistrates in a matter of illegal drinking, however impudent and greedily profit-motivated you consider it to be.

Always ensure that your preliminary observation officers find out the general layout of the premises, so they can draw a sketch plan for you immediately afterwards. Compare this plan with an original plan of the premises. Before they set out tell them you want to know where the switches and fuseboxes are,* and where the till or tills are located. If the lighting inside the premises is reported to be (as so often is the case) subdued and shadowy, you will also want to know from them where convenient light fittings are situated. In such cases, it is good hard-nosed and sensible practice to take two 200-watt bulbs with you when you enter, so if necessary you can illuminate a large area quickly, using or adapting the existing electrical fittings. This applies particularly where you intend to search for dangerous drugs or where, in really depraved premises, it is important to determine accurately and quickly the ages and sexes of young persons, or to look for bruising or other injuries, or the characteristic facial appearances of drug abusers. Intensely bright and unexpected illumination in such sordid surroundings also has a psychological effect upon persons who feel conscious of guilt, or are in some way vaguely ashamed of themselves. It will make them self-conscious *and obviously so*. It is thus an aid in getting to the truth, very much in the long-term interests of the young persons concerned. You have to be forceful and forthright to be truly humane in so many of these circumstances.

However good and experienced your preliminary observation officers are, always warn them to be careful when they leave the premises, certainly never to walk directly back to the station or other police premises—they may be followed. They will groan and say, 'Sir, we know!' but it pays to keep them on their toes. The best of us can become lax in the simple matters. Never assume all officers know the drills brought about by long experience. Now for advice that will be laughed at. *Make sure you take the warrant with you.* If you are a subordinate, make sure your boss takes it with him. He may give you a harsh word for such a reminder, but if you wish genuinely to understudy him with a view one day of being in charge yourself you have willingly to accept such strictures. The fact remains, several raids have taken place where the warrant *was* forgotten, a factor that can cause intense ridicule and severe embarrassment. When the raid is

---

* So that when crowded premises are raided, officers can be sent immediately to prevent any mischievous switching off of lights, which can cause considerable panic and danger, particularly in basements. This is an important part of the briefing.

over, get the notebooks written up there and then, so you can say, on oath if necessary and without the least hesitation, 'All notes were made up as soon after the event as practicable, My Lord, namely at . . .'. Carefully preserve any original notes that, because of the situation prevailing at the time they were made, had to be written on scraps of paper, menus, bills or newspapers. Think carefully how best to present evidence and endeavour to protect the identities of your observation officers. There may be a 'guilty' plea and keeping them out of sight, quickly available on call to give evidence if necessary, may enable their use again with other persistent offenders who were associated with the case in question.

Beware of the attractions of expediency and short-term tactical opportunism in the presentation of your case. The reputation you have for absolute straightforwardness, which has to weather the wear and tear of 30 or more years of duty, is infinitely more important to you and the service than the success or failure of a prosecution. In any event, my experience emphasises repeatedly that, in matters of prosecution, expediency is only rarely truly expedient. This does not alter the desirability for thinking officers to do everything possible, legally and fairly, to make truthful evidence sound both convincing and attractive—not always so easy as it may sound.

Missing youngsters and the search of premises

Different considerations apply when searching premises where lost children are being sought. There is an understandable inclination, when receiving reports of lost or wandering children, to commence the search away from the immediate homes of the children concerned and to go too soon to open country. Experience plainly indicates that there are excellent chances that a child will be found, or in tragic cases the body will be found, by searching premises at or near the child's home. Searching and inquiry at the premises will often reveal clues and pointers to the location of the youngster, if not the child itself.

So, before you embark on major commitment, or recommend to a senior considerable involvement of police, insist that the house(s) must first be searched, and searched thoroughly. Take no excuse from house-proud women who may feel that you have come at a time when untidiness may reflect on their reputations. Search beds—under them, between them, under mattresses, and between mattresses if there are no beds and they have been placed on the floor. Children have been concealed inside boxspring mattresses. Make sure you go inside every room. If there are many people or children sleeping together in one or more rooms, wake them up and make sure the missing child is not in some way being mischievously or (if dead) wickedly concealed. Look everywhere where bedding is stored, including cupboards and chests. Pause and consider where in the house a child's imagination might think there to be a 'secret room' or 'secret passage'. The child may be hiding in such a place, or may have suffocated in such a confined space. Recall your own childhood, when you played in 'dens' and 'forts' or at 'mothers and fathers', both inside and outside premises. Think along this line of consideration in your search of the houses in question, their outbuildings, their lofts, their cellars and barns. Wake other children, and ask them where their imaginary dens, forts, houses and secret passages are. Insist, without bullying, for an answer. Speak to them privately and in a big brother manner. They may not want (in their minds) to betray such locations, especially in the presence of possibly strict parents or foster parents.

Ask every sensible youngster where he thinks the missing person may be. Treat the youngster seriously; give the impression, genuinely, that you value their opinions. Do not patronise.

Are there piles or mounds of rubbish in the vicinity of the premises? Skips for the disposal of rubbish? Dustbins or dustbin sheds? Perambulator sheds? Garages? Is there the remotest chance that the child has been suffocated by carbon monoxide while tampering with a car in a closed garage? What about neighbours' garages or lock-up garages, where the child may previously have found a way to break in through a window or a defective lock? Any old vehicles or old refrigerators abandoned inside or in the vicinity of premises? The boot of every conceivably likely vehicle must be opened and minutely examined *in good light*. A boot can suffocate a live child, or conceal or transport a lifeless one. Think, too, of the attraction to young minds of nearby abandoned outbuildings at brick fields, clay pits, rubbish dumps, railway sidings and abandoned industrial buildings generally. In a child's eyes these resemble ranch-house buildings in Western films, or the no man's land of war films. They will have been the scene of many hours of play and happy imagination. When children are emotionally stretched, they may—without conscious thought—be drawn to conceal themselves in a place where they have previously been happy. Elsewhere, I have said that if you wish to catch thieves, you need to think like a thief. In a similar sense, if you wish to find wandering or absent children, you need to *think like a child*.

Another point of some importance is this—when at innocent play in such places, in their forts and ranches, these children occasionally draw to themselves the attention of perverts and child molesters, mainly because of the remoteness of such buildings and the absence of other adults. You must consider the possibility that the child, previously seen at play by a local unfortunate or inadequate, has been outraged and murdered in such a locale, and the body conveniently concealed there. As a thinking policeman, eventually you will come to realise a frequently forgotten and possibly unpleasant truth about such people. There is compelling evidence to justify what I say, which is this: sexual violators of children are not always disliked by their victims. You see, they listen to children, they flatter children, they give them gifts, they tell stories, they answer questions, in short, *they have time for children as persons.* Of course, it is done with ulterior and lustful sexual motives, but none the less, however distasteful the grasping of this concept may be, genuine affection can develop between such people and the children concerned. The children may consider the irregular sexual intimacies to be trifles, compared with the interest that is shown in them. Why is this important? Because when a child is emotionally stretched, after some disagreement with parents, for example, he may go willingly and secretly to a person he considers his friend, one who understands, quite irrespective of any unnatural sexual proclivities he may have. Thus the experienced policeman must visit and in some way, with consent of course, *search the premises of such people,* without humbling or disgracing them unnecessarily.

In this area of human behaviour remember two things. First, such a person may think you are investigating homosexuality rather than looking for the child, and consequently lie to you and conceal the youngster. He may fear the child has said something to a parent. Secondly, the child may have met such a person when away from home on holiday with a relative, so there is a possibility the child may be safe but some distance away. In any event, if you are a skilful officer, able to speak in a straightforward and transparently honest manner to such people, untrammelled by unthinking prejudice, you may either find the child before real harm comes to it, or at least discover some real clue as to its whereabouts.

Give the child who has left home in a temper, on a temporary basis, a chance to come back voluntarily. In particular, do not have a 'four-ring circus' of police vehicles with flashing lights too near the child's home, which will be counterproductive to a repentant child creeping back hungry and cold to the fold. He may think to himself, 'Look at all the fuss I have caused, they will never forgive me! I'll stay away'. Be discreet when parking vehicles that are obviously police ones.

153

With older youngsters missing from home, subtly different and additional considerations apply to the searching of premises. If the child or young person is of sufficient age to read or write, there is every likelihood that a properly directed and thoughtful search will bring a clue as to their likely whereabouts. Find and read their schoolbooks, read any notes inside their private books and any library books. Look carefully in satchels and brief-cases. Find every letter they may have received by post. Question parents and the postman about deliveries of any letters. Postmarks ? Has the child a post office account ? Find the book, if it has not gone with the youngster, and go through it with the parent. Has any withdrawal taken place at a location surprising to the parent ? That is where the older child may be, at the house of an acquaintance or relative, near that withdrawal of money. Is there any routine or obviously favourite place of withdrawal ? If the pass book you are looking at is an old one, the missing youngster may go to that location for further withdrawals with the current book. It may be worth notifying such a place. Do the youngsters of the house use the phone ? Is there any way of finding out where unusual calls have gone to ? Or come from ? Who have these children been writing to ? Can we find any of the letters ? Letters may be concealed in desks, behind drawers, between the leaves of favourite books or magazines, and in bedding. Any unfinished letters thrown away ? Letters with intimate allusions are the ones which may explain the location of a missing youngster. Any favourite relatives, especially those not too popular with parents ? Ask the parent where the child has said he/she was happiest. Phrase the question so as not to offend. The answer may reveal the youngster's present location. In searching for children, an hour spent thinking through the problem will pay repeated dividends. Do not be unnecessarily hurried or bullied into hurrying.

Successful searching of premises is the key to so much, in so many fields of police endeavour. Never lose an opportunity to take part in any form of search, in the briefing and in administration. Combined with careful thinking through of the individual task or problem, this is a principal way to increase professional skill, so better to serve the public.

14. Criminal violence to children

'Baby battering'—police officers are so often the only persons available to protect these children. How to recognise these difficult cases.

An important area of practical duty, where careful judgement is needed to decide whether action is to be taken at once or if a prompt report should be written, is in the field of the protection of children from violence. A terrible truth is that, today, many infant children are crippled and maimed, even killed, by their parents and step-parents. I am referring to 'baby battering', or as the milky-sounding euphemism now has it, 'non-accidental injuries to infants'. Estimates of the number of really serious assaults per year vary considerably, perhaps because of the falsehoods told to medical men, nurses and to social workers generally by the persons responsible, or by their near relatives. Nevertheless, responsible estimates (*The Observer,** 25 August 1974, for example) place it as high as 4600 per year, with no fewer than 700 deaths resulting. This means, and let us face the truth about it, that *every day* in the UK two children are killed, or rather murdered, by those having charge of them, and that these facts have been accepted not as the terrible crimes they are, but rather as some form of esoteric social problem that will be attended to in due course by conferences, seminars and 'more research'. The mood of general opinion is perhaps at last moving away from this latter attitude.

Nevertheless, my advice to practical peace officers is this—remember first, what Lord Birkett, a most unbigoted even free-minded judge, said many years ago, namely that the Law of England and its officers extend sure protection to babes no less than to any other of the Sovereign's subjects, and second, what it was you declared at your Attestation on joining when, before one of Her Majesty's Justices, you solemnly promised '. . . to cause the Peace to be kept and preserved, and *to prevent all offences against the persons . . . of Her Majesty's subjects'*. Clear your mind of the intellectual

* See also the *Justice of the Peace* (page 501), 14 September 1974.

confusion surrounding this important issue, and regard these deaths as murders, and the crippling assaults as either attempted murder or the 'causing of grievous bodily harm', and act accordingly. There is nothing inconsistent with this and the mutual regard and respect which should exist between our service and social workers. Where interests apparently clash, however, as when social helpers—with the best intentions—are perhaps over-inclined to disregard these matters, wistfully hopeful that the family unit concerned can be 'preserved', it is as well, without heat, to point out that it is a matter of our *sworn duty*, first to protect life and secondly to bring such offences officially to the notice of our chief officer, and that it is he, with the advice of the Director of Public Prosecutions, who has discretion in these serious matters. If you have the least suspicion that such a crime is in progress but only injuring the child cumulatively, or 'little by little', then ensure a senior detective officer is told all the facts, and told promptly.

But what else can ordinary motor and foot patrol men, in uniform or plain clothes, do when their duty takes them through the streets, the play-grounds, into the hospitals and schools of our great cities, and into homes generally? They can keep their eyes and ears open for the signs and symptoms of these crimes, based on an intelligent assessment of the pattern as we know it, and make sure that prompt action is taken where there is reasonable suspicion that such an outrage, for outrage it is, has occurred, or is occurring. As we all know so well, police are frequently called to violent man-and-wife disputes, where the wife has been injured or abused. In some urban areas it is a multi-daily duty for policemen. Therefore

Watch for

▷ The domestic situation where there may well be, in addition to the obvious injury to the woman, criminal violence to the children of the union or previous unions—*particularly the latter*. It could even be the fundamental cause of the dispute between the man and woman. A previous death of a child, even if not thought to be anything other than accidental, should be taken into consideration in assessing whether there is latent danger to other children, or not. Think of the statistical chances against two children of the same household separately being involved in fatal accidents within the household's general area, or even of dying of disease. Coincidences of this nature are rarely found. A pointer can be where the child, if a baby, is referred to by either parent as 'it' in an

otherwise innocuous sentence; in fact, any phrases indicating deperson-
alisation of the child in any turn of expression should make you wary.
The fact that the natural mother does not readily know the child's exact
age may be a pointer towards an unnatural situation developing. If
either parent seems unreasonably to insist that the child is 'mental' or
'dull', you should also take extra care in your assessment. You must be
particularly alert in any of these circumstances to ensure that the children
are not in danger, and make it a matter of disciplined mental drill
always to ask yourself, before you leave such a household, '. . . is every
child accounted for, and are they thriving?' A shrewd officer can speak
affectionately to, and perhaps admire, every child there, possibly
picking them up, tickling or 'chucking' them under the chin, without
arousing the least suspicion or resentment, but making certain all is well.
Remember, a vindictive man or woman may falsely accuse their spouse in
some situations, so you should not act too precipitately. *Injuries to the
child* are what you should act on.

Watch for

▷ Families on your patch, or those to whom you are called or sent, where
the actual structure of the family is both complex and complicated.
Perhaps a near-incestuous relationship is suspected to exist. Unmarried
cousins living together as man and wife? Stepchildren? Is there
habitual and accepted sexual infidelity by either spouse with others? Are
nieces and nephews living cheek by jowl with natural children? Have
any of the children been 'fostered' or 'in care' previously? Has the family
a history of frequent changes of address owing to debt? Is there a prior
mental history, or reputation for violence outside the family? What
about alcoholism? Do they speak resentfully about doctors, nurses,
health visitors and social workers? Do they talk slightingly of the
children's department of local hospitals? Have there been several
admissions to hospitals by various members of the family? A combination of these factors can indicate the type of problem family where
violence to children may be commonplace but concealed.

It seems to me that there are good liberal grounds to argue that it is Her
Majesty's judges who should decide in open court, with all their worldly
knowledge, their independence and balanced mercy, what should be done
concerning really gross offences against children, rather than they be items
on the agenda of a private conference of social workers, however well

intentioned. Courts alone have the facility *to insist* upon medical and mental treatment in non-custodial cases, and all High Court proceedings have a sobering effect, which the informal counselling of a patient sadly lacks.

As a constable, your statutory powers of arrest, and your powers to take such a child to a place of safety—which, of course, includes a hospital—are more than sufficient. (See and know your powers under Section 2 of the Criminal Law Act 1967, and Sections 1 and 28 of the Children and Young Persons Act 1969, so that you can quote them with confidence in any company.)

Experience has shown that there are certain patterns to the injuries sustained by these children, so

Watch for

▷ Toddlers or babies with black eyes. As every footballer knows, it is difficult to get a black eye merely by falling over. A small configuration, the shape of a pointed elbow or fist, is necessary to fit into the area concerned. A child with two black eyes should cause you to have twice as much suspicion. It is straining coincidence to the limit for a fall to cause two black eyes. It is possible for a blow to the rear of the head, for example, to cause black eyes but, in innocent circumstances, there should be other signs to rule out criminal violence.

Watch for

▷ Bruises on top of older bruises; also bruises consistent with fingermarks. Imagine a child's face being grasped violently by a man's right hand (Plate 1). The thumb would bruise the child's right jaw, his forefinger the forehead, the three other fingers the left cheek and jaw. It seems that babies are brutally grasped in this way, which in itself causes injury. Further injuries—concealed by clothing—may be present, remember. Look particularly for similar injuries caused at different times and similar injuries caused to children of different ages.

Watch for

▷ Bite marks. Remember that children bite each other, so the size of the mark may be significant.

Watch for

▷ Frightened appearance. A dog that has been abused and beaten cruelly has a characteristic appearance and an unmistakable attitude towards all

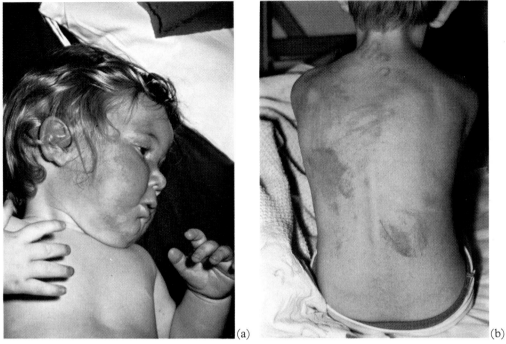

(a)

(b)

Plate 1. (a) Effect of a violent man's grasp. (b) and (c) Appearances of an injury: (b) by hand and shoe; (c) a tear in the fold of skin between the upper lip and gum, suggesting a blow on the upper lip. (Courtesy M. H. Hall, MRCS, LRCP.)

(c)

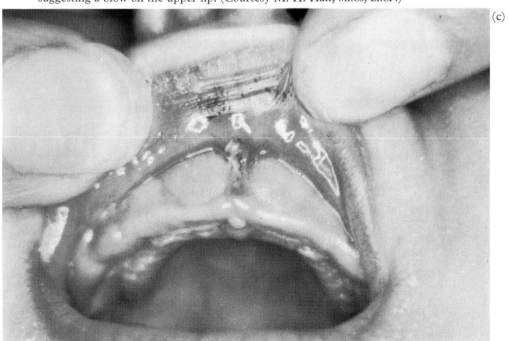

Plate 2. Appearances of an injury. (Courtesy M. H. Hall, MRCS, LRCP.)

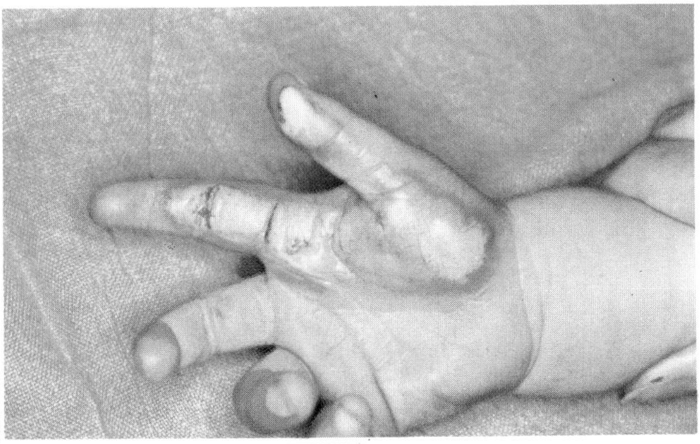

(a) A hand burnt by contact with an electric fire element.

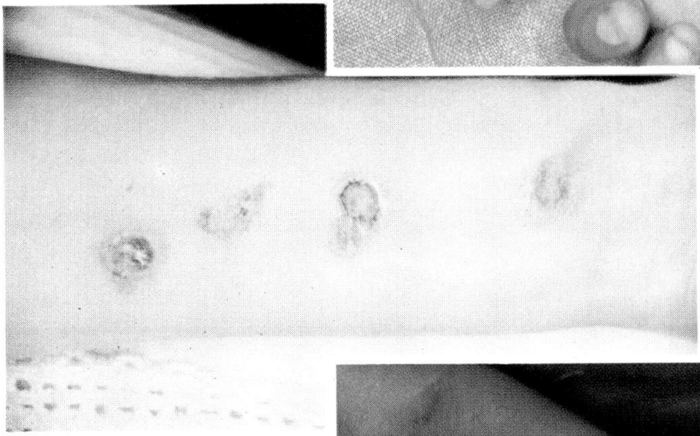

(b) Deep cigarette burns.

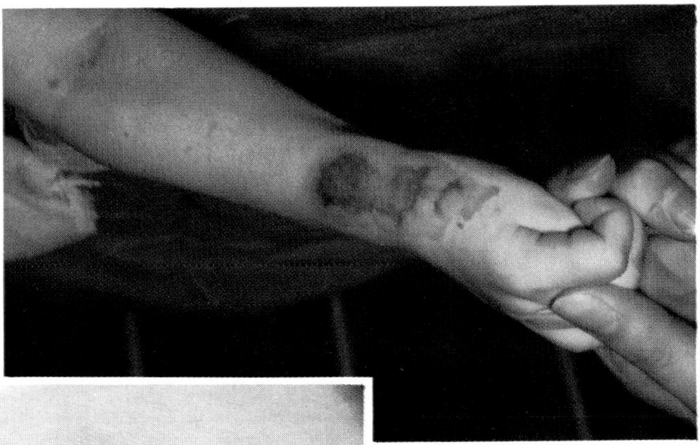

(c) A burn produced by contact with an electric iron.

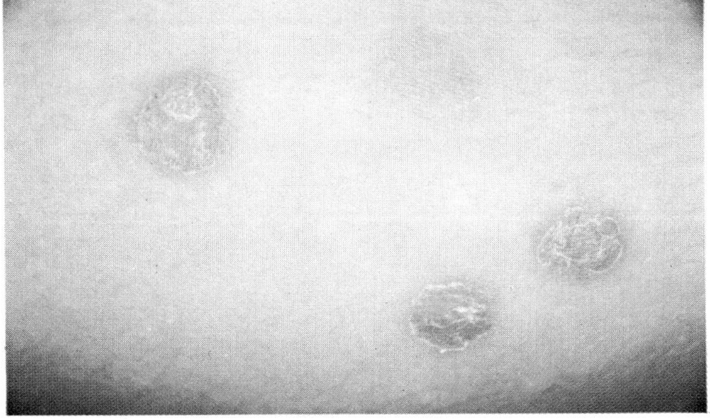

(d) Superficial cigarette burns.

men and women. It is edgy, it is apprehensive, it flinches and avoids even innocent movements by a nearby human being. It retreats, it huddles, it hides. It is hopeless to offer it titbits of food or to speak kindly to it. All these facts concerning the ill-treatment of beasts must be within your own experience of life. Exactly the same occurs with battered infants. Medical consultants frequently refer to it as 'frozen awareness', and this chilling phrase sums it up well. There is often, too, a general apathy about the child. These poor creatures rarely cry, but when they do the sound they make is quite unlike a normal child's squalling. My wife, a nursing officer, emphasises two characteristics: firstly there is no indignant urgency about the sound as with a normally happy child, and secondly, it has the note of an utterly hopeless and crushed whining about it. These low-key continuous sounds are more a commentary on despair than a tearful call for a mother's help, which the normal child knows will be answered. Do what you can to recognise such outward signs. Remember, however, that savage mental bullying, without actual blows, can induce a similar state.

Watch for

▷ or rather listen for, over-rehearsed answers in relation to the explanations of how children received their injuries. These can betray their falseness by their over-fluent, facile, 'pat' sound, and by the frequent repetition of certain key phrases, essential to the explanation. For example, 'He's always falling over', 'He bruises so easily'.* Remember, too, the fact that a child who is well dressed or has good-quality 'cuddly toys', is not necessarily indicative of truly loving care. It has been noticed repeatedly that many of these unfortunate children are clean, well clothed and outwardly well cared for. Social class has little or nothing to do with it.

Watch for

▷ Every opportunity to improve your general knowledge of the appearance of wounds. If you get a chance to see, for example, at a hospital or at the scene of a crime, cigarette burns on human skin—whether upon an adult or not—do so, and note carefully what you see (Plate 2). If you have access to coloured photographs of such injuries previously coming to the notice of police and still attached to prosecution papers, again examine them thoughtfully. These injuries are not unknown upon children, but

---

* Where a suspect parent attributes adult attitudes to a baby ('He has never loved me!') you should be alert.

they can resemble, especially after the lapse of time, innocent skin eruptions. Take the same interest in any sort of wounds that come to police notice. Scalding can happen to children accidentally, and often does. It can also be a terrible assault. If you are called or sent by radio message to such an incident, keep an unprejudiced eye open for other injuries, the sort I have described. Do not over-react, but have a healthy objective and questioning eye at any incident you attend where children are injured, even slightly. When an adult is attacked by a violent person wielding a knife, almost invariably you will see 'defensive cuts' on the hands of the victim. Similar defensive injuries may sometimes be seen on the hands and lower arms of young children.

Remember, you have a professional duty to make yourself as experienced as possible in all criminal matters, so better to protect the public. Beware of making yourself a nuisance but, again generally speaking, paediatricians and pathologists, if they see your interest in wounds is sensible and professional —without a trace of morbid curiosity—will go out of their way to show you the signs that should greatly increase your professional knowledge. You have a plain duty always to get an injured child—however they come under your notice—to a doctor, preferably at a hospital, as quickly as possible. If you suspect grievous assault masquerading as an accident, privately tell the casualty sister or the medical officer. Remember how busy they are and how easy it is for them, without the policeman's eye and his daily awareness of the brutalities of life, to miss certain aspects of these cases and to accept a lying tale of explanation. Rightly so, they are concerned principally with treating the patient; their minds are not slanted, as ours are, towards the criminal law. Whereas their sentiments are to be respected by all sensible policemen, our view, properly explained without heat or emotion, is also entitled to recognition.

Although he is perhaps generally disinclined to speak openly about it, every man who has done any competitive boxing will know that there is something about successfully landing effective blows upon an opponent—a strange, perverse and almost sexual pleasure. It is my view that this pleasurable feeling may well be a hidden cause of violence to defenceless children, especially by inadequate men who are perhaps failures in both the day-to-day work they undertake and in their private lives. The same feelings may perhaps be latent in adult females, especially if they themselves are the subject of violence from a spouse. In their mind's eye they may imagine that the child assumes the identity of the violent partner, and they then revenge themselves on him. It seems, generally speaking, that far more females indulge in 'battering' their children than men, some authorities giving the proportion as high as two to one. Far from being 'cries for help' by the batterers, as some social workers consider these terrible assaults to be, it may be merely the indulging of lustful and resentful feelings.

A balanced enforcement of the criminal law is the first defence in the welfare of children. Police are on duty twenty-four hours a day and, at night or at weekends, are perhaps the only people immediately available to protect children. Other interested parties are not so fortunate, because of their small numbers and their extremely heavy case-loads.

Remember, hospital casualty sisters, district nurses, midwives and health visitors are not infrequently the wives of policemen and, because of their necessarily practical approach to life, nearly all are unlike the permissive type of social worker who mistakenly (but actively) tries to conceal from police the fact that a child is slowly being tortured to death, in the theoretical assumption that a police investigation would 'break up the family'. The nurses concerned may well privately indicate to you long-term suspicious cases, provided they trust you as a reasonable man who would never embarrass them professionally. If you wish for such trust and help, go out of your way to oblige the senior nursing staff of hospitals, particularly in matters of messages at awkward hours, in the disposal of property and in the co-operative handling of hospital trespassers or drunks. Even when such tasks could be avoided by too pedantic an attachment to written regulations, you must attend to them and attend promptly. Remember, you cultivate these persons with the best of intentions—so that they will assist you in the protection of defenceless children.

15. Final comments

How to keep the initiative and avoid unnecessary complaint; also, some courtroom advice in extreme cases.

A 'stop in the street', whether of a motorist or a pedestrian, is really an interview conducted by a police officer, who has chosen his subject, and the time and place to stop him, on reasonable grounds. At the outset the policeman has the initiative. He can decide what line of questioning to follow, and can steer the questions in the direction of his choice, depending on whether the first contact confirms his suspicions or suggests that he is dealing with a law-abiding citizen.

Officers should try, by verbal skill and simple psychology, to retain this initiative in a pleasant and friendly way. The interview will consist of three stages—the approach, the examination and then arrest or disengagement. The officer who makes the approach should conduct the first part of the interrogation. He should not be interrupted by any other officer until he indicates that there may be a break.

Many suspects, innocent and guilty alike, will try to turn you from the subject in hand. Do not allow yourself to be deflected. While remaining courteous and friendly, you must convey firmly the impression that you are examining for a particular reason, without revealing what the reason is at this stage. Never suggest that your inquiries are casual or a matter of mere routine.

Learn to know and counter a number of familiar replies which are obstructive, bearing in mind that they do not necessarily indicate guilt. Remember, too, that innocent people sometimes give conflicting explanations because of nervousness. Never be drawn into a discussion of police powers. When this happens, the wrong party is asking the questions and the peace officer has lost the initiative.

The counter to 'What right have you to stop me like this?' is: 'It would be strange if policemen were forbidden to speak to people. We couldn't protect them or their property at all.' Before the person stopped has time to frame a reply, the original question should be put again in a firm and pleasant voice. Police powers or Acts of Parliament should not be quoted, unless a suspect is being arrested or charged. The street is not the place for the discussion of legal niceties. 'There is nothing personal in this' is always a useful expression. An antagonistic manner is contagious and fatal to the efficient discharge of duty. Allow an innocent interviewee to withdraw without loss of self-respect or 'face', even if it means accepting some unpleasant or harsh remark from him. Do not be thin-skinned. This applies particularly if a man is accompanied by a woman. Some men of absolutely respectable background would rather strike a police officer, with all this may entail in the way of disgrace and financial penalty, than look foolish or be humbled in the presence of a woman. This truth is so frequently overlooked by younger officers. A man unnecessarily humbled, or even merely spoken down to in a patronising manner, when with a woman, feels his manliness—even his virility—is being challenged. Avoid like the plague any desire to be the worldly and witty 'tough cop' of television. A natural and fluent courtesy is the hallmark of the successful professional man.

The counter to 'Why have you stopped me, officer?' is: 'I've good reason for wanting to put some questions to you, and I'll tell you what it is in a minute or two.' The original question should be put again. The counter to the old familiar 'Do I look like a criminal, officer?' is: 'These days, as you see from newspapers and courts, mere appearance counts for little or nothing.' The original question should be put again in a pleasant manner.

An innocent person who has been stopped and interrogated is entitled to a prompt and open-handed apology from the officer stopping him. He should be given a good reason for having been stopped, if he appears to require it, although it may not be appropriate to give him the principal reason on every occasion, as this may be wounding or offensive. Be truthful but discreet. It is as well to record a suspect's name and address while he is not watching. It is often useful to use the suspect's own name when speaking to him, e.g., 'Mr Brown' or 'Mr Jenkins', as this can put the interview on a personal and friendly basis before it closes. If you stop a tradesman, say a plumber or decorator, and he is obviously straightforward, he will be pleased if you speak of his trade favourably and ask for his trade card. Never be familiar in the way you address prostitutes when you have to speak to them. They may have well-known first or nicknames. Never use them. Whatever they may say, you will be the gainer if you remember that all persons, however apparently degraded, desire to be treated in a dignified way. It is not a bad rule with older prostitutes to use the prefix 'Mrs', followed by their surname, whatever their marital state. This will avoid embarrassing them and will be to your advantage in the long run. Both skill and practice are necessary to be truly courteous, and of course there are real dangers of sounding patronising, so let good sense and sincerity guide your use of this advice.

An excellent closing remark to an innocent motorist, whether respectable or not, is: 'If we were able to get back your car undamaged, after it had been stolen, by questioning someone like this, you'd be pleased with us, wouldn't you? As I said just now, there's nothing personal in this.' Only a very churlish person can continue to be offended after an obvious truth like this. Similar remarks can be adapted to cover all property, and they rarely fail.

A skilful officer never willingly offends members of the public. When approaching apparently suspicious persons in stationary vehicles, a wise man opens the interrogation with a friendly inquiry as to whether they have broken down. If it becomes obvious at once that you are dealing with respectable people, they need never know of your original suspicion. When explaining why you have 'stopped' an honest resident, avoid telling him it was because he lives in a 'rough district' and 'should be careful'. He may well have real pride in his home and strong local patriotism towards the area in which he lives. Your remarks, although well intentioned, can still wound and annoy him.

In endeavouring to resolve this difficult problem of assertive policing and the liberty of the subject, the whole of the judgment in the case of McArdle v Egan and others (1933)* should be read.

Remember, reasonable suspicion justifying arrest (in criminal matters) may be founded (a) on matters within your knowledge, including the fact that you know the suspect has in the past been convicted of offences of similar character, and (b) statements made to you by another which you consider worthy of credit. (The fact that a suspect has, in the past, been convicted of similar offences would not *by itself* afford 'reasonable suspicion', but it can legitimately be used with other suspicions quite distinct from bad character.) Whether you had reasonable and probable cause in making the arrest is a matter for the judge and not the jury.

* McArdle v Egan and others (1933) All E.R. 611 (150 L.T.412; 98 J.P. 103; 30 Cox C.C.67).

In the performance of duty, take comfort from the words used by Lord Wright in this famous case (words that many 'liberals' wish had never been uttered!):

It is, no doubt, very important that the liberty of the subject should be preserved from undue interference, and in this case the charge has been withdrawn and it is not suggested that he was guilty of the offence. *On the other hand, it has got to be remembered that, in the public interest, it is very important that Police officers should be protected in the reasonable and proper execution of their duty; they should not be hampered or terrified by being unfairly criticised if they act on reasonable suspicion.* Although the amount here is very small, I think the question of principle is very important. It has to be remembered that Police officers in determining whether or not to arrest are not finally to decide the guilt or innocence of the person arrested. Their functions are not judicial, but ministerial, *and it may well be that if they hesitate too long when they have a proper and sufficient ground of suspicion against an individual they may lose an opportunity to preserve evidence.* I am not saying that as in any way justifying hasty or ill advised conduct. Far from that, but, once there is what appears to be a reasonable suspicion against a particular individual, *the police officer is not bound, as I understand the Law, to hold his hand in order to make further enquiries if all that is involved is to make assurance doubly sure.*

Catching ruthless, proficient thieves in the street, especially those using vehicles, is undoubtedly the most skilled of police duties. To be successful you must, to quote Lord Brampton ('An address to police constables on their duties' 1904): 'When on duty, allow nothing but duty to occupy your thoughts.' The public have a right to expect your best endeavours during this period. Read the *Gazette* and 'Informations' with sensible discernment, look for details of men you know and those likely to be in the areas you are working. It is impossible to read these publications usefully in any other way. The sheer bulk of detail will defeat you. In this connection, once every two or three months, read 'Supplement A' of the *Gazette*. In this publication the case histories and photographs of expert travelling criminals are given. You will get a good knowledge of how the more expert criminals operate, by reading about their past methods of working.

Whether you are in plain clothes or uniform, cultivate a smart appearance; the smarter you are, the greater will be your success in interrogating

165

persons, in giving instructions and in avoiding complaints. Instinctive respect is paid to an immaculate man or woman in any walk of life.

Proper stress and natural pauses are necessary in giving evidence. Some officers give evidence extremely well; listen to them carefully and improve your own ability. Cultivate a genuinely liberal attitude and manner in giving evidence. As I have said before, remember you are usually speaking about your fellow-countrymen and fellow-citizens, and you should not presume to judge them, even in the tone of your voice. In cases where imputations of personal animosity may be made by defendants—for example, 'assault on police'—let another officer, not directly involved, give the antecedents and previous convictions if the man is found guilty. In a 'guilty' plea, let him give 'the facts' as well. Never show what may be interpreted as vindictiveness, no matter how vilely you have been used by the defendant.

If you are active against thieves it is inevitable that eventually false allegations will be made against you. These falsehoods can always be frustrated by intelligent anticipation, accurate note-keeping and transparent honesty in all your dealings.

You must not be thin-skinned in the witness box. In contested cases you are sure, sooner or later, to be accused of being thoughtless or pompous, unskilled, inexperienced and frequently of being 'genuinely mistaken'. Remember, counsel is acting on instructions he has received and is duty bound to test you. It is often sensible to deny insinuations of this sort quietly and with good humour, or even to concede with grace that you may be (if it is true) inexperienced or unskilled and, where it is obvious that you could be mistaken, to say so.

Take this advice, however—never allow an attack on your integrity to pass without prompt, and occasionally fierce, denial. Integrity goes far beyond telling the whole truth. If you are accused of being brutal or of being prejudiced against a minority group, or if it is hinted that you are so obsessed by thoughts of your own advancement that you have the approach of an officious martinet towards suspected law breakers, these are attacks on integrity. Even if it is only hinted that you were thoughtless with a woman or child coming into your care, or carelessly cavalier with important evidence, these too are attacks upon your straightforwardness. In short, any question or statement falsely inferring that you behaved in an unmanly way should be rebutted, and rebutted at the time. Such denials can be courteously phrased.

A very small proportion of both counsel and solicitors are grossly insulting to police witnesses. Why, goodness knows. A charitable view is that possibly because of their unworldliness, when listening to deceitful men instructing them, they are duped by the lies they hear about you. This, combined with a perfectly proper but perhaps too intense desire to right wrongs, causes both impatience and discourtesy. Try to remember that, like social workers and probation officers, lawyers meet professional criminals *after they are caught*. They see them when they are defused and harmless. They hear their explanations when they are contrite, in sober clothes, accompanied by distraught relatives, all of whom are quick to point out alleged police bullying. Policemen, like the victims of crime, see these greedy and sometimes violent thieves at a very different stage. We see them when they are ruthless and aggressive, or confidently arrogant; when they are fat and comfortable on the fruits of crime, telling us in obscene phrases to 'prove it if you can'. A very different sight to the subdued detected criminal, who seems to a naive and forgiving eye to be respectful sweet reason itself, so deserving of 'another chance'. With an even smaller proportion of lawyers, the reason is more sinister—they are as dishonest as the profit-motivated criminals they defend and justify. The motives of this tiny proportion are plain enough—they abuse you because they think it good tactics in the frustrating of justice and the making of money.

Although we can weather the usual cut and thrust of cross-examination, there are limits. When a really vindictive-tongued attorney does all he can to sting you, with contrived lies and insults, into making ill-judged replies you must beware. Do not enter into argument or long answers. If the man deliberately mispronounces your name, for example, or provocatively sneers as he addresses you by a rank either less than you have or perhaps over-high (a not uncommon courtroom ploy) keep a cool head. Let it go the first and second time. To be thin-skinned over rank and the pronunciation of your surname can sound conceited. Nevertheless, you can, after the third time, say to the Bench something like, 'My Lord, perhaps the shorthand writer should know my police ranking is that of Constable'.

The best cure for such counsel is to reply to their questions perfectly civilly, but through the Bench. Listen to the question, consider it and your reply, then turn your head to the Bench and reply to the judge or presiding magistrate. This will give you the lever to control the rate of questions. The sort of lawyers I have in mind will see that you have the measure of them, and realise that you have taken the initiative. It is likely that they will then cease the more malevolent of their attacks. Remember, courtesy and willing subordination to the authority of the Queen's Courts does not mean you must behave like a servile doormat in the witness box.

When giving evidence in disputed and defended cases, you may be pressed, and pressed hard, for a 'yes' or 'no' answer in cross-examination when such an answer would *never adequately or truthfully reflect what occurred*. Remember, you have a duty, as a witness of truth, to tell the *whole truth* and you must not be bullied or browbeaten into such answers, when the interests of Justice plainly require otherwise. Of course, you must beware of being loquacious, or of endeavouring to introduce opinion into an answer, or even of bumptiousness, nevertheless duty is duty, and plain, direct speaking may be called for. In most cases it will be best for younger officers to ask the presiding Chairman of Justices, the Magistrate, or the Judge, at the hearing in question, for permission to answer more fully, saying perhaps '. . . the question cannot truthfully or adequately be answered by "yes" or "no" in the circumstances as I know them . . .' or '. . . I do not think I can give an answer which will be accurate and truthful by saying "yes" or "no" . . .'. However, I recall a friend of mine, engaged over many months of hard work with me in an intensely difficult case of alleged criminal corruption, when pressed 'Will you answer my question "yes" or "no"?' saying, 'The question may be yours, sir, but the answer *must be mine*'. While not suitable for every case, this answer has considerable shrewdness and impact.

Remember, too, a fundamental fact about the dignity and wholesomeness of even the humblest of peace officers. Evidence in criminal cases is given as a matter of duty, without consideration of monetary reward. Our rate of pay remains the same whether we go to court or not. Further, court attendances have little or nothing to do with promotion, as we all know. In London particularly, competitive written examination, open to all, decides promotion to the grade of inspector. On the other hand, lawyers appear in court for specific fees, sometimes so high that open disclosure would make many men gasp! To be blunt about it, there is no escaping it, they are there for money; they are *hired* by one of the contesting sides, and the size of their annual income depends upon their reputation for success. Take comfort and confidence from these often-forgotten truths, but do not remind lawyers from the witness box of their special and biased interest, it can do no good. Just let these facts fortify your resolve when your integrity is unfairly attacked.

Really malignant insults—I mean something really vile—should never be passed over, but must be answered directly. Consider coldly and quietly saying, 'A cowardly insinuation, and I deny it absolutely'. If a certain style of lawyer repeatedly says, for example, 'I put it to you that you are a liar and perjurer', or 'I put it to you that you coached, trained and rehearsed this woman witness in lying for you', say in reply, after the second time, after the first sober denials, 'Do you, sir?' This can be an unexpected and disconcerting reply and it may well leave your questioner speechless. To use the word 'sir' need never indicate the least feeling of inferiority. If you have made an honest mistake and it is unfairly harped upon, after courteously admitting it, say, 'I acted with good intention, in what I thought then was the public interest'.

Occasions will arise when you will have to strike with hand or baton, and sometimes unavoidably to wound, law breakers who are frenziedly violent to yourself or to defenceless persons. In the witness box, at a criminal or coroner's court, never attempt to gloss over or to diminish the seriousness of such an incident. Nothing sounds worse or more suspect than an inference that such injuries, fatal or otherwise, were in some way caused unintentionally or accidentally. Be frank. *Be frank.* There is nothing shameful in using reasonable force to do your duty. Reasonable force has sometimes to be deadly force. You are an agent and officer of the Crown, of our 'Sovereign Lady The Queen', and you have taken an oath or declaration that you will protect her subjects, and those other persons under her protection, to the very limit of force, if it is necessary. Yours is thus a post of great trust and dignity. Bear all this in mind and regard any equivocation or avoidance of responsibility as beneath contempt.

When questioned in a serious case consider saying, with a quiet firmness, 'In my judgement I had to subdue him. It was absolutely necessary to restore quiet, and there was no other way. Of course I regret it, but it was a matter of duty, of obedience to instructions, and the protection of the public.' If you are then asked why you regret it, say something after this style, 'All violence, even lawful and necessary violence, is never welcomed. That is what I mean when I say I regret it. I would rather it had ended quietly.'

In the past 30 years there have been tremendous technological advances in the field of police work. As the result of careful study and evaluation there have been improvements, too, in techniques of interrogation, in the allocation of resources and in the matter of better office management of large-scale inquiries. Records are on instant retrieval computer, there is microfilm storage of bulky papers, individual trouble-free radio, more rapid search of single-fingerprint collections—forensic science is now universally available and in many new fields. There are electronic listening, recording and surveillance contrivances that are nothing short of amazing. Nevertheless, they are nothing without integrity and a wholesome motivation, for otherwise oppression and injustice are merely made more efficient.

Therefore, despite these improved tools, for that is all they are, be aware of the undoubted fact that sophisticated and brutal criminals will continue to be caught, *in the first instance*, not by devices but by the trained, discriminating and humane eye, the persevering determination and the dedication of ordinary police officers, determined to keep the streets as free from the obscenity and eventual degradation of crime as is possible. Get to the truth, then; it stands all tests.

Glossary of words and phrases commonly used by thieves, cheats and ponces

Some of the words and phrases listed in this glossary are offensively racist, some are reactionary and sexist, a considerable number are obscene or at least unpleasant.

It goes without saying that they do not reflect in the least way the views of the compiler; he merely reports what he considers a genuine vocabulary, detestable though it may be.

In addition to many expressions taken from Cockney rhyming slang there are also several Yiddish terms included. Whereas these latter are common in both the respectable and dubious sections of the jewellery, clothing, fur and antique trades (and, of course, with long firm frauds generally) they are also commonly used by non-Jews, especially by those persons on the edge of the criminal field who wish to be considered worldly wise and commercially sharp. Some phrases are used almost as a private 'in' language, and their use is increasing. In many ways this is a considerable compliment to the expressiveness of Yiddish.

Acid	(a) Cheekiness (especially in a child), (b) LSD (lysergic acid diethylamide—the hallucinatory drug).
Acid, to come the old	Either to be officious or to throw one's weight about.
Acid, to put in the	To inform against, or to say something unpleasant about someone in his absence.
Acid rock	Modern music which, when accompanied by unusual lighting and extreme amplification, is evocative of LSD hallucinations.
Across the pavement	A street situation, e.g., 'Let's do one across the pavement' may mean 'Let's commit a robbery in the street'.
Adam (and Eve) it, to	To believe it.
Afro	Having the hair in a spherical, bushy and tightly curled mass, in the style of certain Negroes.
Aggro	Aggravation, trouble.

Aggro belt, or aggro boots	Articles of clothing adapted for rough-house fighting: belt heavily studded or adorned with several (army) heavy brass badges; boots studded, capped and heeled with metal.
Alias man	A criminal, especially a morally worthless cheat or hypocrite (West Indian term, originally an eighteenth century English expression).
All that, giving it	Bragging or showing off.
Almonds (rocks)	Socks.
Alphonse (ponce)	Man living on the earnings of prostitution.
Andrew, the	The Royal Navy.
Apples (and pears)	Stairs.
Arthur (Rank)	Bank; *see also* J. Arthur.
Artist	Term often used ironically in conjunction with other words, e.g., 'con-artist'—fraudsman; 'piss-artist'—a man addicted to alcoholic drink; 'skid-artist'—a bad driver.
As it is, telling it as it is	Speaking the unvarnished truth.
Babylon	The police, or any allegedly repressive government agency (West Indian term, also used in hippy communes).
Back-ah-yard	The Caribbean generally; an expression, roughly translated as 'back home', used by homesick West Indians.
Bald-tyre bandits	Traffic patrol police.
Ball (of chalk)	A walk: 'I'm going for a ball.'
Balloon, the	The saloon of a public house.
Balls	Testicles. Masculine courage, 'He's got balls, all right', and by extension masterfulness. The term can be used to describe a dominant woman in a home, e.g., 'She's the one with the balls in that family'. An exclamation meaning 'Rubbish'.
Bandit	A term sometimes used ironically in conjunction with other words, e.g., 'piss-hole bandit'—a homosexual who importunes in lavatories; 'knickers bandit'—clothes line thief; 'light ale bandit'—a beer scrounger; 'gas meter bandit'—a paltry thief; 'one of a gang of international milk bandits'—near-vagrant labourers, who steal milk left outside dwellings, especially when down on their luck.
Bang	Sexual intercourse.
Bang to rights, caught	Caught red-handed.
Banged-up	Locked in a cell, and thus in any place where one cannot conveniently leave, and thus, by extension: for a female—pregnant; for a male—infected with venereal disease. Not used in mixed company in the latter senses.

172

Banger	Dilapidated motor car.
Barker	Pistol, especially a small pistol.
Bat phone	Policeman's small personal radio set.
Battle cruiser	Public house (boozer).
Battyman	A male homosexual. South London expression, of West Indian origin.
Bazey cheyeh	Savage and violent criminal ('wild beast', Yiddish).
Beaver	Hat, also a salute as a soldier would give to an officer: 'I threw the old captain up a beaver.'
Beer belly	Fatness induced by over-indulgence in ale, used particularly of any young man with a large belly.
Be like Dad! (unsaid—'and keep Mum')	Keep quiet!
Belly rubbing	Dancing. Not used in mixed company.
Bends his elbow	Drinks heavily.
Bent	Description of something stolen or dishonest; less commonly, of a homosexual.
Bent as a butcher's hook	Stolen or dishonest.
Bent my ear	Talked interminably about an uninteresting subject.
Berk(eley Hunt)	A fool. After a gross reference to the female sexual organ.
Bertie, doing a	Giving evidence against accomplices in a criminal trial; turning 'Queen's evidence'.
Bicycle	See Bike.
Biggest f . . .-up since Dunkirk	A disaster (Second World War).
Biggest f . . .-up since Mons	A disaster (First World War).
Bike	A woman of accommodatingly promiscuous attitude, not a prostitute, usually a local woman; a not unkindly meant phrase: 'Nice woman, bit of a bike, you know.'
Bill	Taxi driver's licence.
Bill, or Old Bill	Specifically, the Metropolitan Police and, generally, all police: 'Is he Bill?' means 'Is he a police officer?'
Bill from the Hill, a	Specifically, a Notting Hill police officer (once a very busy and active police station) and generally a very energetic policeman.
Bill oh!	A shouted warning, 'Look out!' (presumably from 'Bill', the police). Pronounced 'below'.
Bill shop	Police station.
Billig	Cheap (Yiddish).
Bin	Cell, or pockets in clothes.
Bins	(a) Prismatic binocular glasses, or ordinary spectacles. (b) Pockets.
Bint	Young woman (originally Arabic).

173

Bird	Term of imprisonment, also a girlfriend.
Birdlime	Time (in prison).
Bit of mess	Prostitute's male lover who is neither her ponce nor a paying client. A completely non-commercial relationship, but not the same as a 'tin soldier' (q.v.).
Blower	Telephone.
Blowing down (his/my) ear	Whispering.
Blue foot	Prostitute (used in hippy communes and probably of West Indian origin).
Blues	An illegal drinking house (shebeen), especially one where amplified dance music is also provided.
Bluey	(a) Lead, (b) a red-headed man (originally solely an Australian term).
Boffing	Term for sexual intercourse.
Bogey	A detective officer.
Boiler	A mature woman, especially one who dresses or acts in a fashion younger than her years. Can be a term of abuse towards such a woman.
Bollocking	A severe telling off.
Bollocko	Naked : 'There he was bollocko.'
Bolo	Friend or 'mate' (hippy term).
Bombed	Intoxicated by drug abuse.
Bonce	Head.
Boned	Hit on the head hard.
Boot	To hurt severely by blows or words after having obtained the advantage over a person : to 'put the boot in'. Unnecessary cruelty after victory.
Boozer	Public house.
Boracic (lint)	Penniless (skint).
Bottle	Courage, forceful character or nerve : 'He has plenty of bottle', or 'He has lost his bottle'. A variation is where something of no value, moral or material, is said to be 'no bottle'.
Bounce	A word used among dishonest shop employees to describe the system of falsely adjusting invoices, delivery notes and price tags, so as to cover up the theft of stock either by the employees themselves or by accomplices who enter the shop during business hours.
Bounced	Ejected from premises.
Bouncer	A man employed to throw out trespassers and undesirables from premises.
Bow, on the	Variation of 'on the elbow' meaning scrounging.
Box, a	A guitar.
Box, the	Television generally.
Brains, the	Ironic term for the CID.
Brass	Prostitute.

174

Brass balls	Something severe or testing, 'a brass balls job', or someone tough and unyieldingly masculine.
Bread	Money. Once exclusively hippy, now common.
Brewer's droop	A large belly brought on by beer, and by extension a reference to alleged impotence in a male. Can be a most insulting phrase to use to a man in this latter meaning as it impugns his virility. Not to be used in jest.
Brief	(a) A warrant to arrest or search, a police warrant card (or any other identity document). (b) Generally, any lawyer; specifically, a barrister.
Bristols	Woman's breasts. (Bristol City, titty.)
Broads	A pack of playing cards (a little archaic), also identity documents and, recently, credit cards. Women of easy virtue.
Broadsman	Card sharp.
Brooming-off	The unscrupulous or 'sharp' cab driver's practice, when he is at the head of a cab rank (at the 'pin position', q.v.), of refusing an unprofitable hiring and passing the intended hirer back along the cab line to a driver who will take the hiring. A practice often causing extreme bad feeling between cab drivers.
Browncoat	Junior examiner at the (taxi) Police Public Carriage Office.
Brownhatter	Generally, any male homosexual; specifically, one of wealth or position.
BSHs	Ironically humorous play on an official sounding but mock abbreviation, in this case meaning a woman's bosom—'British Standard Handfuls'; becoming a common expression.
Bubble (and squeak)	To inform (speak) against: 'Put the bubble in' or 'Bubble him'.
Bucket gaff, or bucket job	Fraudulent company.
Budgie	A talkative man, especially of small stature, also used as a nickname; can be used by police to refer to a minor informer—one who has details of only 'gas meter jobs' (unimportant local cases).
Bull (and cow)	Violent disagreement (row).
Bulldike	Masculine type of lesbian woman.
Bum	Vagrant type, any person without credibility or reputation.
Bunco	Fraud generally; sometimes false and flattering 'chat' by a man to a woman. Originally exclusively an American expression, brought into use by 'hippy' persons and by West Indians who have previously lived in the USA: 'Don't give me that, man—I've been buncoed by experts!' means 'Don't try to deceive me!'

175

Buncum	*See* Bunco.
Bung, a	A gratuity of an almost legitimate nature, not quite a bribe.
Bung, to	To give secretly (often used to describe the actual passing of corrupt money).
Bunkum	*See* Bunco.
Bunty	Affectionate term for a small person, especially a small woman of middle age.
Burke	*See* Berk.
Burton, gone for a	Gone away; in some circumstances can infer death or fatal injury (Burton-on-Trent, went).
Burton(-on-Trent)	Rent.
Business girl	Prostitute.
Business with, do	Has the innocent meaning but also means to have corrupt transactions with.
Busted	Arrested, almost exclusively a hippy expression, gradually becoming current.
Bustle-punching	The practice, not uncommon in dense crowds, of a male rubbing his penis against the buttocks of females. The penis may or may not be exposed.
Busy	A CID officer.
Butch	Masculine type of lesbian woman. Also used to describe manliness in any woman, especially in a derogatory sense: 'She's too butch for me.'
Butcher's (hook)	Look: 'Let's have a butcher's.'
Butter boy	Newly licensed cab driver, or very young policeman.
Button mob, the	Uniformed police officers, especially in large numbers, at a political demonstration for example.
Buttoner	Assistant in three-card trick 'firm' who brings customers to the game, and thus any bringer of dupes to a fraud.
Buyer	Euphemism for a receiver of stolen goods. 'Go in as a buyer' means to pretend to be a receiver so as to identify thieves or to discover the whereabouts of stolen property.
Buzz	Information: 'I've heard a buzz that . . . .'
Buzzing	(a) A near-archaic term for stealing by picking pockets; nevertheless, still used by old East Londoners. (b) Circulating, as in a crowded public house.
Caddy	A hat.
Calloh	*See* Kollah.
Came his cocoa	The act of ejaculation, or to make a complete confession of guilt. Taboo words, never used in mixed company.
Came his fat	*See* Came his cocoa; a taboo expression.

Came his lot	*See* Came his cocoa; again, a taboo expression.
Camp	This term originally meant to be inclined **towards** male homosexuality in a tolerant and friendly manner, without necessarily being homosexual oneself. Currently has the loose meaning of anything or anybody with homosexual overtones.
Canary, sing like a	Give information under pressure.
Caper, a	A large-scale crime (once exclusively an American term, now quite common).
Card, go through the	To cover comprehensively, or to have everything that is on offer (on a menu, for example); originally meant to back every winning horse at a meeting.
Car park	Informer (nark): 'Been at the old car park have you ?', or 'Watch what you say, he's car park you know'.
Carl Rosa	A poser. Someone who is not what he seems. The name refers to a well-known operatic society. Fraud or deceit is sometimes referred to as 'the old Carl Rosa'.
Carpet	Three months imprisonment.
Carrot crunchers	Country visitors to London.
Case	Brothel.
Cat	Hippy term for any male within the hippy world or the drug scene. 'He's a cool cat' would mean 'He is a self-assured, "knowing" man who is one of us'.
Chalk (Farm)	Arm (London district).
Chapper	Policeman (Yiddish). *See also* Shamez.
Charge	Cannabis.
Charged	Stimulated, but not intoxicated, with drink or cannabis.
Charming wife	Knife.
Cheaters	Eyes. Sometimes spectacles or sunglasses.
Chedar	Jewish for a prison cell, sometimes pronounced 'heeder'; originally meant a small room or a study.
Cherries (cherry-hogs)	Dog racing tracks.
Chevy (Chase)	Face.
Chick	Young woman.
Chicken	(a) A young runaway schoolboy, likely to be preyed on by homosexuals. The male equivalent of a 'mystery' (q.v.). (b) A coward.
Chicken shit	Anything unworthy, paltry or worthless. Once an American expression, now not uncommon because of hippy influence.
China (plate)	Mate, particularly used to mean a highly regarded husband or wife.

Chiv	A knife, particularly one made up by grinding and sharpening a piece of waste metal, or by sharpening a file or screwdriver.
Choppers	(a) Teeth, (b) bicycles.
Chutzpah	Extreme nerve or gall, a skill in pretence or in playing a part, or in selling shoddy goods. Clever or bold explaining away of guilt. Old East End Yiddish expression, pronounced 'hootspah'. Often used in grudging admiration.
Claret	Blood (especially common in South London).
Clean wheels	A motor vehicle to be used in crime that has never been previously stolen or come under prior police suspicion in any way.
Cleaned out	To have lost all one's money (usually by betting or gaming).
Cleaners, sent to the	Completely outwitted and (usually) substantially defrauded.
Clipping	Pretending to be a prostitute, obtaining cash, but absconding before any intimacy occurs.
Clock, on the	Journeyman cab driver hiring a cab and paying the owner for it by a percentage of what is recorded on the meter. Significant because it usually precludes the dishonest practice of 'stalking' (q.v.). Also called 'jobbers' (q.v.).
Clock, to	To look at intently, e.g., 'Clock his suit!'
Clock and a half, guv'nor ?	Unscrupulous cab drivers' term for the metered fare plus an extra half. Unknowing or foreign fares are sometimes duped into paying this unlawful excess.
Clockwork orange	A male homosexual: 'He's as queer as a clockwork orange.'
Coating, give a	Reprimand.
Cobblers (awls)	Testicles (balls), also a contemptuous term for rubbish, or a sceptical view taken of an explanation, 'It's a load of cobblers', i.e., 'It's untrue'.
Cock	A man who buys more than his share of drinks in a public house or club so as to have company pleasing to him. A man easy to sponge upon.
Cocking a deaf 'un	Pretending not to hear.
Cock-up, a	A disaster or badly organized situation.
Cocoa, came his	See under Came his cocoa.
Cocoa, I should	'I should think so!'
CO lot, that	The Special Patrol Group (the letters 'CO' meaning 'Commissioner's Office' are on these officers' shoulder straps). The Special Patrol Group is a squad of experienced, uniformed officers, skilled in thief taking, deployed tactically to deal with outbreaks of street crime. Often operating in plain clothes.

178

COs	Taxi drivers' term for police officers engaged in enforcing the laws affecting cabs and the prosecuting of illegal or dishonest cab practices.
Confusion	A street fight (West Indian origin).
Con, a	(a) A deceitful story, (b), a confidence trickster or 'con-man' and a convicted person.
Conning	To cheat by first obtaining the confidence or trust trust of the victim.
Cool	(a) Hippy expression for confidence or self-assuredness, (b) look (backslang, 'take a cool at that').
Cool (keep your)	Keep calm, keep your temper.
Cool it!	Quieten down!
Cooneh, or cooneh lemel	A 'mug' or a person likely to be defrauded easily (Yiddish).
Cop (verb)	To receive corrupt payments: 'Did he cop?' means 'Did he receive a gratuity (or bribe)?'
Cop out	A pretext for avoiding responsibility.
Copping	The criminal practice of receiving corrupt payments or bribes.
Corner, it's your	It is your time to pay.
Corner, to; or cornering	The criminal practices of (a) selling shoddy goods by pretending falsely they are high-class stolen property, or (b) selling genuinely stolen goods to a greedy and foolish tradesman, receiving his money for the stolen goods and leaving his premises. By arrangement the seller then signals other corrupt persons who, pretending to be honest police officers, enter and search the 'mug's' premises and find the goods. The tradesman will be threatened with a charge of 'receiving', the property seized and privily returned to the first conspirator to be re-sold or used again for another 'cornering'. The tradesman will then be blackmailed, by a middleman or stakeholder, who alleges he is able to bribe and influence the police or even the courts. He will skilfully play this part, posing as the friend of the dupe. This style of conspiracy is also called 'lawing', and has many variations, including the middleman or stakeholder, already referred to, 'steering' (falsely recommending) the dupe to a dishonest solicitor (who knows of the conspiracy) so that more effective blackmail demands can be made and any likelihood of complaint by the dupe to the authorities can be blocked or at least discouraged.
Cottage	Public lavatory.
Council houses (i.e., government-aided housing)	Trousers.

Crash	To 'put your head down' (sleep), particularly during the day. Also to write off or cancel inquiries into an unsubstantiated complaint or allegation of crime (in this sense, almost exclusively police): 'The Smith housebreaking has been crashed.'
Creaming	Stealing from an employer in such a way as not to be obvious. Similar to 'weeding' (q.v.). *See also* Bounce and Mark-up.
Crows	Lookout men in the three-card trick.
Crumpet	Sexually attractive woman or girl.
Crumpet man	A womanizer.
Cutting gear	Oxyacetylene apparatus when used to break into safes.
Dabs	Fingerprints.
Daily Mail (newspaper)	Buttocks (tail): 'He fell on his Daily Mail'; also bail, 'Guvnor, what's the chances of the old Daily Mail?'; also tale, 'He spun me a Daily (Mail) I just couldn't believe'; also sexual proclivity, e.g., 'She's Daily Mail all right' (she is accommodating in the sexual sense).
Daisy chain	The 'brotherhood'—the special relationship that exists between all males, of every and any social position, who are homosexual.
Damager	Manager (boxing and theatrical use also).
Dancers, had it on his	He ran away.
Dancing	Stealing from offices above ground level where one must use stairways. Stairs—Fred Astaire—dancing.
Darby (Kelly)	Belly, frequently 'Darby Kel'.
Decko	To see: 'Let's have a decko.'
Dekko	*See* Decko.
Delo	*See* Dillo, but also a shortened form of 'delonammon' (q.v.).
Delonammon	Wife (backslang, 'old woman').
Dickery (dock)	Clock.
Diddicoy	Gypsy, or associate of gypsies.
Diddiki	*See* Diddicoy.
Didn't ought	Port (wine).
Didn't oughter	Daughter.
Dig	(a) To understand: 'Do you dig this?' (hippy expression). (b) To punch (Cockney expression).
Dike	Lesbian woman, *see also* 'Bulldike'.
Dillo	Old (backslang).
Dinky	Attractively small.
Dip, a	Pickpocket.

180

Dip, the	That part of Piccadilly (the thoroughfare) adjoining St James's Park, where male prostitutes once importuned wealthy homosexuals. A term known to many homosexuals throughout the UK and even abroad.
Dipping	Stealing as a pickpocket.
Do as you like	A bicycle (bike).
Dock asthma	Pretended gasps of surprise by accused persons when incriminating evidence is given against them. Used generally to describe the reaction to any unpleasant surprise, whether in court or not.
Dodgy	Unreliable, doubtful or dishonest.
Dog driver	Policeman, used in an insulting or contemptuous context (West Indian).
Doggo, to lie	To remain under cover, to keep still and thus be unobserved.
Doing the party	A ploy in the three-card trick where a confederate of a card sharp pretends to be a winning player so as to encourage 'mugs' to stake heavily and, of course, to lose.
Dolly (Varden)	Garden: 'Ted's in the dolly.' (Dickens character.)
Donnah	An attractive woman; also the queen in a pack of playing cards, particularly in the three-card trick.
Double carpet	Six months imprisonment: 'Did he get bird?'; reply, 'Yes, a double carpet'.
Doubles	Streets.
Down to	Responsible for (a crime).
Down to Larkin	Free: 'Who is paying for this round?'; reply, 'Shush! It's down to Larkin'.
Drag	(a) A street, (b) a van or motor car, (c) clothes, of the opposite sex, (d) to steal, (e) deep inhalation of cigarette or cannabis smoke, (f) a cigarette, e.g., 'Have a drag'. 'Main drag' means the principal thoroughfare; 'Get in the drag' means get in the car; 'He was in drag' means he was dressed in woman's clothes; 'van dragging' means stealing from motor vehicles. Additionally means anything boring, 'What a drag!'
Dreck	Low Yiddish word meaning excrement, and used to describe anything or anybody shoddy or unpleasant. Taboo word, never used in polite company.
Dreykop	Yiddish word (literally 'twisted head') for a fraudsman or trickster.
Drink	Euphemism for blackmail payment or a money bribe. 'There's a drink in it for you' may mean there will be such payments; 'Does he drink?' may mean 'Is he willing to be bribed?'
Drop	A covert address or place where messages or money can be left for a third person.

181

Dropper	Passer of worthless cheques.
Drops	Money (or messages) left in a secret place for collection by another party. Ironically, money left for one's wife as housekeeping expenses.
Dropsy	Near-archaic word for corrupt payments.
Drum	House, flat or any living apartment.
Drum-up	Effort to obtain results.
Drumming	Calling at dwellings to see if temporarily unoccupied so as to facilitate breaking and entering. Sometimes used to describe honest door-to-door salesmanship.
Dublin University graduate	A particularly dense person, or a person unable to read and write. Intended to be humorously ironic.
Duke of Kent	Rent.
Dukes	Fists.
Dummy, a	Deaf and dumb person.
Dummy up	To keep silent. Sometimes used as a command to an over-talkative accessory in dangerous company: 'Dummy up!'
Dutch (plate)	*See* China.
Earhole, on the	Scrounging.
Earn	To make a corrupt or dishonest profit. A thief might say about a proposed fraud or illegal scheme: 'We can all *really earn* on this one!'
Earner, an	Any circumstances that thieves can turn to corrupt or dishonest advantage: 'We are on to an earner here!'
Earwig	To listen.
Edna (May)!	On your way! (command to 'clear off').
Einstein's mate	A dense person, especially in relation to faulty calculations.
Elbow, on the	Scrounging.
Electric	Efficient, weird, sudden or marvellous.
Elephant (& Castle)	Anus.
Emag	Game (London backslang) but usually in the sense of disgust: 'What a bleeding emag this is!'
Esclop	Policeman (London backslang).
Faces	A term for notorious cab drivers (fortunately few in number) who quite unscrupulously make their own rules and take only profitable hirings or those where they can more easily extort from fares, e.g., 'airport faces', 'hotel faces', 'abortion faces'. Also used in a general sense for known criminals.

Factory	Specifically, a large Metropolitan police station of severe appearance (the Old Commercial Street 'nick', for example); generally, any police station. Not now so common an expression as it once was, perhaps because police stations are not now quite as stark and forbidding as they once were.
Fag	Hippy expression for a young, passive homosexual; originally exclusively an American term, not now uncommon in West London.
Fair-weather drink	Small celebration with intimates before some enterprise or holiday.
Family	Closely related. Used in this sense: 'Don't say things like that about Gert, she's family.' Also, in an ironic sense it means dishonesty generally: 'He's a family man' may mean 'He's a thief' or 'He is one of us'; in other words, similarly dishonest.
Fan	To feel clothes for valuables, to pass one's hands quickly over such clothing and, by extension, any quick body search.
Fanning	Stealing as a pickpocket.
Fanny	(a) A false story, (b) the female sexual organ. American-influenced hippies use the expression for buttocks, male or female.
Fat, came his	*See under* Came his cocoa.
Feel his collar	To arrest a person.
Feet muddy, get your	To have been in trouble, especially with the criminal law, e.g., 'He got his feet muddy before he had straight work.'
Fell off a lorry	Ironic explanation, given more humorously than seriously, when asked to account for the possession of valuable property, obviously stolen.
Filth	Specifically, dishonest policemen; generally, any police. Used only by confirmed and embittered criminals. Any extreme hypocrite, not necessarily in the police sense, might be so referred to.
Firm	A gang of card sharps or criminals; also humorously used to describe a particular squad of detective officers, especially a closely knit and comradely band.
Fit up	Falsely (but cleverly and effectively) to accuse; also to plant incriminating evidence upon. *See also* Stitch up.
Flap	Panic (noun or verb).
Flapping track	Small (and unlicensed) dog track.
Flappings	Small race meetings.
Flaps	Ears. Often a nickname for a man with large ears.

Flash	Smart or 'snappy' in appearance but unmistakably vulgar and showy; not a compliment, and usually descriptive of males rather than females.
Flasher	One who exposes his penis to females.
Flats	Playing cards and, recently, credit cards.
Flatties	Uniform police officers (flatfeet); has a derogatory sense and is thus not used to the face of such an officer.
Flops	Houses or garages where escaping thieves can safely offload weapons, implements or stolen property, thus leaving their own homes free of incriminating articles.
Flossed up	Made attractive by paint and powder—another expression for 'tarted up'.
Flour mixer	(a) Yiddish rhyming slang for 'shikse' (girl domestic or shop assistant). (b) An inoffensive man, particularly a clerk.
Flowery (dell)	Cell.
Fly	Smart, quick to see any advantage : 'He's a fly boy.'
Fonfen	The spurious stories of fraudsmen (common Yiddish word in the world of commercial fraud or near-fraud).
Fork	To give. Sometimes a single word of command, 'Fork!'.
Fork out	To give.
Forks	Fingers.
Form	Previous convictions: 'What's his form ?'
Frame, in the	Suspected, with some good reason, of being concerned in a serious crime; 'Well in the frame' is even stronger.
Frazer, Ted	Cut-throat razor.
Freak out	Hippy expression to lose control of oneself.
Freaky	Sexually deviant.
Frig	Sexual intercourse (taboo word).
Frog (and toad)	Road.
Front, the	Oxford Street.
Front, to	To confront; to face in challenge.
Front-wheel (skid) or front-wheeler	Jew (yid).
Full house	To have both syphilis and gonorrhoea. To have more than one form of body infestation with parasites, e.g., both head and body lice.
Funky	Descriptive of modern music when played with great feeling (hippy).
Fuzz	Police (hippy and liberal political). Rarely used by thieves.
Gaff	A house, flat or shop.

184

Gam	Taboo word for fellatio. Never used in mixed company.
Game	Generally used to describe courage, particularly in a small man. Occasionally used to indicate a willingness to engage in either violently dishonest or deceitfully corrupt practices, e.g., 'Is he game then?' might mean either 'Has he enough courage?' or, on the other hand, 'Can he be bribed?'
Game, on the	Engaged in prostitution.
Gamerouche	Taboo word for fellatio. Never used in mixed company.
Gammy	(a) Unreliable, counterfeit, likely 'to let you down'. (b) Lame.
Ganef	A thief (Yiddish).
Ganev	*See* Ganef.
Gang bang	Depraved sexual orgy between several pairs, or a violent multi-rape of one female; also in a humorous ironic sense of, say, a garden party or a vicarage fete—'a real gang bang'.
Ganja	Cannabis.
Gas meter bandit	Ironic term of contempt for a small-time thief. Stealing from gas meters being considered a petty crime.
Gate fever	The unsettled feeling convicted men have towards the end of their prison sentences, and thus used to describe any show of impatience before an event.
Gateway to the South	Ironic term for the Balham district of South London.
Gazlon	Sneak thief, especially a timid thief. One big-time thief might use it as an insulting term to a rival. A Yiddish term.
Gear, bent	Stolen property.
Geezer	A male stranger. Sometimes used more loosely to mean any male person.
Gelt	Money.
Gelt gait zu gelt	Money makes money (Yiddish saying common in the underworld of commercial fraud).
Gin and Jaguar belt	The upper class districts of Surrey, and a fruitful area for worth-while housebreaking.
Gin and Jaguar bird	A wealthy (usually married) woman from this area and in some senses likely to be 'racy', 'with it' or sexually accommodating.
Ginger (beer)	Queer (i.e., a male homosexual).
Give them away with a pound of tea, they	Ironic explanation when asked to account for the possession of an obviously stolen and valuable article.
Give me outers	Allow me a way of escape or a way of avoiding responsibility. For example: 'Give me outers, guv'nor, and I'll tell you where the gear it.'

185

Give your arse/ears a chance	Stop talking and listen (a terse command), or sometimes a form of complaining comment about an over-talkative person. 'Why doesn't he give his arse a chance?' i.e., 'Why doesn't he shut up?'
Giving it all that	*See* All that, giving it.
Glassed	Jabbed in the face with broken glass.
Glick	Luck (Yiddish).
Glim	A torch, especially a miniature torch.
Glimmer	A beggar.
Glimming	Begging.
God forbids	Children (kids).
Going down south	Taboo expression for the practice of cunnilingus; common but never used in mixed company.
Goitre	A large number of banknotes, usually kept in fob pocket of trousers.
Gold watch	Scotch whisky: 'What are you having? Gold watch?'
Gonaiva	Yiddish word meaning theft generally, or the act of theft—sometimes used as a collective noun for stolen property.
Gonivim	A plural word for thieves. 'Yockele gonivim' would mean a group of non-Jewish thieves.
Gonk, a	A prostitute's term for a client. Used contemptuously.
Gonnoph	Male thief (Yiddish).
Gonnophta	Female thief, particularly a skilled woman shoplifter.
Goy	Yiddish term for a non-Jew; *see also* Yockele.
Graduate from Dublin University	*See* Dublin university graduate.
Grafting	Working hard, either honestly or otherwise.
Grand, a	One thousand pounds
Grass	An informer, or to inform.
Great unwashed, the	Hippies, male or female.
Greedy pigs	Contemptuous term used by card sharps for the public they cheat.
Greens (gages)	Wages.
Groin/groyne	A ring with some form of stone in it.
Groupie	A young girl associating promiscuously with members of rock music groups (originally hippy slang).
Grove, the	West Indian slang for Notting Hill (possibly from Ladbroke or Westbourne Grove).
Guiver, put on the	To pretend gentility or affect a 'well-bred' voice.
Gunja	Cannabis.
Gunsel	A transatlantic term (now not uncommon because of American hippy influence) for a passive adolescent male homosexual. Nothing whatsoever to do with firearms or their use.

Guntz, go the	Go all the way (East End Jewish expression).
Guy (Fawkes)	A walk: 'Let's do a guy' means 'Let's go for a walk'.
Gypsy's (kiss)	Urination (piss): 'Watch my drink, I'm going for a gypsy's.'
Had her over	Outwitted or seduced her.
Had him over	Outwitted him.
Had it off	Successful attempt at theft, or successful attempt at seduction.
Hairies	Male hippies.
Hairy	Dangerous: 'That was a hairy job.'
Half a bar	50p (once a 10s note).
Hampton (Wick)	Penis (prick) and, by extension, a fool—'He's a right Hampton'; also to express dislike, 'Doesn't he get on my Hampton!'.
Handful, a	(a) Five pounds, (b) troublesome person, usually a young person.
Handful, to have a	To fondle a woman's bosom or other sexual parts (taboo expression).
Hands up, put his	Surrendered or admitted all the crimes put to him.
Hanging-up	Unscrupulous cab driver's illegal practice of deliberately failing to move up on an official (or unofficial) cab rank and not taking hirings in rotation. Done to enable obtaining more favourable hirings. Cause of disputes and bad feeling between cab drivers. See also Brooming-off.
Hang-up	A problem.
Happening, a	Hippy expression for an event.
Hassle	Hippy expression for any form of nuisance or disagreement.
Hawkshaw	CID officer. A derisive term, originally exclusively US, but used by West Indians.
Heads!, or Heads up!	Warning shout.
Hearts (of oak)	Penniless (broke): 'Coming down to Brighton for for the races?'; reply, 'What's the point, we are all hearts'.
Heavies	Police officers from either the Flying Squad or the Special Patrol Group.
Heder	See Chedar.
Hedge	Crowd around a street card sharp or street trader.
Hit (and miss)	A kiss: '. . . and give us a hit, love' is an impertinent phrase which might be used to an attractive barmaid when drinks are ordered.
Hit and missed (in full)	Drunk (pissed): 'On the hit and miss' means going out drinking.
Hoister	Female shoplifter.

Hoisting	Shoplifting.
Hollow tooth, the	Ironic and disgruntled term for New Scotland Yard, used by some police, and thus by certain knowledgeable criminals. Very much an 'in' term.
Home and Colonial	The London-based Regional Crime Squad office, comprising Metropolitan detectives ('Home') and provincial officers ('Colonial'). Expression comes from the name of a chain of grocery shops.
Honky	Racist negro expression (unpleasant) for a white person (usually male).
Hook	North Country slang for a thief, rarely heard in London.
Hooker	Transatlantic term for a prostitute becoming current here, probably because of American hippy influence.
Hooking	A dishonest informer attempting to entangle public officials or police officers in a proposed crime, for his own benefit.
Hop the wag	To play truant from school.
Horse (and trap)	Gonorrhoea (clap): 'Got a dose of horse.' Also, hippy slang for heroin.
Hot lot	Flying Squad or the Special Patrol Group. The Flying Squad are comprised of experienced detectives. Special Patrol Group are, in a similar fashion, experienced uniformed officers both used in team and group situations.
House, to	To follow secretly to a person's home or living quarters, or to locate property. 'The Sweeney has housed that whisky lot' means 'The Flying Squad have found where the stolen whisky was hidden'.
Hurry up, on the	Very quickly, perhaps taking action before there was time to prepare.
Hustler	Prostitute.
Hustling	Prostitution.
Ice cream freezer	Geezer (male person).
Iffy	Doubtful or dishonest. An 'iffy brief' would mean a dishonest lawyer, an 'iffy motor' would mean a (probably) stolen car.
Ignorant, make	Make angry (South London).
In, have an	To have a contact in a place to be robbed or in a place where secret negotiations would be advantageous.
International (milk thief/gas meter screwsman)	Ironic terms for a petty thief.
Interrupter	A court interpreter.

Iron	Male homosexual (said to originate from 'iron hoof', rhyming with 'poof').
Iron lung	Old-fashioned street urinal with iron fixtures.
Isle of Wight	All right, 'OK'.
Ivan (and Ivanovitch), an	Peasant-like person who is good natured but a little dense. Used by anglicised East Europeans sometimes as a mock insult: 'You believed that? You Ivanovitch!'
Ivan the Terrible, an	An evil or harsh East European person.
Jack (Jones)	Alone: 'He's all on his Jack.'
Jack tar	A bar, of licensed premises: 'He's in the Jack.'
Jacks	North Country term for junior CID officers.
Jacks (alive)	Five pounds or a £5 note.
Jam jar	Motor car.
Jargoon	Counterfeit or worthless 'diamond' ring.
J. Arthur (Rank)	(a) A bank, (b) to masturbate (wank) and, by extension, a fool: 'What a J. Arthur he is!'
Jelly	Gelignite.
Jewish Joanna, or Jewish piano	Ironic term for a cash register.
Jew's typewriter	Ironic term for a cash register.
Jigglers	Skeleton keys for pin tumbler locks.
Jimmying	(a) Obtaining entry into cinemas, theatres, dog tracks and enclosures at race meetings by subterfuge and without paying. (b) Urinating.
Jims, or jimmies	The 'men in raincoats' who watch prostitutes at work in an unhealthy but quite inactive manner.
Jobbers	Journeymen cab drivers who operate 'on the clock'. *See also* Clock, on the.
Jockey	*See* John.
John	Prostitutes' term for a client or for a sheath contraceptive. The term is used contemptuously in both cases. A ponce might say to a prostitute: 'Don't you treat me like a john or I'll mark your face.' Also a urinal.
John Law	Policeman, especially a popular or respected policeman; sometimes used to identify the senior policeman of a locality: 'He's John Law here.'
Joint	(a) Cigarette containing cannabis, (b) illegal drinking shebeen.
Juice	(a) Petrol, (b) alcohol, 'On the juice' means drinking heavily, (c) corrupt payments, (d) money generally.
Jump	Sexual intercourse.
Jumper	(a) Device consisting of a single-stranded insulated wire, with a crocodile clip at each end, used to short out the ignition system of a vehicle. Carried by car thieves. (b) A bus inspector.

189

Jump-up man	Lorry hijacker (one has to 'jump up' on to the rear of a lorry).
Junction, the	Clapham area of South London.
Jungle bunny	Patronising and unpleasant racist expression for a Negro, never used in black company.
Kaker	Yiddish for excrement and thus anything unpleasant, particularly unsavoury words or exaggerated stories.
Kaker demah	*See* Kaker.
Kalloh	*See* Kollah.
Kansas cocoa	Coca cola.
Karzi	Water closet style lavatory.
Kate (Karney)	The (British) Army.
Keep mum!	Keep quiet! (rhyming slang for 'Keep stumm'. *See also* Stumm.
Kennetseeno	Smelly, the stench of decomposition; sometimes said when a person breaks wind: 'Kennetseeno!' (London backslang for 'stinking'.)
Khyber (Pass)	The buttocks or anus (arse).
Kibbitzer	Generally, one who interferes or gives unwanted advice in an annoying fashion, but especially as an onlooker at a gambling situation, usually a card game (common Yiddish East End expression).
Kife	Bed.
Kifering	Act of sexual intercourse, sometimes specifically an act of adultery.
Kike	Unpleasantly racist expression for a Jew; never used by Jews.
Kilburn (Priory)	Diary, especially a plain clothes officer's official diary (which may be examined in court).
Kinky	Sexually deviant.
Kip, to	To sleep.
Kip, the	Common lodging house.
Kip house	Common lodging house.
Kisser	Face; sometimes used in an ironic sense to indicate the anus.
Kite	Cheque: 'Flying kites' means encashing fraudulent cheques.
Knickers	A (usually) not unfriendly rebuff. For example: 'Jack, lend me a quid'; reply, 'Knickers!'
Knocker, on the	Visiting houses to sell or purchase goods, but particularly seeking antiques from elderly spinsters and widows who can be bullied into selling cheaply.
Knockers	Low expression meaning either a woman's bosom or a man's testicles.

Knock off	To steal, to arrest, or to sexually seduce.
Kollah	Yiddish for young woman, or a bride.
Kosher	Genuine, reliable, orthodox. (Hebrew for permissible, the opposite—'traifa'.) Very common expression.
Kremlin	New Scotland Yard.
Kurva	Prostitute (Yiddish).
Lah-di-dah	Cigar (sometimes just 'lardy').
Lakes (of Killarney)	Insane (barmy).
Lamps	Eyes.
Lardy	*See* Lah-di-dah.
Larkin, down to	Free: 'The next round of drinks are down to Larkin.'
Lay, to	To seduce sexually.
Lay down	A remand in custody.
Law, the	The police.
Lawing	*See* Corner, to.
Leery	Bad tempered, disagreeable or cheeky.
Levy (& Frank), to	To masturbate (wank). (Brewing firm.)
LF	*See* Long firm fraud.
LF gear	The proceeds of a long firm fraud often offered at very low prices; often, too, quite honestly obtained property of low quality is falsely described at 'LF gear' to explain cheapness and stimulate customer interest.
Lilley & Skinner	Dinner: 'I'm going home for my lilley.' (Name of well-known firm of shoe shops.)
Linen (draper)	Newspaper: 'I'm nipping out to get the linen.'
Lloyd (Harold)	*See* Loid.
Loaded	Drunk, or having plenty of money.
Loaf (of bread)	Head: 'Use your loaf!' means 'Be sagacious!'
Loid (Harold Lloyd)	Celluloid (or, nowadays, plastic pieces) used to slip door catches when housebreaking: 'When they nicked him he had loid in his pocket.'
Lollied	Informed against: 'He was lollied. The Law found the gear in his garage and he got a five stretch.'
Long firm fraud	A type of fraud where a great deal of property is ordered on credit through legitimate channels and then sold at 'knock-down' prices. Suppliers are not paid and fraudsmen abscond.
Long-tailed 'un	£10 or £20 Bank of England note.
Loop-the-loop	Soup.
Lot, came his	*See under* Came his cocoa.
Lug around (a person)	To have an unpleasant person in one's company because of orders received or a sale to be made.
Lugs	Ears.

Lumbered — Left holding the baby. Sometimes used in the sense of arrested when others have gone free. Often used as an expletive when faced with an unavoidable and unpleasant task brought about by others, e.g., 'I've been lumbered!'

Lush — Alcoholic drink itself and (less usually, except in the USA) an alcoholic.

Lushington — An alcoholic.

Macer — Thief or cheat.

Machine — Hypodermic syringe.

Machismo — Hippy expression, used particularly by hippy females (originally Mexican/Spanish), meaning excessive masculine pride. Came to the UK via Californian hippy talk. Pronounced with a soft 'c'.

Macho (masho) — Machismo.

Macing — Stealing or cheating (especially at the three-card trick).

Madam — (a) Loquacious deceit, usually skilfully put across. Flattery in general. (b) Female brothel-keeper.

Magflying — Playing pitch and toss.

Magsmen — See Megsmen.

Main liner — Confirmed 'hard' drug addict who injects drugs directly into a vein.

Main lining — The practice of injecting drugs directly into a vein.

Mama, a (real) — A promiscuous female.

Manor — Police area: 'He's Superintendent of this manor.'

Mare — Unpleasant and bad-tempered woman. 'Bitch' connotes contrariness in addition to slight bad temper; 'cow' the next degree of unpleasantness. 'Mare' is easily the worst and most insulting.

Marie (Correlli) — The television (telly). (Authoress.)

Mark-up, at the — Secretly taking more than your 'rightful' share of a bribe or blackmail payment. Often done by the middleman or stakeholder who actually receives the total money from the briber or victim, or their agents. It is an illusion to believe there is a sense of 'fair shares' or honour with corrupt persons. Also referred to as 'creaming'. Frequently the cause of intense bad feeling, sometimes violence, and even betrayal to police.

Mauley — Handwriting, also one's signature: 'I put my mauley on it.'

McAlpine Fusilier — Irish labourer employed in the construction business (from the name of the famous building firm).

Meat rack, the	Pavement beside railings under the colonnade of the County Fire Office, Piccadilly Circus, where male prostitutes gather.
Meet, a	In most cases a place of meeting with a friend or informer, but sometimes with undertones of clandestine irregularity. For example, 'Make the meet' can mean to go to the place where a corrupt and secret transactions will be made. 'Don't make the meet!' would be a warning of a likely trap. Emphasis upon the word itself often indicates this clandestine second meaning.
Megsmen	Petty thieves and cheats, in a small way of business, and used contemptuously.
Mess, bit of	See Bit of mess.
Meter thief	Term of contempt for a petty thief.
Metziyah	A bargain (Yiddish).
Mezuzah	Small metal container holding a prayer, often seen on the upper frame of the front door of Jewish homes.
Mick's, at the	Causing trouble.
Mince (pies)	Eyes: 'His minces are blue.'
Minder	A man used as an 'enforcer', or to extract money from persons making regular extortion payments; a person who 'minds' or looks after stolen property and, less commonly, a milder term for a ponce.
Mix, at the	See Mick's, at the.
Molly (Malone)	The telephone.
Monkey	Five hundred pounds.
Monnicker	Signature.
Monte	The three-card trick.
Moody or old moody	Lies, deceit and, in another sense, something that goes wrong. 'What he said was just a load of old moody'. means it was deceitful and false, and 'It went moody on us' would mean that the expected successful result did not materialise.
Moon	Month.
Mother f . . . er	Once entirely American, now often used by London hippies as abuse, especially to police. A term never used ironically or humorously.
Mouth music	A taboo and gross expression meaning the practice of cunnilingus. Never used in mixed or family company.
Mouth and trousers, all	Noisy and worthless bluff: 'He's all mouth and trousers.'
Mouthpiece	Lawyer.
Muff diving	Another taboo and gross expression meaning the practice of cunnilingus. Never used in mixed or family company.

193

Mug	Anyone other than a thief, a policeman, a physician, a lawyer or a journalist. Any member of the honest general public.
Mug punters	Gullible fools. Contemptuous term used by fraudsmen and card sharps for the persons they cheat.
Mug's ticker	*See* Patacca.
Mum	One's wife or long-established mistress, and *not* one's mother, unless it is plainly made to sound so by the addition of such words as 'my dear old mum'.
Mump, to	To scrounge or to beg.
Mumper	A beggar or a scrounger.
Mush	Low expression used by South Country thieves for friend or mate. 'Hello, my old mush' would be a friendly greeting. Originally Romany, heard in South London. Pronounced like 'bush'.
Mushie, a	Taxi driver who owns his cab.
Mushter	As Mush.
My old guv'nor	One's father.
My old lady	One's mother.
Mystery	An adolescent female absent from her home, approved school or Borstal and 'floating' around the streets. 'Chicken' (q.v.) is the male equivalent.
Mystery mad, or mystery punter	A ('girl crazy') man who spends time obsessively on the look-out for such young girls, so that he can live with them for a short period.
Naftkeh	Prostitute (Yiddish).
Nan (and Nanna)	Grandmother.
Nancy	Buttocks, or (apparently by extension) a male homosexual.
Narna	A fool.
Ned, a	A young Scots hooligan, a member of a Glasgow gang of roughs, not necessarily criminals (used slightly contemptuously).
Neddy	A cosh.
Needle, the	Resentment: 'It's plain he's got the needle to me.'
Nemmo	Woman (London backslang).
Nervo (and Knox)	Syphilis (pox): 'A dose of the old Nervo.' (Names of an old music hall duo of comedians.)
Newington (Butts)	Stomach (guts), especially a large corporation; not used to mean courage, but rather as follows: 'I've got a pain in my newington' or 'What a newington!' (Name of London street.)
Nick, the	Police station or, less commonly, prison.
Nicked	Arrested.
Nicker, a	£1 note.
Nigerian lager	Guinness stout.

194

Nit	The egg of the head louse and, by extension, a fool.
Nit-picking	Making a fuss over trifles and, more rarely, the practice of the alcoholic derelict going through the pockets of another alcoholic derelict while the latter is unconscious, when in search of the price of drink.
No way!	Originally hippy, now becoming common, meaning 'I refuse' or 'No, definitely'.
Nommus!	Costermongers' and pitch and toss players' warning cry upon the approach of police (London backslang).
Nookey	Sexual intercourse. Considered a 'naughty but nice' expression that could be used in mixed company.
North and south	Mouth. Sometimes used to indicate loquaciousness: 'What a north and south!'
Nosper	A person (London backslang).
Nut, did his	Lost his temper.
Nuts	Testicles.
Oishe(r)	Rich man (Yiddish).
Old Bill	*See* Bill.
Oliver (Twist) on, put the	To put an incorrect entry in any ledger but particularly in a betting ledger, and to do it covertly. A dishonest bookmaker might, when taking a bet, say to his equally dishonest clerk, 'Put the oliver on that', meaning that the entry (which might win handsomely) must be altered.
Once a week	Cheek, in the sense of impertinence: 'He's got plenty of once a week.'
Oncer, a	A £1 note (pronounced 'wun-cer').
On the pension	A person receiving regular bribes or blackmail payments, acting as a 'leech'.
Out front	Same meaning as 'Up front' (q.v.).
Outers	A way of escape, or a way to escape responsibility, or to avoid conviction at court. For example, in this sense: 'Give me outers, guv'nor, and I'll help you get the gear back.'
Outside man	Lookout man for criminals but particularly for a 'firm' of card sharps engaged in the three-card trick. Such lookout men may be posted as far as 200 yd (183 m) away from the venue of the 'action'.
Overs	Surplus of property or money after a theft that can itself be stolen by trusted persons.

Pad	Hippy slang for room or bed, now becoming a commonly used term in non-hippy company.
Patacca	Italian slang term, pronounced 'pataka', meaning worthless rubbish, but now particularly used in the dubious jewellery trade, and amongst air stewards, to describe a counterfeit Swiss watch. For example, a cheap mass-produced (usually Italian or Russian) movement, with a false famous Swiss proprietary name (e.g., Rolex, Omega, Longines, Patek Phillip) on the dial, and false hallmarks and manufacturers' emblems on the back of the case. Some are skilfully forged using genuine precious metal. Great profit is made in their unlawful sale to tourists here and abroad. Also referred to as a 'ramped watch' or 'mug's ticker'.
Pattacche	Plural of patacca.
Percher	An easy arrest, or an easy victim.
Peter	A safe or a cell, less frequently a large suitcase or a trunk.
Peterman	A skilled safe-cutter, often it seems a Scot.
Phone freaks	Persons who electronically and fraudulently manipulate international calls.
Pigs	Hippy slang for police, becoming commonly used in extreme political circles, but not by thieves.
Pig's (ear)	Beer.
Pig's ear, never in a	Never (rhyming 'year').
Pimp	Man living on the earnings of prostitutes, particularly by procuring and soliciting men clients for them.
Pin or Pin position	First cab on an authorised standing.
Pinky	(a) One's little finger. (b) Negro racist expression for a white person, not used in white company. Originally an expression for a light-coloured Negro.
Pirates	Motorised traffic police, in cars and on motor cycles; also unlicensed cab drivers.
Piss (broken) glass, to	Descriptive phrase referring to gonorrhoea or any urinary infection. Also to anything particularly unpleasant. A boring conversation, possibly, or an unexpected disappointment in a sexual encounter.
Piss off!	Clear off!
Piss-artist	Man addicted to alcoholic drink.
Pissed off	Bored.
Pit	An inside pocket in a jacket, also a bed.
Pitch	(a) Sales talk, (b) street site used by pavement salesmen or three-card trick men, (c) a prostitute's territory.

196

Pitch fly	A person who uses another's street selling position without permission.
Placer	Person who negotiates for thieves the 'placing' of stolen property with a receiver interested in the class of property concerned.
Plastic, on the	Defrauding persons, banks and stores with false credit or bank cards.
Plater	A male homosexual prepared only for oral sexual connections. Sometimes used in a heterosexual sense.
Plot	Card sharps' term for the venue in the street or on waste land where illegal gaming can and often does take place. A three-card trick card sharp's pitch.
Poggler	Purse, sometimes a wallet.
Pogue	*See* Poggler.
Point, point position	*See* Pin position.
Poke	*See* Poggler.
Ponce	Man living on the earnings of prostitution.
Pontoon	Twenty-one months imprisonment.
Pony	Twenty-five pounds.
Pony (and trap)	Act of defaecation (crap): 'I'm off for a pony.'
Poof	Male homosexual.
Poppy	Money.
Porridge	Imprisonment: 'He's done his porridge.'
Prick teaser	*See* PT.
Promise, on a	Awaiting a gift or personal services; sometimes used in anticipation of sexual favours to come.
Prop up, to	Originally and most commonly short for 'proposition'. Still used in that sense but also to suggest or arrange, particularly through a third person: 'we must prop up a story over this.'
PT	A 'prick teaser', a woman who pretends an interest in sexual affairs, but deliberately does not 'follow through'. Often used as an insult to such a woman, or a gross insult to a completely innocent and virtuous woman who has caused annoyance, when both words and not the abbreviation would be used.
Pulled	Stopped by the police either when on foot or when driving a car.
Punce	Variation, by pronunciation of, 'ponce' (q.v.).
Punter	Originally a man who bet at race meetings. Has now become synonymous with 'mug', and the phrase 'mug punter' emphasises the contempt in a single term.
Push	Crowd.
Push up, at the	Stealing by picking pockets in crowds.
Puss	Feminine type of female lesbian.

197

Pussies	Furs.
Pussy	The female sexual organ. 'He's mad on pussy' would mean a man fond of the company of accommodating females. Not used in mixed company, but not in the extreme taboo area.
Put him away	Gave information against him so that he is convicted and sentenced: 'Tommy put him away.'
Put his hands up, he	He surrendered or he admitted all the crimes put to him.
Put it around	Let it be known.
Put yourself about	To circulate.
'Q' boat	Nondescript police radio car with plain clothes crew (named after the disguised naval vessels of the First World War).
Queer	Male homosexual.
Queer as a nine-bob note	Something very unusual or suspicious, or extreme feminine behaviour by a male.
Queer bashing	Assaulting male homosexuals either for gain or for perverse pleasure.
Queer rolling	Robbing male homosexuals.
Queer street, in	In trouble, usually financial trouble; possibly from Carey Street, the bankruptcy court location.
Rabbit (and pork)	Talk too much (talk).
Raddie	An Italian, particularly an Anglo-Italian domiciled in London. Originally a term descriptive of Italian families in Clerkenwell.
Ramped watch	*See* Patacca.
Randy	Sexually potent or inclined.
Rasputin, a proper	Ironic phrase for a meek-looking and unworldly clergyman.
Rattler	(a) The railway or the underground railway, (b) a promiscuous young woman.
Raver	A young woman who is enthusiastically promiscuous or merely of a passionate (but not promiscuous) nature.
Ready-eyed	Knowing the full story, awareness of the real 'low-down' of the situation.
Red stuff	Gold.
Reeb	Beer (London backslang).
Reggae	West Indian dance music. Usually greatly amplified.

Reload	To ensnare a 'mug' by letting him think he is winning (at the three-card trick, for example) or has gained a smallish profit or advantage (in a confidence trick, for example), and then, while he is in the mood of false confidence and with his appetite whetted, to cheat him of all he possesses, or as the term has it 'to send him to the cleaners'.
Reschit	Jewish for prison.
Rhubarb	Nonsense. Sometimes the word is used three times thus, 'Rhubarb, rhubarb, rhubarb' as emphasis. (From the muttering of actors when simulating the sound of a crowd.)
Ribby	(a) Short of cash, (b) substandard.
Right finger	Clever thief.
Right on	'I agree', or 'very good', or 'well put'. (Originally hippy slang.)
Ringer	Man who steals vehicles and alters their appearance skilfully for sale here or abroad; also, such an altered vehicle. Originally meant horses or greyhounds that had been similarly disguised. Not so common in this sense now. Also used to describe any genuine-appearing fake.
Rip-off	Hippy slang for an act of theft, becoming not uncommon in thieves' slang.
Rod	Overcoat.
Rolling	Stealing from a man bemused by drink, from an unconscious person, or from one engaged in sexual intimacies.
Ronson	Ponce.
Rory (O'More)	Short of cash (rhymes with 'on the floor').
Rouf	Four (London backslang).
Rough trade, the	Male street prostitution in the West End, especially when frequenting the colonnade in Piccadilly Circus.
Rub-a-dub	Public house or club (pub).
Rumble	Brixton West Indian phrase for a street fight.
Rumbled	To become aware of: 'The doorman has rumbled us all right.'
Rung it on us, they have	They have outwitted us.
Runner	A person, arrested by police, likely to abscond if given bail.
Sackwah	Place where drinking, usually illegal or irregular, takes place (West Indian).
Sally (Ann)	The Salvation Army. Used also to refer to the common lodging houses managed by this organisation.
Salmon (and trout)	Tobacco (snout) and less commonly, gout (the disease).

Sam	To cheat or deceive.
Scam	A 'long firm fraud' (q.v.).
Scamming	Taking part in a long firm fraud.
Scarper	Run away.
Schainer yid	An honest and absolutely trustworthy Jewish man (Yiddish).
Schikse	Slightly derogatory Yiddish term for a non-Jewish girl domestic servant or shop assistant.
Schlepper	Scrounger (Yiddish).
Schlock	Cheaply shoddy or useless (Yiddish).
Schmaltz	Flattery, insincere pleasantries, or 'bull' (Yiddish).
Schmeer	Bribe.
Schmock	Unpleasant fool (Yiddish, taboo word).
Schmutter	Clothing, or rags, or rubbish (Yiddish), but especially a suit: 'That's a nice schmutter you've got.'
Schnoink	Unpleasant and insulting term used by a non-Jew for a Jew (not a Yiddish or Hebrew word).
Schonk	*See* Schnoink.
Schvegg!	Stop talking! (Common Yiddish.)
Schwartzer	Negro (an expression used by people familiar with Yiddish).
Scran	Food.
Scratch	Banknotes, or pretended banknotes.
Screw, a	A prison warder.
Screw, to	(a) To take part in sexual intercourse, (b) to break into premises, (c) to look at intently, 'Look at that geezer screwing us', (d) to deal harshly with, 'I'll screw the rat!'
Screwsman	Housebreaker of some skill.
Scrubber	Low-class woman, or an amateur (and usually pathetic) young prostitute.
Sent down	Imprisoned.
Shagetz	Young Christian (or rather non-Jewish) male.
Shamez	Synagogue official used as a slang word for policeman (Yiddish).
Shant	A drink, principally an alcoholic drink.
Shebeen	Illegal drinking establishment.
Sheenie, a	Unpleasantly racist term for a Jew (not used in Jewish company).
Sheol	Hell (East End Jewish).
Sherbert (the old)	Alcoholic drink, particularly beer.
Shicer (sheister)	A cheat or 'welsher'.
Shill	A decoy, particularly in fraud or the three-card trick, who lures or encourages a victim.
Shiv	*See* Chiv.
Shoobin	Pronunciation variation of 'shebeen' (q.v.).
Shooter	Commonest expression for a firearm, usually but not exclusively a pistol.

Shop, to	To betray or to inform against.
Shtook	Counterfeit Yiddish-sounding expression meaning an unpleasant situation: 'I've been left in shtook all right!'
Shubeen	Pronunciation variation of 'shebeen' (q.v.).
Side, bit on the	Having an extramarital affair.
Side, over the	Absent from place of duty, or home.
Sightseers	Card sharps' term for the 'hedge' or crowd of members of the public around the action of a three-card trick conspiracy, each such undecided person being regarded as a potential 'mug'.
Skid artist	Get-away car driver.
Skimmish	Beer.
Skin pop, to	Inject narcotic drug (heroin, for example) into the skin rather than into a vein ('main lining', q.v.): the words 'skin popper' may be used as a term of patronising contempt by a confirmed addict to one just starting.
Skint	*See* Boracic (lint).
Sky(rocket)	Pocket.
Slag, a	A low-class hooligan or a hippy person, or a contemptuous term for a prostitute: 'Look at that old slag.'
Slag, to	To admonish in violent terms.
Slaughter, a	A place temporarily to hide property recently stolen.
Smoke, the	London.
Smother	Overcoat (probably from Yiddish 'schmutter', q.v.).
Snide	Anything worthless, unpleasant or counterfeit.
Snorer	Scrounger (Yiddish).
Snout	(a) Tobacco, (b) informant.
Solo creeper	Sneak thief operating absolutely alone.
Sounds man	Person providing amplified reggae music at illegal drinking establishment.
Spade	A Negro.
Spare	An unattached female.
Spare, to go	To react violently.
Spare, to have a bit of	Sexual liaison outside marriage, adultery.
Sparkers	Unconscious or deeply asleep: 'She was sparkers.'
Sparklers	Diamonds.
Speak to you ?, can I	The commonest euphemism for 'Are you willing to listen to a corrupt proposal I am about to put to you ?' The phrase is used with intensity and a 'knowing' glance.
Special Branch again, the	Ironic phrase used when an eccentrically dressed or filthy person is seen.
SP	Starting price. Used in non-racing conversation in this sense: 'What's the SP on this ?', meaning 'What is the inside story ?'

201

Spiel, to	(a) To gamble, (b) to spin a yarn or to 'patter'.
Spieler	(a) A gambler or a gambling house, (b) a person who spins a yarn or 'patters'.
Spike, the	Originally the workhouse, now used to describe any common lodging house whether managed by the local authority or by a charity.
Spin (someone's drum)	To search a house.
Split	To leave (originally hippy, now becoming common). Used in this sense: 'What a bore this place is. Come on, let's split.'
Spreading broads	Playing or cheating at cards. Manipulating the three-card trick.
Squeeze (noun)	Silk.
Squirreled away	Hidden away.
Stage fright	Light ale: 'What's yours?'; reply, 'Stage fright'.
Stalk	Male sexual propensity, courage or cheek: 'He's got plenty of stalk'; also, an erection of the penis.
Stalking	The practice by unscrupulous owner cab drivers, and those drivers who hire the cab for a fixed period, of leaving their meters set 'hired' while unhired, so that they can cruise or loiter about 'stalking' worthwhile hirings (e.g., long trips to airports, 'steering' dupes to expensive night clubs, young foreign girls to abortion touts, etc.). They thus have a cast-iron excuse, 'I am already hired, guv'nor', if an attempt is made to hire them for an unprofitable or short journey. It also enables dishonest drivers to grossly over-charge foreign visitors and, if there is a dispute, to point to the fare registered on the meter.
Stand to (attention)	Pension: I'm off to draw my stand to.'
Starkers	Naked.
Starters	Opening gambits: 'How's that for starters?'
Stash, a	Concealed drugs.
Stash (away), to	To hide (drugs).
Steamer	A mug or fool (steam tug).
Stick	Cigarette containing cannabis.
Stick him on!	Charge him with a crime, or summons him.
Stick one on (him/her)	Hit him/her on the chin.
Sticker	A prisoner who must remain in custody while on remand or awaiting appearance at court.
Stickman	The confederate of a pickpocket or skilled shop-lifter to whom stolen property is handed and whose other task is 'accidentally' to impede pursuit of the actual thief if he is detected by the loser.
Sticksing	Picking pockets (West Indian).
Stiff, to	To kill.

202

Stir	Prison.
Stitch up	To deal effectively with a situation, but usually unscrupulously. 'Let's stitch up old Bill' might mean 'Let's give overwhelming but perjured evidence against that policeman'. *See also* Fit up.
Stonikey	A cosh.
Straight up	Telling the truth: 'It's straight up, guv'nor.'
Straighten	To avoid trouble by a blackmail payment or a bribe: 'Don't worry—he can be straightened, I know.'
Straightener	Money, blackmail payment or a bribe.
Strap, to	To interrogate strongly.
Stretch	Once meant specifically twelve months imprisonment, now means any long term of imprisonment. 'Half a stretch' still means six months imprisonment; 'five stretch' means five years.
Strokes	Unfair actions.
Strokes, pulling	Using skill at deceit and unfair actions to gain advantage: '. . . talk about Oxford and Cambridge!' (involved allusion to 'strokes' in the University Boat Race).
Strum	Fuse.
Stuffy	Wealthy.
Stumm	Silent. Pronounced *Sch*tumm. 'Keep stumm!' is an urgent command—'Stop talking!' (Yiddish.)
Stumm and crum	Emphatic version of 'stumm'.
Sus	Suspected generally, or specifically a person arrested for 'being a suspected person loitering . . .'.
Sussed	Arrested as a suspected person loitering.
Sussed me out	Guessed correctly who I was, or what I was doing.
Swailer	Cosh.
Swank	Pretend: 'Let's swank that Tommy here isn't married and the . . ..'
Sweeney (Todd), the	The Flying Squad (named after an apocryphal nineteenth-century criminal barber who butchered his victims and sold their corpses to a meat-pie maker).
Sweet as a nut	An easy facility, for example: 'We went in sweet as a nut.'
Sweet FA	Nothing (originally Sweet Fanny Adams, a famous nineteenth-century female murder victim, but now more commonly 'sweet f . . . all').
Sweetman	Man living on the earnings of one prostitute. A prostitute's regular 'man'.
Swift, a bit	Unfair advantage was taken: 'Guv'nor, now that was a bit swift.'

Swift 'un, a	An arrest for 'being a suspected person loitering' (*see also* Very swift) with undertones of unfair advantage being taken.
Swiss watch, went like a	Went smoothly.
Switch, at the	Stealing property from a shop and subsequently exchanging it for cash at the same shop.
Switched on	Aroused by music or by sexual overtures. Can be used in female company.
Syrup (of figs)	Wig (term originates from the name of a commercial laxative). A common criminal expression, as wigs are not infrequently used as disguises and are often worn by prostitutes.
Table, under the	Dishonestly or corruptly.
Taig	A Roman Catholic
Tail	Sexual intercourse in a general sense: 'He loves tail.'
Tailed off	Followed.
Talent, the	Attractive young women: 'Let's look at the talent.'
Tallahwah	Decent, straightforward and honourable. Complimentary adjective (West Indian).
Tapping	Begging or scrounging.
Tatts	Dice.
Tea, go for your	To die.
Tea leaf	Thief.
Tea with, take	Act with covert impertinence towards someone (usually someone in authority), or to take advantage of someone; to outwit a clever person (not used in respect of 'mugs').
Team	Gang of criminals and, by extension, a posse of police.
Tekram	Any street market, once only the Covent Garden or Finsbury markets (London backslang).
Thieves' kitchen	The Stock Exchange (taxi drivers' slang).
Three-card monte	The three-card trick.
Ticket	Warrant to arrest or search.
Tickle	Successful crime or a worthwhile arrest, especially if unexpected. Sometimes, a medium-sized betting success: 'A nice little tickle!'
Tin soldier	(a) To be impertinent or obstructive, as in '. . . don't come the old tin soldier with me!' (b) A voyeur-type male, usually of middle- or upper-class background, who voluntarily acts as a prostitute's 'slave' or companion for no apparent reward (prostitutes' slang).
Tit for (tat)	Hat. Pronounced 'titfer'.
Toby	Area, or Police Division: 'Keep off this toby!'

Toches	A low, almost taboo, Yiddish expression for buttocks.
Tod (Sloan)	All alone: 'He's on his tod.'
Toff	Gentleman (in every sense), including a complimentary description of an honourable and upright man.
Toffee	Nonsense or flattery: 'You don't believe that load of toffee, do you?', or 'He's full of the old toffee!'
Tom	Prostitute.
Tom(foolery)	Jewellery.
Tom and Dick	Sick: 'Where's Roy?'; reply, 'He's tom and dick'.
Tom Mix	Predicament (fix): 'She's in a bit of a tom mix.'
Tomtit	Act of defaecation: 'I must go for a tomtit.'
Ton, a	One hundred pounds or 100 m.p.h. (160 km per hour).
Tonsorials, a touch of the	Haircut.
Tookus	Buttocks (Yiddish).
Tool	A jemmy.
Tooled up	Armed, or in possession of housebreaking implements.
Tootoo(s)	Excrement.
Topped	Hanged.
Topped up	Any container full 'to the brim' and, by extension, drunkenness.
Touch of the seconds	Fear of consequences, second thoughts: 'He had a touch of the seconds.'
Trick	(a) Prostitutes' term for one transaction with a client: 'I've done six tricks so far today.' (b) Unpleasant or demanding period of work, usually of short duration, for example: 'I've done my trick (at the wheel of a car or cab) and now it's your turn.'
Trot, on the	Wanted by police.
Trotter	A deserter from HM Armed Forces.
Trumpet	The telephone.
Tsitskes	Woman's breasts (taboo Yiddish word not used in polite company).
Tumble, give it a	Try it; experiment with it.
Tumble, to	To become aware of, in this sense: 'We had to call it off—they tumbled us straight away.'
Turkey	A disaster or resounding failure : 'My God, what a turkey!'
Turking	Low expression for sexual intercourse, not used in mixed company.
Turn over	A house search or a search in the street of a person or vehicle: 'My motor was turned over by the Law today.'

Turned on	Aroused by music or by sexual overtures. Can be used in female company.
Turtle (doves) or turtles	Gloves (commoner than may be expected, used to refer to housebreakers' and safe-cutters' gloves).
Twat	Female sexual organ, but more commonly a fool: 'What a twat he is!'
Tweedler	A stolen vehicle disguised for 'honest' sale to a respectable dupe.
Tweedling	Selling stolen property, or selling non-existent property, or selling shoddy and worthless articles.
Twig	Recognise: '. . . the manager twigged what we was up to as soon as we was in the shop'.
Twirl	Any key, but especially a stolen, duplicate or skeleton key.
Two and eight	State (of nervous tension): 'After the accident she was in a bit of a two and eight!'
Twot	*See* Twat.
Umbrella Brigade	Ironic police term for the Special Branch.
Uncle Dick	Same as Tom and Dick (q.v.).
Uncle's	A pawnbroker's shop.
Under the table	Dishonestly or corruptly.
Undertaker's job	Specifically, a horse or greyhound not intended to win; generally, any hopeless proposition.
Up front	Straightforward and honest. 'He's up front' is a great compliment.
Up the road	Committed for trial before a judge and jury.
Up the steps	*See* Up the road.
Uppers, on his	Down and out.
Verbals	Oral statements of admission made at the time of arrest by criminals, and very frequently denied when in court. It is often said that police invent them. However, they are usually not denied until legal aid is granted to the criminals.
Very swift	Grossly unfair advantage taken.
Vibes	Pleasurable 'vibrations': 'She gave me the old vibes, all right.'
Voker?	Do you understand?
'W', a	A warrant to arrest or search.
Wash, at the	Stealing as a pickpocket from washrooms of public lavatories in airports, railway stations, hotels, etc.

Wash, the	Shebeen proprietors' term for the mash of cheap grain and sugar (for example) cooked before distillation into illegal drinking spirit alcohol. Has a very distinctive and repulsive super-sweet smell.
Weakheart	West Indian slang for police. Meant to be offensive.
Weasel (and stoat)	Coat.
Wedge	Large number of banknotes folded once.
Weeding	Stealing, especially from an employer, or at the scene of a crime already committed.
Weighed off	Sentenced.
West Ham (Reserves)	Nerves: 'Mum's got the West Ham's.'
Wet foot	Naïve and innocent person.
Wheelman	Expert driver of a motor car.
Whistle (and flute)	Suit (of clothes).
Whistle on, blow the	Stop someone suddenly, or give information to the police about someone which results in his arrest.
Whitecoat	The senior examiner at the (taxi) Police Public Carriage Office.
Whitey	A racist Negro term for a white person (usually male), not said in a pleasant manner.
Whiz, the	The craft of the pickpocket: 'Tom has been at the whiz these last ten years at least.'
Wick (Hampton)	Penis (prick).
Wide	Experienced, cunning.
Wind and piss, all	Bragging: 'He's all wind and piss' or, more politely, 'He's all wind and water'.
Wino	Alcoholic, particularly one who drinks cheap domestic wine.
Yancing or yencing	Yiddish term for sexual intercourse; although not usually used in mixed company it it not considered completely taboo.
Yarmelka	Orthodox Jewish skull cap. Word often used in bantering humour amongst East End of London thieves.
Yennap	A penny (London backslang).
Yob	Low-class young hooligan (London backslang).
Yockele	East End Yiddish for Christian (commoner than 'goy'), often used in a slightly derogatory sense.
You and me	Tea, i.e., the evening meal: 'I am off for my you and me.'
You know how it is ...	A frequently heard excuse or explanation when nothing specific comes to mind. Very common.
Zaftig	Yiddish term literally meaning 'juicey'. Often used to describe a curvaceous and attractive woman. Not used in mixed company, but not completely taboo.

Appendix 1

Recognition and sighting by witnesses

By repeated tests it is safe to assume that a witness of normal intelligence and vision, of or above 5 ft 6 in (1·7 m) in height, in good daylight, can recognise:

A person seen once before up to about	18 yd (16 m)
A person seen on several prior occasions up to about	30 yd (27 m)
A person intimately known up to about	100 yd (91 m)
A person with minor deformities or at least somewhat unusual characteristics up to about	115 yd (105 m)
A person with particularly marked deformities up to about	170 yd (155 m)
At night, in bright moonlight or under good street lighting, a little-known person can only rarely be recognised beyond about	20–30 yd (18–27 m)

In the absence of heat haze, large bodies of people, troops for example, can be made out with the naked eye at 2000 yd (1830 m) and both men and vehicles will resemble varied dots; movements can just be distinguished at 1000–1300 yd (914–1190 m) and at 750 yd (686 m) one can just separate arms and legs. At 600 yd (550 m) a man's head can be distinguished as resembling a minute oval sphere. At 500 yd (457 m) colour of clothing can be seen. At 400 yd (366 m) movements of legs can more easily be made out, at 300 yd (275 m) faces can be seen, and at 200 yd (183 m) details of clothing, e.g., collar, overcoats, skirts, can be made out. At 100 yd (91 m) the eyes resemble two black dots, and at 50 yd (46 m) the mouth and eyes can be distinguished plainly.

VEHICLE INDEX PLATES

By repeated tests it is safe to assume that a witness of normal intelligence and vision, of or above 5 ft 6 in (1·7 m) in height, can read an index plate:

In good daylight

Ideally fitted and clean, up to about   70 yd (64 m)

Badly fitted (e.g., bad angle, facing down or of a reflective surface type which, in certain angles or light, can be obliterated by side reflection, but in all cases clean) up to about   60 yd (55 m)

Ideally fitted American or Canadian-style licence plates in good daylight up to about   45 yd (41 m)

In good street lighting

Ideally fitted, clean and illuminated, up to about   60 yd (55 m)

Badly fitted, but clean, up to about   50 yd (46 m)

Ideally fitted American or Canadian-style licence plates, clean and illuminated, up to about   30 yd (27 m)

You should carefully test (without being offensive) claims to have recognised persons, or to have read index plates, beyond these distances. There is no substitute in any disputed case, or one involving any fatality, of quietly and privately checking the likelihood of a statement of recognition or extreme observation by reconstructing (as far as practicable) the scene and testing it against your own eyesight.

Appendix 2

Some constants, conversions and approximations which may be useful generally, but also in gauging the accuracy of witnesses' recollection of observed incidents

Time between tides, approx. 12 h 24 min.

1 gal of watery liquid weighs about 10 lb (4·5 kg).

To convert millimetres to inches (useful for rapid mental calculation in respect of firearm calibres) multiply by 4 and divide by 100. To convert inches to millimetres, multiply by 100 and divide by 4. (Reason: 1 mm = 0·03937 in = (approx.) $\frac{4}{100}$ in. or $\frac{1}{25}$ in.)

Using a pocket calculator you can quickly convert

inches to millimetres multiply by 25·4   or divide by 0·039 37
inches to centimetres multiply by   2·54   or divide by 0·393 7

feet	to centimetres	multiply by	30·48	or divide by	0·032 8
feet	to metres	multiply by	0·304 8	or divide by	3·280 8
yards	to metres	multiply by	0·914 4	or divide by	1·093 6
miles	to kilometres	multiply by	1·609	or divide by	0·621 4
sq. in	to sq. cm	multiply by	6·45	or divide by	0·155 729
cu. in	to cu. cm	multiply by	16·387	or divide by	0·610 24
f.p.s.	to m.p.h.	multiply by	0·681 8	or divide by	1·466 6
m.p.h.	to f.p.s.	multiply by	1·466 6	or divide by	0·681 8

A cheap electronic calculator (if possible one with a square root facility) is as much a useful tool for a thinking police officer as a pair of handcuffs or your baton—more so, in fact. If any of your calculations are to form part of evidence tendered in court, ensure that all unavoidable errors or estimates made favour the accused.

Appendix 3

Time, speed and distance

During inquiries into those crimes associated with the use of vehicles, and into reckless or negligent use of motor vehicles, you may well need to know quickly

1. The time taken to travel a known distance at a known or estimated speed, or
2. The average speed of a vehicle or person cycling or on foot, over a known distance in a known period of time, or finally
3. How to calculate the distance travelled by a vehicle or person at a known average speed in a known period of time.

A useful and universal formula for these calculations can be expressed as follows:

$$\frac{\text{Distance (miles)}}{\text{m.p.h.}} = \frac{\text{Time taken (sec)}}{3600 \ (\text{i.e., the number of seconds in an hour})}$$

By simple transposition this formula can answer each of the above queries, as follows:

$$1. \qquad \text{Time taken (sec)} = \frac{3600 \times \text{Distance (miles)}}{\text{m.p.h.}}$$

2. $$\text{Average speed (m.p.h.)} = \frac{3600 \times \text{Distance (miles)}}{\text{Time (sec)}}.$$

and finally

3. $$\text{Distance travelled (miles)} = \frac{\text{m.p.h.} \times \text{Time (sec)}}{3600}$$

Problems

To illustrate the usefulness of these formulae, see how rapid are the solutions to the following practical problems:

1. How long would it take the accused to travel 440 yd (0·25 of a mile), in his car, but not to exceed 50 m.p.h. ?

$$\text{Answer} = \frac{3600 \times 0\cdot25}{50} = \frac{3600}{200}$$
$$= 18 \text{ sec.}$$

2. Is it possible for a young male housebreaker, with access to a pedal cycle, to cover $7\frac{1}{4}$ (7·25) miles in half-an-hour (1800 sec)?

$$\text{Average speed} = \frac{3600 \times 7\cdot25}{1800}$$
$$= 14\tfrac{1}{2} \text{ m.p.h.}$$
$$\text{Answer} = \text{Yes, it is possible}$$

3. How far along the motorway could the accused's wife travel in this stolen Rover car (which we know is capable of a sustained 102 m.p.h.) in 1 hr 45 min?

$$\text{Distance (miles)} = \frac{\text{m.p.h.} \times \text{time (sec)}}{3600}$$

$$= \frac{102 \times 1\cdot75 \times 3600}{3600} = 178\cdot5$$

$$\text{Answer} = \text{The accused's wife could travel a maximum of 178 miles 880 yd}$$

To find speed, in m.p.h., when time for a measured distance is known:

$$\text{m.p.h.} = \frac{45 \times \text{Distance (yd)}}{22 \times \text{Time for that distance (sec)}}.$$

The following speed table gives the average speed per hour against the time occupied to traverse 1 mile:

Time for 1 mile		Speed per hour		Time for 1 mile		Speed per hour	
min	sec	mile	yd	min	sec	mile	yd
4	0	15	0	1	28	40	1660
3	50	15	1148	1	26	41	1514
3	40	16	640	1	24	42	1509
3	30	17	251	1	22	43	1588
3	20	18	0	1	20	45	0
3	10	18	1667	1	18	46	271
3	0	20	0	1	16	47	648
2	50	21	311	1	14	48	1142
2	40	22	880	1	12	50	0
2	30	24	0	1	10	51	754
2	20	25	1257	1	8	52	1656
2	10	27	1218	1	6	54	960
2	0	30	0	1	4	56	440
1	50	32	1280	1	2	58	113
1	48	33	587	1	0	60	0
1	46	33	1694	0	59	61	50
1	44	34	1083	0	58	62	121
1	42	35	518	0	57	63	278
1	40	36	0	0	56	64	503
1	38	36	1298	0	55	65	800
1	36	37	880	0	54	66	1173
1	34	38	524	0	53	67	1627
1	32	39	158	0	52	69	406
1	30	40	0	0	51	70	1035

To convert m.p.h. to f.p.s. (within an error of $2\frac{1}{2}$ per cent) multiply by $1\frac{1}{2}$ (e.g., 60 m.p.h. halved = 30. 60 + 30 = 90 f.p.s.) (actually 88 f.p.s.). This conversion is most convenient for rapid mental calculations in the witness box. With an electronic calculator you can, with great accuracy, convert m.p.h. to f.p.s. by multiplying by 1·4666, and similarly can convert f.p.s. to m.p.h. by multiplying by 0·6818.

This is not the place for the more detailed formulae concerned in serious accident investigation, but it is useful to have two approximate formulae for quick calculation at the scene of an accident.

In relation to measured skid marks (taking an approximate and general* braking efficiency of 66·8 per cent, for the convenience of calculation):

$$\text{Speed} = \frac{\sqrt{(\text{Skid mark length (ft)} \times 66\cdot8)}}{3\cdot34}$$

or

$$\text{Speed} = \sqrt{(\text{Skid mark length (ft)} \times 20)}$$

Take a skid mark of 45 ft, then:

$$\text{Speed will have been in the region of} = \sqrt{(45 \times 20)}$$
$$= \sqrt{(900)}$$

(i.e., the square root of 20 times the skid mark.)

$$= 30 \text{ m.p.h.}$$

To work out *braking* distance for a given speed, transposition of the original formula gives

$$\text{Distance} = \frac{V^2}{20}$$

where $V =$ the given speed in m.p.h.

This will enable you to give a rough but reasonable approximation in answer to the sort of questions you should ask yourself at the scene of serious accidents where criminal neglect or recklessness may be involved, e.g.: 'What braking distance is reasonable if this man was driving at 30 m.p.h. as he says?'

$$\text{Braking distance} = \frac{30 \times 30}{20} = 45 \text{ ft} = 15 \text{ yd}$$

This latter calculation does not include any approximation of 'thinking time' (about 1 ft for every mile per hour), and it is emphasised they are all *approximate* to facilitate only rough calculations in the field or for rapid mental calculation in the witness box under cross-examination. No consideration has been given to the variations of road surface.

---

* These formulae are based on the skidding vehicle being decelerated at $0\cdot66g$. This figure is used to calculate the stopping distances quoted in the *Highway Code*. It is a reasonable estimate for skidding on *dry roads*; however, the formulae are not applicable if the vehicle is forcibly brought to rest during the skid by colliding with an obstruction. Nevertheless, if still used the errors *favour an accused*. Vehicles skidding on *wet roads* may be retarded at less than $0\cdot66g$, but will not usually leave marks. Lastly, certain vehicles fitted with *anti-lock* braking systems can decelerate at over $1\cdot0g$ on dry roads without skidding.

Sensible use of these calculations may also protect an accused person from the over-estimations of speed made by emotionally charged witnesses at the scene of fatal or serious accidents, who can materially mislead you without intending to tell lies. I am indebted to E. W. Eastmond, a former Metropolitan Police Officer of great practical experience, for permission to quote his 'on street' formulae.

Appendix 4

Other observed approximations helpful in establishing truth

The initial flash of a lighted match can be seen in otherwise total or near-total darkness at a distance of no less than 900 yd (823 m). The glow of a cigarette, when positive inhalation is made by the smoker, can be seen in similar circumstances for approximately 300 yd (275 m).

An approximate method of determining the distance, in miles, to the visible horizon is to obtain the square root of $1\frac{1}{2}$ times the height, in feet, of the observer above sea level.

A trained man or woman, mounted on a healthy horse, can walk at between 3 and 4 m.p.h.,* trot at between 7 and 9 m.p.h., canter or 'trot out' at about 10 m.p.h. and gallop at approximately 15 m.p.h. Walking and trotting alternately, on a regular basis, can produce 6 m.p.h. or more. Endurance of a horse is an intensely variable consideration, but they can be force-ridden to collapse by determined persons. A first-rate racehorse can cross country at about 21 m.p.h. The Derby, for example, is run at about 35 m.p.h., the Grand National—a steeplechase, of course—at about 28 m.p.h. More usual steeplechases are run at approximately 25 m.p.h. In 1963, a measured mile was covered by a quality thoroughbred at a speed of between 39 and 40 m.p.h.

On foot, a fit man (or an unfit determined man) can cover 100 yd (91 m) per min or slightly more (approximately 3 m.p.h., including occasional halts) for several hours over flat roads or good paths. Rough or hilly cross-country may halve this rate. A fit man, running and walking alternately, can cover 7 m.p.h., or about 200 yd (183 m) per min in similar conditions.

* 1 m.p.h. = 1·6093 kilometres per hour.

A cyclist on a standard pedal cycle usually covers about 10 m.p.h. over reasonable roads, but can reach up to 13 or 14 m.p.h. A racing cycle, with a young adult, can cover 14 m.p.h. at a standard pace, but can reach up to 19 m.p.h. and, in extreme cases, even up to 25 m.p.h.

A pedal cycle can be useful in 'making time' in even very rough country as there will inevitably be portions of the route where cycling will be possible.

Women are about seven-eighths of this efficiency in walking, running or cycling. Many, however, can ride a horse more efficiently than a male.

The possible physical effort of either a very determined person of either sex, or one emotionally or obsessively charged, should not be under-estimated. Such persons may exceed substantially the norms described: 'Powerful motives increase the force of will.'

Appendix 5

Useful mnemonics

To recall quarter days promptly:

March 25	(March has 5 letters)
June 24	(June has 4 letters)
September 29	(September has 9 letters)

Bones of the shoulder, arm and hand

'Some cheats have underestimated Royal Canadian Mounted Policemen':

Scapula, clavicle, humerus, ulna, radius, carpals, metacarpals, phalanges

Bones of the hip, leg and foot

'Handy for Police to find the missing pieces':

hip, femur, patella, tibia, fibula, tarsals, metatarsals, phalanges

Appendix 6

Footprints and other traces

Well-indented footmarks at the toe end of the footprint, in widely spaced marks, indicate the person concerned was running. If the marks are spaced in accordance with a normal walking pace, but still deeply toe-indented, the person concerned was heavily laden. Footprints made in wet ground will have muddy water within the indented print; in the absence of other considerations, this muddied water will clear within an hour. In drier areas, clear water in footprints indicates they were made before rain. Rain flattens edges of footmarks very quickly. Sunlight quickly affects the sharpness of dry prints and disintegrates edges. Always measure, as well as photograph, footprints. It may sound obvious but remember it is the last person in a single file that leaves well-indented prints. Plated surfaces of abandoned food tins will not rust, but the tin-opener cut edges of the lid will rust within 12–14 hours.

Appendix 7

Cold exhaustion in river, canal, reservoir or sea water

At just over freezing temperatures unconsciousness will follow rapidly after 12–14 min immersion, and survival is unlikely beyond 45 min. This is due to rapid body heat loss. Children cool the most rapidly, adult females the slowest. Clothing, specifically of natural fibres, tends to retard heat loss even when saturated.

At temperatures up to 40 °F (4·4 °C), unconsciousness will usually follow half an hour's immersion, at 50 °F (10 °C) about an hour, at 60 °F (15·6 °C) up to two hours and in an ascending curve to reasonable comfort (as far as body heat is concerned) in the region of 70–80 °F (21–27 °C).

Speed is of the essence in the recovery of all accidental casualties or intending suicides reported or found in reservoirs, canals or rivers, *particularly in winter*. It is worth while remembering that the inflated spare tyre and wheel in the boot (trunk) of the police car (or any other vehicle) will float and will support an immersed conscious person temporarily. Such a wheel, frequently immediately to hand, is relatively easy to negotiate both over rough ground and down the inclined sides of a reservoir.

Appendix 8

How far can a gun shoot?

In general terms, at the *best elevation* (angle of the barrel above the ground at the time of discharge, about 29° or 30°), a modern firearm using modern smokeless (nitro) propellant will discharge its projectiles as follows:

Firearm	Yards (approx.)	Metres (approx.)
0·22 'long rifle' (as used in miniature ranges), to about	1500	1370
0·38 Special (revolver), to about	1800	1650
9 mm Parabellum, the British—and many other—Service pistol and submachine gun round, to about	1900	1740
Service rifle round (varying very much according to type and whether fired from a rifle, carbine or a machine gun), from about	3400–5600	3110–5120

(Modern tendency is to have less powerful rounds in Service 'assault rifles'—the Soviet Kalashnikov AK 47, for example—than was used in the Service rifles of 1914 and 1939. This should be taken into account when considering extreme ranges.)

Firearm		Yards (approx.)	Metres (approx.)
12-bore shotgun	solid round ball	1400	1280
	buckshot	720	658
	pellets	220	201

If you multiply the shotgun pellet diameter, in inches, by 2200 you have the approximate distance, in yards, the pellet will travel (Journee's formula).

Appendix 9

What is reasonable protection against rifle fire ?

The following table (taken from a 1914 manual) gives the maximum penetration of the high-powered pointed, fully loaded, powerful Service rifle bullet. It can still be regarded as an up-to-date general guide. Pistol and submachine gun bullets have nothing like this penetration, and one can safely consider approximately 30 per cent effectiveness in their case, which may be on the generous side.

Material	Maximum penetration		Remarks
	(in)	(mm)	
Steel plate, best hard	$\frac{7}{16}$	(11)	At 30 yd (27 m) normal to plate
Steel plate, ordinary mild or wrought iron	$\frac{3}{4}$	(19)	$\frac{3}{16}$ in (5 mm) is proof at not less than 600 yd (550 m), unless the plate is set at a slope of 3/2; then $\frac{3}{16}$ in is proof at 250 yd (232 m)
Shingle	6	(152)	Not larger than 1 in (25 mm) ring gauge
Coal, hard	6	(152)	
Brickwork, cement mortar	9	(228)	150 rounds concentrated on one
lime mortar	14	(355)	spot will breach a 9 in (228
Chalk	15	(381)	mm) brick wall at 200 yd (183 m)

Table, *continued*

Sand, confined between boards or in sandbags	18	(45)	Very high velocity bullets have less penetration in sand at short than at medium ranges
Sand, loose	30	(76)	
Hard wood, e.g., oak, with grain	38	(96)	
Earth, free from stones (unrammed)	40	(101)	Ramming earth reduces its resisting power
Soft wood, e.g., fir, with grain	58	(147)	Penetration of brickwork and timber is less at short than at medium ranges
Clay	60	(152)	Varies greatly. This is maximum for greasy clay
Dry turf or peat	80	(203)	

Note—Experiments at which the writer has been present have shown that:

Walls of broken brick, 2 in by 3 in (51 mm by 76 mm), between corrugated iron, are proof if 8 in (203 mm) thick.

Walls of broken-up road-making material, 2 in by 3 in (51 mm by 76 mm), between corrugated iron, are proof if 8 in (203 mm) thick.

Walls of screened gravel, 1½ in (38 mm), between corrugated iron, are proof if 6 in (152 mm) thick.

Walls of hand-picked Thames ballast, 1½ in (38 mm), between corrugated iron, are proof if 6 in (152 mm) thick.

Appendix 10

How far away were those shots?

The velocity of sound in still air (varying according to ambient temperature) is about 1128 feet per second or 344 metres per second (or 376 yards per second), which is about 770 miles per hour. As stated, variations in ambient temperature will affect the velocity of sound, but in the sort of approximate field calculations of use to practical police officers, this can be ignored. The velocity of light—186 284 *miles* per sec—which necessarily enters into these calculations, can also be ignored because of its sheer immensity.

Nevertheless, using the sweep second hand of your wristlet watch (ideally a stop-watch) you can estimate the distance from your position to a man using modern firearms, by noting the seconds and fraction of seconds that elapse between seeing the flash of gunfire and hearing the report of the weapon. Multiply this by 376 to give you the distance in yards, by 344 to give the distance in metres. If you have no access to a calculator, or the time to do complicated manual calculations, multiply the time in seconds by $3\frac{3}{4}$ and add two noughts to your answer. This will give a rough estimation of the distance in yards; $3\frac{1}{2}$ will give the result in metres.

Remember, however, that with modern projectiles (certainly those from an old-style Service rifle, machine gun or even the modern less powerful 'assault rifle') which travel initially at speeds of about 2000–2500 f.p.s. (approximately 1360–1700 m.p.h.) the projectile or bullet is more likely to strike its target area before you hear the sound of the report. It is important, too, not to confuse the whiplash-like sound, made by a bullet still travelling in excess of 770 m.p.h., in other words faster than, and breaking the 'barrier' of, sound when it passes over or near your head, and the much duller sound of the weapon's report. The sequence of events will probably be flash—*crack*—duller crack. It is the time, in seconds, between the flash and the duller crack that forms the basis of these calculations.

The distortions of sound (as far as pinpointing a position are concerned) are generally so confusing that should you see a flash but then hear a report which your hearing considers to be from a different direction, *rely on your eyes* rather than your ears.

Appendix 11

Which binoculars are right for police observations?

In binocular specifications, e.g. 6×30, 7×35, 8×30, 7×50, 12×50, 16×50, etc., the first figure indicates the magnification and the second figure the diameter, in millimetres, of the object lens (i.e. the lens farthest from the eye).

If the second number is divided by the first the diameter is obtained, in millimetres, of the 'exit pupil', that bright bundle of light rays seen in the centre of the eyepieces of binoculars when held at arms' length. Thus 6×30 glasses have an exit pupil diameter of 5 mm, 7×35 also 5; 8×30 are only 3·7 mm, 12×50 slightly better at 4·2 mm, but 16×50 goes to the very low 3·1 mm. Note that 7×50 glasses have a massive 7·1 mm exit pupil.

The pupil of the human eye has a diameter of about 2 mm in bright sunlight, but opens to 7 mm (approximately) at dusk to gather as much light as possible. This is the time when 7×50 glasses come into their own and the glasses with small exit pupils are nearly useless. In adverse conditions of heat haze, mist or, of course, night time, the 7×50's light-gathering qualities are superlatively good. The best test of the truth of this is to compare a 16×50 glass with a 7×50 one at dusk—it will absolutely convince you. Needless to say a 7×50 glass is also efficient in good light conditions.

Do not be over-fascinated by high magnification specification. Remember, natural hand vibrations make the use, unsupported by a tripod or other fixture, of any glass of over 8 diameters magnification very difficult. The best buy is, therefore, a 7×50, even though they are bulky. Shop around; the cheaper new and secondhand ex-Service glass of this specification can be obtained for about £15–£20. Make sure there is not the least trace of double image by looking at a distant television aerial or flagpole. Reject any glass that gives the slightest double vision, or you will suffer eyestrain and headache after prolonged viewing. If the circumstances of your observation require high magnification beyond 7 diameters, the answer is a telescope mounted upon a tripod.

Appendix 12

Perpetual calendar

When checking documents of some age that may be false, when endeavouring to verify a stated date of birth, or that a given date of marriage or dates of sale and the like are correct, or to assist a straightforward witness in pinpointing a past event of some importance, it is useful to have immediate access to a perpetual calendar. Here is one.

EASY REFERENCE CALENDAR

for any year between 1753 and 2000 together with the dates of Easter in each of those years
TO SELECT THE CORRECT CALENDAR FOR ANY YEAR consult the INDEX below

INDEX TO CALENDARS

Year		Cal	Year		Cal	Year		Cal	Year		Cal	Year		Cal
1753	..	C				1836	..	L*	1877	..	C	1918	..	E	1959	..	I
1754	..	E	1795	..	I	1837	..	A	1878	..	E	1919	..	G	1960	..	L*
1755	..	G	1796	..	L*	1838	..	C	1879	..	G	1920	..	J*	1961	..	A
1756	..	J*	1797	..	A	1839	..	E	1880	..	J*	1921	..	M	1962	..	C
1757	..	M	1798	..	C	1840	..	H*	1881	..	M	1922	..	A	1963	..	E
1758	..	A	1799	..	E	1841	..	K	1882	..	A	1923	..	C	1964	..	H*
1759	..	C	1800	..	G	1842	..	M	1883	..	C	1924	..	F*	1965	..	K
1760	..	F*	1801	..	I	1843	..	A	1884	..	F*	1925	..	I	1966	..	M
1761	..	I	1802	..	K	1844	..	D*	1885	..	I	1926	..	K	1967	..	A
1762	..	K	1803	..	M	1845	..	G	1886	..	K	1927	..	M	1968	..	D*
1763	..	M	1804	..	B*	1846	..	I	1887	..	M	1928	..	B*	1969	..	G
1764	..	B*	1805	..	E	1847	..	K	1888	..	B*	1929	..	E	1970	..	I
1765	..	E	1806	..	G	1848	..	N*	1889	..	E	1930	..	G	1971	..	K
1766	..	G	1807	..	I	1849	..	C	1890	..	G	1931	..	I	1972	..	N*
1767	..	I	1808	..	L*	1850	..	E	1891	..	I	1932	..	L*	1973	..	C
1768	..	L*	1809	..	A	1851	..	G	1892	..	L*	1933	..	A	1974	..	E
1769	..	A	1810	..	C	1852	..	J*	1893	..	A	1934	..	C	1975	..	G
1770	..	C	1811	..	E	1853	..	M	1894	..	C	1935	..	E	1976	..	J*
1771	..	E	1812	..	H*	1854	..	A	1895	..	E	1936	..	H*	1977	..	M
1772	..	H*	1813	..	K	1855	..	C	1896	..	H*	1937	..	K	1978	..	A
1773	..	K	1814	..	M	1856	..	F*	1897	..	K	1938	..	M	1979	..	C
1774	..	M	1815	..	A	1857	..	I	1898	..	M	1939	..	A	1980	..	F*
1775	..	A	1816	..	D*	1858	..	K	1899	..	A	1940	..	D*	1981	..	I
1776	..	D*	1817	..	G	1859	..	M	1900	..	C	1941	..	G	1982	..	K
1777	..	G	1818	..	I	1860	..	B*	1901	..	E	1942	..	I	1983	..	M
1778	..	I	1819	..	K	1861	..	E	1902	..	G	1943	..	K	1984	..	B*
1779	..	K	1820	..	N*	1862	..	G	1903	..	I	1944	..	N*	1985	..	E
1780	..	N*	1821	..	C	1863	..	I	1904	..	L*	1945	..	C	1986	..	G
1781	..	C	1822	..	E	1864	..	L*	1905	..	A	1946	..	E	1987	..	I
1782	..	E	1823	..	G	1865	..	A	1906	..	C	1947	..	G	1988	..	L*
1783	..	G	1824	..	J*	1866	..	C	1907	..	E	1948	..	J*	1989	..	A
1784	..	J*	1825	..	M	1867	..	E	1908	..	H*	1949	..	M	1990	..	C
1785	..	M	1826	..	A	1868	..	H*	1909	..	K	1950	..	A	1991	..	E
1786	..	A	1827	..	C	1869	..	K	1910	..	M	1951	..	C	1992	..	H*
1787	..	C	1828	..	F*	1870	..	M	1911	..	A	1952	..	F*	1993	..	K
1788	..	F*	1829	..	I	1871	..	A	1912	..	D*	1953	..	I	1994	..	M
1789	..	I	1830	..	K	1872	..	D*	1913	..	G	1954	..	K	1995	..	A
1790	..	K	1831	..	M	1873	..	G	1914	..	I	1955	..	M	1996	..	D*
1791	..	M	1832	..	B*	1874	..	I	1915	..	K	1956	..	B*	1997	..	G
1792	..	B*	1833	..	E	1875	..	K	1916	..	N*	1957	..	E	1998	..	I
1793	..	E	1834	..	G	1876	..	N*	1917	..	C	1958	..	G	1999	..	K
1794	..	G	1835	..	I										2000	..	N*

* Leap Year

A

	January		May		September
Su.	...1 8 15 22 29		7 14 21 28		3 10 17 24
M.	...2 9 16 23 30		1 8 15 22 29		4 11 18 25
Tu.	...3 10 17 24 31		2 9 16 23 30		5 12 19 26
W.	...4 11 18 25		3 10 17 24 31		6 13 20 27
Th.	...5 12 19 26		4 11 18 25		7 14 21 28
F.	...6 13 20 27		5 12 19 26	1 8 15 22 29
S.	...7 14 21 28		6 13 20 27	2 9 16 23 30

	February		June		October
Su.	... 5 12 19 26		4 11 18 25	1 8 15 22 29
M.	... 6 13 20 27		5 12 19 26	2 9 16 23 30
Tu.	... 7 14 21 28		6 13 20 27	3 10 17 24 31
W.	...1 8 15 22		7 14 21 28	4 11 18 25
Th.	...2 9 16 23	1 8 15 22 29	5 12 19 26
F.	...3 10 17 24	2 9 16 23 30	6 13 20 27
S.	...4 11 18 25	3 10 17 24	7 14 21 28

	March		July		November
Su.	... 5 12 19 26	2 9 16 23 30		5 12 19 26
M.	... 6 13 20 27	3 10 17 24 31		6 13 20 27
Tu.	... 7 14 21 28	4 11 18 25		7 14 21 28
W.	...1 8 15 22 29	5 12 19 26	1 8 15 22 29
Th.	...2 9 16 23 30	6 13 20 27	2 9 16 23 30
F.	...3 10 17 24 31	7 14 21 28	3 10 17 24
S.	...4 11 18 25	1 8 15 22 29	4 11 18 25

	April		August		December
Su.	...2 9 16 23 30		6 13 20 27	3 10 17 24 31
M.	...3 10 17 24		7 14 21 28	4 11 18 25
Tu.	...4 11 18 25	1 8 15 22 29	5 12 19 26
W.	...5 12 19 26	2 9 16 23 30	6 13 20 27
Th.	...6 13 20 27	3 10 17 24 31	7 14 21 28
F.	...7 14 21 28	4 11 18 25	1 8 15 22 29
S.	...1 8 15 22 29	5 12 19 26	2 9 16 23 30

Easter Days

March 26.	1758	1769	1815	1826	1837	1967	1978
April 2.	1809	1893	1899	1961.			[1989.
April 9.	1871	1882	1939	1950.			
April 16.	1775	1786	1797	1843	1854	1865	1911
April 23.	1905.				[1922	1933	1995.

B (Leap year)

	January		May		September
Su.	...1 8 15 22 29		6 13 20 27	2 9 16 23 30
M.	...2 9 16 23 30		7 14 21 28	3 10 17 24
Tu.	...3 10 17 24 31		1 8 15 22 29	4 11 18 25
W.	...4 11 18 25		2 9 16 23 30	5 12 19 26
Th.	...5 12 19 26		3 10 17 24 31	6 13 20 27
F.	...6 13 20 27		4 11 18 25	7 14 21 28
S.	...7 14 21 28		5 12 19 26	1 8 15 22 29

	February		June		October
Su.	... 5 12 19 26		3 10 17 24	7 14 21 28
M.	... 6 13 20 27		4 11 18 25	1 8 15 22 29
Tu.	... 7 14 21 28		5 12 19 26	2 9 16 23 30
W.	...1 8 15 22 29		6 13 20 27	3 10 17 24 31
Th.	...2 9 16 23		7 14 21 28	4 11 18 25
F.	...3 10 17 24	1 8 15 22 29	5 12 19 26
S.	...4 11 18 25	2 9 16 23 30	6 13 20 27

	March		July		November
Su.	... 4 11 18 25	1 8 15 22 29		4 11 18 25
M.	... 5 12 19 26	2 9 16 23 30		5 12 19 26
Tu.	... 6 13 20 27	3 10 17 24 31		6 13 20 27
W.	... 7 14 21 28	4 11 18 25		7 14 21 28
Th.	...1 8 15 22 29	5 12 19 26	1 8 15 22 29
F.	...2 9 16 23 30	6 13 20 27	2 9 16 23 30
S.	...3 10 17 24 31	7 14 21 28	3 10 17 24

	April		August		December
Su.	...1 8 15 22 29		5 12 19 26	2 9 16 23 30
M.	...2 9 16 23 30		6 13 20 27	3 10 17 24 31
Tu.	...3 10 17 24		7 14 21 28	4 11 18 25
W.	...4 11 18 25	1 8 15 22 29	5 12 19 26
Th.	...5 12 19 26	2 9 16 23 30	6 13 20 27
F.	...6 13 20 27	3 10 17 24 31	7 14 21 28
S.	...7 14 21 28	4 11 18 25	1 8 15 22 29

Easter Days

April 1.	1804	1888	1956.
April 8.	1792	1860	1928.
April 22.	1764	1832	1984.

1977]   *Reference Calendar*

CALENDAR TABLES

C – F

C

	January		May		September
Su. ..	7 14 21 28		6 13 20 27	2	9 16 23 30
M. ..	1 8 15 22 29		7 14 21 28	3	10 17 24
Tu. ..	2 9 16 23 30	1	8 15 22 29	4	11 18 25
W. ..	3 10 17 24 31	2	9 16 23 30	5	12 19 26
Th. ..	4 11 18 25	3	10 17 24 31	6	13 20 27
F. ..	5 12 19 26	4	11 18 25	7	14 21 28
S. ..	6 13 20 27	5	12 19 26	1 8	15 22 29

	February		June		October
Su. ..	4 11 18 25	3	10 17 24	7	14 21 28
M. ..	5 12 19 26	4	11 18 25	1	8 15 22 29
Tu. ..	6 13 20 27	5	12 19 26	2	9 16 23 30
W. ..	7 14 21 28	6	13 20 27	3	10 17 24 31
Th. ..	1 8 15 22	7	14 21 28	4	11 18 25
F. ..	2 9 16 23	1 8	15 22 29	5	12 19 26
S. ..	3 10 17 24	2	9 16 23 30	6	13 20 27

	March		July		November
Su. ..	4 11 18 25	1	8 15 22 29	4	11 18 25
M. ..	5 12 19 26	2	9 16 23 30	5	12 19 26
Tu. ..	6 13 20 27	3	10 17 24 31	6	13 20 27
W. ..	7 14 21 28	4	11 18 25	7	14 21 28
Th. ..	1 8 15 22 29	5	12 19 26	1	8 15 22 29
F. ..	2 9 16 23 30	6	13 20 27	2	9 16 23 30
S. ..	3 10 17 24 31	7	14 21 28	3	10 17 24

	April		August		December
Su. ..	1 8 15 22 29	5	12 19 26	2	9 16 23 30
M. ..	2 9 16 23 30	6	13 20 27	3	10 17 24 31
Tu. ..	3 10 17 24	7	14 21 28	4	11 18 25
W. ..	4 11 18 25	1	8 15 22 29	5	12 19 26
Th. ..	5 12 19 26	2	9 16 23 30	6	13 20 27
F. ..	6 13 20 27	3	10 17 24 31	7	14 21 28
S. ..	7 14 21 28	4	11 18 25	1 8	15 22 29

Easter Days

March 25.	1883	1894	1951.			
April 1.	1866	1877	1923	1934	1945.	
April 8.	1787	1798	1849	1855	1917.	
April 15.	1759	1770	1781	1827	1838	1900 1906
	1979	1990.				
April 22.	1753	1810	1821	1962	1973.	

D (Leap year)

	January		May		September
Su. ..	7 14 21 28	5	12 19 26	1	8 15 22 29
M. ..	1 8 15 22 29	6	13 20 27	2	9 16 23 30
Tu. ..	2 9 16 23 30	7	14 21 28	3	10 17 24
W. ..	3 10 17 24 31	1	8 15 22 29	4	11 18 25
Th. ..	4 11 18 25	2	9 16 23 30	5	12 19 26
F. ..	5 12 19 26	3	10 17 24 31	6	13 20 27
S. ..	6 13 20 27	4	11 18 25	7	14 21 28

	February		June		October
Su. ..	4 11 18 25	2	9 16 23 30	6	13 20 27
M. ..	5 12 19 26	3	10 17 24	7	14 21 28
Tu. ..	6 13 20 27	4	11 18 25	1	8 15 22 29
W. ..	7 14 21 28	5	12 19 26	2	9 16 23 30
Th. ..	1 8 15 22 29	6	13 20 27	3	10 17 24 31
F. ..	2 9 16 23	7	14 21 28	4	11 18 25
S. ..	3 10 17 24	1 8	15 22 29	5	12 19 26

	March		July		November
Su. ..	3 10 17 24 31	7	14 21 28	3	10 17 24
M. ..	4 11 18 25	1	8 15 22 29	4	11 18 25
Tu. ..	5 12 19 26	2	9 16 23 30	5	12 19 26
W. ..	6 13 20 27	3	10 17 24 31	6	13 20 27
Th. ..	7 14 21 28	4	11 18 25	7	14 21 28
F. ..	1 8 15 22 29	5	12 19 26	1	8 15 22 29
S. ..	2 9 16 23 30	6	13 20 27	2	9 16 23 30

	April		August		December
Su. ..	7 14 21 28	4	11 18 25	1	8 15 22 29
M. ..	1 8 15 22 29	5	12 19 26	2	9 16 23 30
Tu. ..	2 9 16 23 30	6	13 20 27	3	10 17 24 31
W. ..	3 10 17 24	7	14 21 28	4	11 18 25
Th. ..	4 11 18 25	1	8 15 22 29	5	12 19 26
F. ..	5 12 19 26	2	9 16 23 30	6	13 20 27
S. ..	6 13 20 27	3	10 17 24 31	7	14 21 28

Easter Days

March 24.	1940.			
March 31.	1872.			
April 7.	1776	1844	1912	1996.
April 14.	1816	1968.		

E

	January		May		September
Su. ..	6 13 20 27	5	12 19 26	1	8 15 22 29
M. ..	7 14 21 28	6	13 20 27	2	9 16 23 30
Tu. ..	1 8 15 22 29	7	14 21 28	3	10 17 24
W. ..	2 9 16 23 30	1	8 15 22 29	4	11 18 25
Th. ..	3 10 17 24 31	2	9 16 23 30	5	12 19 26
F. ..	4 11 18 25	3	10 17 24 31	6	13 20 27
S. ..	5 12 19 26	4	11 18 25	7	14 21 28

	February		June		October
Su. ..	3 10 17 24	2	9 16 23 30	6	13 20 27
M. ..	4 11 18 25	3	10 17 24	7	14 21 28
Tu. ..	5 12 19 26	4	11 18 25	1	8 15 22 29
W. ..	6 13 20 27	5	12 19 26	2	9 16 23 30
Th. ..	7 14 21 28	6	13 20 27	3	10 17 24 31
F. ..	1 8 15 22	7	14 21 28	4	11 18 25
S. ..	2 9 16 23	1 8	15 22 29	5	12 19 26

	March		July		November
Su. ..	3 10 17 24 31	7	14 21 28	3	10 17 24
M. ..	4 11 18 25	1	8 15 22 29	4	11 18 25
Tu. ..	5 12 19 26	2	9 16 23 30	5	12 19 26
W. ..	6 13 20 27	3	10 17 24 31	6	13 20 27
Th. ..	7 14 21 28	4	11 18 25	7	14 21 28
F. ..	1 8 15 22 29	5	12 19 26	1	8 15 22 29
S. ..	2 9 16 23 30	6	13 20 27	2	9 16 23 30

	April		August		December
Su. ..	7 14 21 28	4	11 18 25	1	8 15 22 29
M. ..	1 8 15 22 29	5	12 19 26	2	9 16 23 30
Tu. ..	2 9 16 23 30	6	13 20 27	3	10 17 24 31
W. ..	3 10 17 24	7	14 21 28	4	11 18 25
Th. ..	4 11 18 25	1	8 15 22 29	5	12 19 26
F. ..	5 12 19 26	2	9 16 23 30	6	13 20 27
S. ..	6 13 20 27	3	10 17 24 31	7	14 21 28

Easter Days

March 24.	1799.				
March 31.	1771	1782	1793	1839	1850 1861
April 7.	1765	1822	1833	1901	1985.
April 14.	1754	1805	1811	1895	1963 1974.
April 21.	1867	1878	1889	1935	1946 1957.

(Note: [1907 1918 1929 1991 appears with March 31.)

F (Leap year)

	January		May		September
Su. ..	6 13 20 27	4	11 18 25	7	14 21 28
M. ..	7 14 21 28	5	12 19 26	1	8 15 22 29
Tu. ..	1 8 15 22 29	6	13 20 27	2	9 16 23 30
W. ..	2 9 16 23 30	7	14 21 28	3	10 17 24
Th. ..	3 10 17 24 31	1	8 15 22 29	4	11 18 25
F. ..	4 11 18 25	2	9 16 23 30	5	12 19 26
S. ..	5 12 19 26	3	10 17 24 31	6	13 20 27

	February		June		October
Su. ..	3 10 17 24	1	8 15 22 29	5	12 19 26
M. ..	4 11 18 25	2	9 16 23 30	6	13 20 27
Tu. ..	5 12 19 26	3	10 17 24	7	14 21 28
W. ..	6 13 20 27	4	11 18 25	1	8 15 22 29
Th. ..	7 14 21 28	5	12 19 26	2	9 16 23 30
F. ..	1 8 15 22 29	6	13 20 27	3	10 17 24 31
S. ..	2 9 16 23	7	14 21 28	4	11 18 25

	March		July		November
Su. ..	2 9 16 23 30	6	13 20 27	2	9 16 23 30
M. ..	3 10 17 24 31	7	14 21 28	3	10 17 24
Tu. ..	4 11 18 25	1	8 15 22 29	4	11 18 25
W. ..	5 12 19 26	2	9 16 23 30	5	12 19 26
Th. ..	6 13 20 27	3	10 17 24 31	6	13 20 27
F. ..	7 14 21 28	4	11 18 25	7	14 21 28
S. ..	1 8 15 22 29	5	12 19 26	1 8	15 22 29

	April		August		December
Su. ..	6 13 20 27	3	10 17 24 31	7	14 21 28
M. ..	7 14 21 28	4	11 18 25	1	8 15 22 29
Tu. ..	1 8 15 22 29	5	12 19 26	2	9 16 23 30
W. ..	2 9 16 23 30	6	13 20 27	3	10 17 24 31
Th. ..	3 10 17 24	7	14 21 28	4	11 18 25
F. ..	4 11 18 25	1 8	15 22 29	5	12 19 26
S. ..	5 12 19 26	2 9	16 23 30	6	13 20 27

Easter Days

March 23.	1788	1856.	
April 6.	1760	1828	1980.
April 13.	1884	1952.	
April 20.	1924.		

Reference Calendar [1977

CALENDAR TABLES
G – J

G

	January	May	September
Su. ..	5 12 19 26	4 11 18 25	7 14 21 28
M. ..	6 13 20 27	5 12 19 26	1 8 15 22 29
Tu. ..	7 14 21 28	6 13 20 27	2 9 16 23 30
W. .. 1	8 15 22 29	7 14 21 28	3 10 17 24
Th. .. 2	9 16 23 30	1 8 15 22 29	4 11 18 25
F. .. 3	10 17 24 31	2 9 16 23 30	5 12 19 26
S. .. 4	11 18 25	3 10 17 24 31	6 13 20 27

	February	June	October
Su. ..	2 9 16 23	1 8 15 22 29	5 12 19 26
M. ..	3 10 17 24	2 9 16 23 30	6 13 20 27
Tu. ..	4 11 18 25	3 10 17 24	7 14 21 28
W. ..	5 12 19 26	4 11 18 25	1 8 15 22 29
Th. ..	6 13 20 27	5 12 19 26	2 9 16 23 30
F. ..	7 14 21 28	6 13 20 27	3 10 17 24 31
S. .. 1	8 15 22	7 14 21 28	4 11 18 25

	March	July	November
Su. .. 2	9 16 23 30	6 13 20 27	2 9 16 23 30
M. .. 3	10 17 24 31	7 14 21 28	3 10 17 24
Tu. .. 4	11 18 25	1 8 15 22 29	4 11 18 25
W. .. 5	12 19 26	2 9 16 23 30	5 12 19 26
Th. .. 6	13 20 27	3 10 17 24 31	6 13 20 27
F. .. 7	14 21 28	4 11 18 25	7 14 21 28
S. .. 1 8	15 22 29	5 12 19 26	1 8 15 22 29

	April	August	December
Su. ..	6 13 20 27	3 10 17 24 31	7 14 21 28
M. ..	7 14 21 28	4 11 18 25	1 8 15 22 29
Tu. .. 1	8 15 22 29	5 12 19 26	2 9 16 23 30
W. .. 2	9 16 23 30	6 13 20 27	3 10 17 24 31
Th. .. 3	10 17 24	7 14 21 28	4 11 18 25
F. .. 4	11 18 25	1 8 15 22 29	5 12 19 26
S. .. 5	12 19 26	2 9 16 23 30	6 13 20 27

Easter Days

March 23.	1845	1913.				
March 30.	1755	1766	1777	1823	1834	1902 1975
	1986	1997.				
April 6.	1806	1817	1890	1947	1958	1969.
April 13.	1800	1873	1879	1941.		
April 20.	1783	1794	1851	1862	1919	1930.

H (Leap year)

	January	May	September
Su. ..	5 12 19 26	3 10 17 24 31	6 13 20 27
M. ..	6 13 20 27	4 11 18 25	7 14 21 28
Tu. ..	7 14 21 28	5 12 19 26	1 8 15 22 29
W. .. 1	8 15 22 29	6 13 20 27	2 9 16 23 30
Th. .. 2	9 16 23 30	7 14 21 28	3 10 17 24
F. .. 3	10 17 24 31	1 8 15 22 29	4 11 18 25
S. .. 4	11 18 25	2 9 16 23 30	5 12 19 26

	February	June	October
Su. ..	2 9 16 23	7 14 21 28	4 11 18 25
M. ..	3 10 17 24	1 8 15 22 29	5 12 19 26
Tu. ..	4 11 18 25	2 9 16 23 30	6 13 20 27
W. ..	5 12 19 26	3 10 17 24	7 14 21 28
Th. ..	6 13 20 27	4 11 18 25	1 8 15 22 29
F. ..	7 14 21 28	5 12 19 26	2 9 16 23 30
S. .. 1	8 15 22 29	6 13 20 27	3 10 17 24 31

	March	July	November
Su. .. 1	8 15 22 29	5 12 19 26	1 8 15 22 29
M. .. 2	9 16 23 30	6 13 20 27	2 9 16 23 30
Tu. .. 3	10 17 24 31	7 14 21 28	3 10 17 24
W. .. 4	11 18 25	1 8 15 22 29	4 11 18 25
Th. .. 5	12 19 26	2 9 16 23 30	5 12 19 26
F. .. 6	13 20 27	3 10 17 24 31	6 13 20 27
S. .. 7	14 21 28	4 11 18 25	7 14 21 28

	April	August	December
Su. ..	5 12 19 26	2 9 16 23 30	6 13 20 27
M. ..	6 13 20 27	3 10 17 24 31	7 14 21 28
Tu. ..	7 14 21 28	4 11 18 25	1 8 15 22 29
W. .. 1	8 15 22 29	5 12 19 26	2 9 16 23 30
Th. .. 2	9 16 23 30	6 13 20 27	3 10 17 24 31
F. .. 3	10 17 24	7 14 21 28	4 11 18 25
S. .. 4	11 18 25	1 8 15 22 29	5 12 19 26

Easter Days

March 29.	1812	1964.
April 5.	1896.	
April 12.	1868	1936.
April 19.	1772	1840 1908 1992.

I

	January	May	September
Su. ..	4 11 18 25	3 10 17 24 31	6 13 20 27
M. ..	5 12 19 26	4 11 18 25	7 14 21 28
Tu. ..	6 13 20 27	5 12 19 26	1 8 15 22 29
W. ..	7 14 21 28	6 13 20 27	2 9 16 23 30
Th. .. 1	8 15 22 29	7 14 21 28	3 10 17 24
F. .. 2	9 16 23 30	1 8 15 22 29	4 11 18 25
S. .. 3	10 17 24 31	2 9 16 23 30	5 12 19 26

	February	June	October
Su. .. 1	8 15 22	7 14 21 28	4 11 18 25
M. .. 2	9 16 23	1 8 15 22 29	5 12 19 26
Tu. .. 3	10 17 24	2 9 16 23 30	6 13 20 27
W. .. 4	11 18 25	3 10 17 24	7 14 21 28
Th. .. 5	12 19 26	4 11 18 25	1 8 15 22 29
F. .. 6	13 20 27	5 12 19 26	2 9 16 23 30
S. .. 7	14 21 28	6 13 20 27	3 10 17 24 31

	March	July	November
Su. .. 1	8 15 22 29	5 12 19 26	1 8 15 22 29
M. .. 2	9 16 23 30	6 13 20 27	2 9 16 23 30
Tu. .. 3	10 17 24 31	7 14 21 28	3 10 17 24
W. .. 4	11 18 25	1 8 15 22 29	4 11 18 25
Th. .. 5	12 19 26	2 9 16 23 30	5 12 19 26
F. .. 6	13 20 27	3 10 17 24 31	6 13 20 27
S. .. 7	14 21 28	4 11 18 25	7 14 21 28

	April	August	December
Su. ..	5 12 19 26	2 9 16 23 30	6 13 20 27
M. ..	6 13 20 27	3 10 17 24 31	7 14 21 28
Tu. ..	7 14 21 28	4 11 18 25	1 8 15 22 29
W. .. 1	8 15 22 29	5 12 19 26	2 9 16 23 30
Th. .. 2	9 16 23 30	6 13 20 27	3 10 17 24 31
F. .. 3	10 17 24	7 14 21 28	4 11 18 25
S. .. 4	11 18 25	1 8 15 22 29	5 12 19 26

Easter Days

March 22.	1761	1818.			
March 29.	1807	1891	1959	1970.	
April 5.	1795	1801	1863	1874 1885 1931 1942
	1953.				
April 12.	1789	1846	1857	1903 1914 1925 1998.
April 19.	1767	1778	1829	1835 1981 1987.

J (Leap year)

	January	May	September
Su. ..	4 11 18 25	2 9 16 23 30	5 12 19 26
M. ..	5 12 19 26	3 10 17 24 31	6 13 20 27
Tu. ..	6 13 20 27	4 11 18 25	7 14 21 28
W. ..	7 14 21 28	5 12 19 26	1 8 15 22 29
Th. .. 1	8 15 22 29	6 13 20 27	2 9 16 23 30
F. .. 2	9 16 23 30	7 14 21 28	3 10 17 24
S. .. 3	10 17 24 31	1 8 15 22 29	4 11 18 25

	February	June	October
Su. .. 1	8 15 22 29	6 13 20 27	3 10 17 24 31
M. .. 2	9 16 23	7 14 21 28	4 11 18 25
Tu. .. 3	10 17 24	1 8 15 22 29	5 12 19 26
W. .. 4	11 18 25	2 9 16 23 30	6 13 20 27
Th. .. 5	12 19 26	3 10 17 24	7 14 21 28
F. .. 6	13 20 27	4 11 18 25	1 8 15 22 29
S. .. 7	14 21 28	5 12 19 26	2 9 16 23 30

	March	July	November
Su. ..	7 14 21 28	4 11 18 25	7 14 21 28
M. .. 1	8 15 22 29	5 12 19 26	1 8 15 22 29
Tu. .. 2	9 16 23 30	6 13 20 27	2 9 16 23 30
W. .. 3	10 17 24 31	7 14 21 28	3 10 17 24
Th. .. 4	11 18 25	1 8 15 22 29	4 11 18 25
F. .. 5	12 19 26	2 9 16 23 30	5 12 19 26
S. .. 6	13 20 27	3 10 17 24 31	6 13 20 27

	April	August	December
Su. .. 4	11 18 25	1 8 15 22 29	5 12 19 26
M. .. 5	12 19 26	2 9 16 23 30	6 13 20 27
Tu. .. 6	13 20 27	3 10 17 24 31	7 14 21 28
W. .. 7	14 21 28	4 11 18 25	1 8 15 22 29
Th. .. 1	8 15 22 29	5 12 19 26	2 9 16 23 30
F. .. 2	9 16 23 30	6 13 20 27	3 10 17 24 31
S. .. 3	10 17 24	7 14 21 28	4 11 18 25

Easter Days

March 28.	1880	1948.
April 4.	1920.	
April 11.	1784	1852.
April 18.	1756	1824 1976.

1977] Reference Calendar

CALENDAR TABLES
K – N

K

	January	May	September
Su.	3 10 17 24 31	2 9 16 23 30	5 12 19 26
M.	4 11 18 25	3 10 17 24 31	6 13 20 27
Tu.	5 12 19 26	4 11 18 25	7 14 21 28
W.	6 13 20 27	5 12 19 26	1 8 15 22 29
Th.	7 14 21 28	6 13 20 27	2 9 16 23 30
F.	1 8 15 22 29	7 14 21 28	3 10 17 24
S.	2 9 16 23 30	1 8 15 22 29	4 11 18 25

	February	June	October
Su.	7 14 21 28	6 13 20 27	3 10 17 24 31
M.	1 8 15 22	7 14 21 28	4 11 18 25
Tu.	2 9 16 23	1 8 15 22 29	5 12 19 26
W.	3 10 17 24	2 9 16 23 30	6 13 20 27
Th.	4 11 18 25	3 10 17 24	7 14 21 28
F.	5 12 19 26	4 11 18 25	1 8 15 22 29
S.	6 13 20 27	5 12 19 26	2 9 16 23 30

	March	July	November
Su.	7 14 21 28	4 11 18 25	7 14 21 28
M.	1 8 15 22 29	5 12 19 26	1 8 15 22 29
Tu.	2 9 16 23 30	6 13 20 27	2 9 16 23 30
W.	3 10 17 24 31	7 14 21 28	3 10 17 24
Th.	4 11 18 25	1 8 15 22 29	4 11 18 25
F.	5 12 19 26	2 9 16 23 30	5 12 19 26
S.	6 13 20 27	3 10 17 24 31	6 13 20 27

	April	August	December
Su.	4 11 18 25	1 8 15 22 29	5 12 19 26
M.	5 12 19 26	2 9 16 23 30	6 13 20 27
Tu.	6 13 20 27	3 10 17 24 31	7 14 21 28
W.	7 14 21 28	4 11 18 25	1 8 15 22 29
Th.	1 8 15 22 29	5 12 19 26	2 9 16 23 30
F.	2 9 16 23 30	6 13 20 27	3 10 17 24 31
S.	3 10 17 24	7 14 21 28	4 11 18 25

Easter Days

March 28.	1869	1875	1937.			
April 4.	1779	1790	1847	1858	1915	1926 1999.
	1982	1993.				
April 11.	1762	1773	1819	1830	1841	1909 1971
April 18.	1802	1813	1897	1954	1965.	
April 25.	1886	1943.				

L (Leap year)

	January	May	September
Su.	3 10 17 24 31	1 8 15 22 29	4 11 18 25
M.	4 11 18 25	2 9 16 23 30	5 12 19 26
Tu.	5 12 19 26	3 10 17 24 31	6 13 20 27
W.	6 13 20 27	4 11 18 25	7 14 21 28
Th.	7 14 21 28	5 12 19 26	1 8 15 22 29
F.	1 8 15 22 29	6 13 20 27	2 9 16 23 30
S.	2 9 16 23 30	7 14 21 28	3 10 17 24

	February	June	October
Su.	7 14 21 28	5 12 19 26	2 9 16 23 30
M.	1 8 15 22 29	6 13 20 27	3 10 17 24 31
Tu.	2 9 16 23	7 14 21 28	4 11 18 25
W.	3 10 17 24	1 8 15 22 29	5 12 19 26
Th.	4 11 18 25	2 9 16 23 30	6 13 20 27
F.	5 12 19 26	3 10 17 24	7 14 21 28
S.	6 13 20 27	4 11 18 25	1 8 15 22 29

	March	July	November
Su.	6 13 20 27	3 10 17 24 31	6 13 20 27
M.	7 14 21 28	4 11 18 25	7 14 21 28
Tu.	1 8 15 22 29	5 12 19 26	1 8 15 22 29
W.	2 9 16 23 30	6 13 20 27	2 9 16 23 30
Th.	3 10 17 24 31	7 14 21 28	3 10 17 24
F.	4 11 18 25	1 8 15 22 29	4 11 18 25
S.	5 12 19 26	2 9 16 23 30	5 12 19 26

	April	August	December
Su.	3 10 17 24	7 14 21 28	4 11 18 25
M.	4 11 18 25	1 8 15 22 29	5 12 19 26
Tu.	5 12 19 26	2 9 16 23 30	6 13 20 27
W.	6 13 20 27	3 10 17 24 31	7 14 21 28
Th.	7 14 21 28	4 11 18 25	1 8 15 22 29
F.	1 8 15 22 29	5 12 19 26	2 9 16 23 30
S.	2 9 16 23 30	6 13 20 27	3 10 17 24 31

Easter Days

March 27.	1796	1864	1932.	
April 3.	1768	1836	1904	1988.
April 17.	1808	1892	1960.	

M

	January	May	September
Su.	2 9 16 23 30	1 8 15 22 29	4 11 18 25
M.	3 10 17 24 31	2 9 16 23 30	5 12 19 26
Tu.	4 11 18 25	3 10 17 24 31	6 13 20 27
W.	5 12 19 26	4 11 18 25	7 14 21 28
Th.	6 13 20 27	5 12 19 26	1 8 15 22 29
F.	7 14 21 28	6 13 20 27	2 9 16 23 30
S.	1 8 15 22 29	7 14 21 28	3 10 17 24

	February	June	October
Su.	6 13 20 27	5 12 19 26	2 9 16 23 30
M.	7 14 21 28	6 13 20 27	3 10 17 24 31
Tu.	1 8 15 22	7 14 21 28	4 11 18 25
W.	2 9 16 23	1 8 15 22 29	5 12 19 26
Th.	3 10 17 24	2 9 16 23 30	6 13 20 27
F.	4 11 18 25	3 10 17 24	7 14 21 28
S.	5 12 19 26	4 11 18 25	1 8 15 22 29

	March	July	November
Su.	6 13 20 27	3 10 17 24 31	6 13 20 27
M.	7 14 21 28	4 11 18 25	7 14 21 28
Tu.	1 8 15 22 29	5 12 19 26	1 8 15 22 29
W.	2 9 16 23 30	6 13 20 27	2 9 16 23 30
Th.	3 10 17 24 31	7 14 21 28	3 10 17 24
F.	4 11 18 25	1 8 15 22 29	4 11 18 25
S.	5 12 19 26	2 9 16 23 30	5 12 19 26

	April	August	December
Su.	3 10 17 24	7 14 21 28	4 11 18 25
M.	4 11 18 25	1 8 15 22 29	5 12 19 26
Tu.	5 12 19 26	2 9 16 23 30	6 13 20 27
W.	6 13 20 27	3 10 17 24 31	7 14 21 28
Th.	7 14 21 28	4 11 18 25	1 8 15 22 29
F.	1 8 15 22 29	5 12 19 26	2 9 16 23 30
S.	2 9 16 23 30	6 13 20 27	3 10 17 24 31

Easter Days

March 27.	1785	1842	1853	1910	1921.	
April 3.	1763	1774	1825	1831	1983	1994.
April 10.	1757	1803	1814	1887	1898	1955 1966
April 17.	1870	1881	1927	1938	1949.	[1977.
April 24.	1791	1859.				

N (Leap year)

	January	May	September
Su.	2 9 16 23 30	7 14 21 28	3 10 17 24
M.	3 10 17 24 31	1 8 15 22 29	4 11 18 25
Tu.	4 11 18 25	2 9 16 23 30	5 12 19 26
W.	5 12 19 26	3 10 17 24 31	6 13 20 27
Th.	6 13 20 27	4 11 18 25	7 14 21 28
F.	7 14 21 28	5 12 19 26	1 8 15 22 29
S.	1 8 15 22 29	6 13 20 27	2 9 16 23 30

	February	June	October
Su.	6 13 20 27	4 11 18 25	1 8 15 22 29
M.	7 14 21 28	5 12 19 26	2 9 16 23 30
Tu.	1 8 15 22 29	6 13 20 27	3 10 17 24 31
W.	2 9 16 23	7 14 21 28	4 11 18 25
Th.	3 10 17 24	1 8 15 22 29	5 12 19 26
F.	4 11 18 25	2 9 16 23 30	6 13 20 27
S.	5 12 19 26	3 10 17 24	7 14 21 28

	March	July	November
Su.	5 12 19 26	2 9 16 23 30	5 12 19 26
M.	6 13 20 27	3 10 17 24 31	6 13 20 27
Tu.	7 14 21 28	4 11 18 25	7 14 21 28
W.	1 8 15 22 29	5 12 19 26	1 8 15 22 29
Th.	2 9 16 23 30	6 13 20 27	2 9 16 23 30
F.	3 10 17 24 31	7 14 21 28	3 10 17 24
S.	4 11 18 25	1 8 15 22 29	4 11 18 25

	April	August	December
Su.	2 9 16 23 30	6 13 20 27	3 10 17 24 31
M.	3 10 17 24	7 14 21 28	4 11 18 25
Tu.	4 11 18 25	1 8 15 22 29	5 12 19 26
W.	5 12 19 26	2 9 16 23 30	6 13 20 27
Th.	6 13 20 27	3 10 17 24 31	7 14 21 28
F.	7 14 21 28	4 11 18 25	1 8 15 22 29
S.	1 8 15 22 29	5 12 19 26	2 9 16 23 30

Easter Days

March 26.	1780.		
April 2.	1820	1972.	
April 9.	1944.		
April 16.	1876.		
April 23.	1848	1916	2000.

Appendix 13

Drinking club inquiries

Here is a detailed list of questions you may find useful for inquiries in the more plush of clubs. They are based on a list I used when engaged full time on such duties. You will, of course, vary the questions according to the style of premises concerned. Be reasonable, and adapt to circumstances. My advice, however, is this—have such a list of questions with you. It goes without saying that you will get the best results if you are scrupulously courteous in the manner you question.

Bear in mind the desirability or otherwise of taking with you a typed-out blank authority (to be signed upon request by some person in authority at the club) for the police plan drawer to come and measure up the premises concerned within 7 days of the visit or 'raid'.

Always note *full* name. Question so as to get all forenames. Certain Christian or forenames are often 'left out' by interviewees—especially if they have an over-religious or otherwise embarrassing sound. For easy identification you should get them. Note a short description. Ask yourself, 'What is the most striking thing about his/her appearance?' Estimate height and weight. Obtain exact place and date of birth. Ask for these particulars again at the end of the interview (to check the answers given first). Ask for occupation and previous occupation. Obtain address, and get home and secondary telephone numbers.

1. Is this a proprietary club? (If not, what is the purpose and object of the club—a negative answer here from the official of the club may be most revealing evidentially.)

2. What is your position here? When was it gained?

3. When were you last confirmed in office?

4. Have you a committee?

5. What are the names of the committee members?

6. When did the committee last meet?

7. When was the annual general meeting held?

8. Have you a wine committee?

9. What are the names of the wine committee members?

10. When did the wine committee last meet?

11. What other meetings have you attended in the past 12 months?

12. Who owns the premises?

13. Who is the tenant?

14. What are the rent and rates?

15. Who pays the rent and rates?

16. Who holds the lease (full particulars)?

17. Who orders the liquor?

18. Who has authority to sign cheques? (Are two signatures required? Who is the other person signing?)

19. What accounts are kept?

20. Who keeps the accounts?

21. How are the profits shared?

22. What staff have you?

23. What wages do they get?

24. Who pays their wages?

25. What wages do you get? (Any other allowances?)

26. Do you serve meals?

27. Are there any shareholders?

28. Who owns the furniture and fittings? (Is payment made to anyone for their own use?)

29. What instructions did you give about closing tonight?

30. From whom do you get your liquor?

31. Is your minute book up to date?

32. May I see the minute book?

33. Are all visitors accounted for in the visitors' book?

34. Are all the persons here either members or signed in the visitors' book?

35. May I see the visitors' book?

36. What is the cost of membership?

37. Under what circumstances are temporary members allowed to purchase drinks?

38. What are your weekly takings?

39. What was the profit from liquor last month/year?

40. What insurance do you pay?

41. Where are your nomination forms for membership displayed?

42. Who are your bankers? (Get full address.)

43. How many members are there?

Check the stock till in the presence of subject and another police officer. Detail any foreign currency. After obtaining full particulars of name, etc., frequenters should be asked the following questions:

1. Are you a member?

If the answer is yes:

2. When did you become a member?

3. Have you your membership card?

4. What is your drink?

5. Who paid for it?

6. How much did it cost?

7. From whom was it purchased and when?

8. What membership fees have you paid, if any?

If the answer to the first question is no:

9. Who introduced you?

10. Did you sign the visitors' book?

11. Who bought your drink?

12. Have you ever been here before?

13. When?

Bibliography

Books in print

UK
Gross, H., *Criminal Investigation*, 5 edn, Sweet & Maxwell, 1962.
Williams, W. J., *Moriarty's Police Law*, 22 edn, Butterworth, 1974.
Willett, T. C., *Criminal on the Road*, Tavistock Publications, 1971.

USA
Bristow, A. P., *Field Interrogation*, 2 edn, C. C. Thomas, 1972.
Harney & Cross, *The Narcotic Officer's Notebook*, 2 edn, C. C. Thomas, 1975.
Holcomb, R. L., *Police Patrol*, C. C. Thomas, 1971.
Horgan, J. J., *Criminal Investigation*, McGraw-Hill, 1974.
Iannone, N. F., *Principles of Police Patrol*, McGraw-Hill, 1975.
Nelson, A. T. and Smith, H. E., *Car Clouting: The Crime, The Criminal and the Police*, C. C. Thomas, 1958.
O'Hara, C. E., *Fundamentals at Criminal Investigation*, 3 edn, C. C. Thomas, 1975.
Ward, R. A., *Introduction to Criminal Investigation*, Addison–Wesley, 1975.
Weston, P. B. and Wells, K. M., *Criminal Investigation: Basic Perspectives*, 2 edn, Prentice-Hall, 1974.

Magazine and journal articles

Pilcher, D., 'The law and practice of field interrogation', *Journal of Criminal Law, Criminology and Police Science*, vol. 58, no. 4, 1968.
Schwartz, H., 'Stop and frisk?' *Journal of Criminal Law, Criminology and Police Science*, vol. 58, no. 4, 1968.
Thomas, D. A., 'The law of search and seizure: Further ground for rationalisation', *Criminal Law Review*, 3, 1967.
Williams, G., 'Statutory powers of search and arrest on the grounds of unlawful possession', *Criminal Law Review*, 598, 1960.

Police service publications

Commissioner of Metropolitan Police:
(a) *Vehicle Identification*, 1967.
(b) *Traffic Accident Investigators' Manual*, 1972.
(c) *Notes on Criminal Law* (earlier known as *Keech's Notes*,) 1976 (annual).
(d) *Instruction Book*, amended 1969 edition.

West Yorkshire Metropolitan Police Notes on Criminal Law and Procedure, Staff of Detective Training School, 1976.

Special Investigation Branch—Royal Corps of Military Police, *Manual of Instruction—Crime* (especially chapter on use of dyes in thief taking, page 137 *et seq.*), 1953.

Publications not in print in UK, but recommended if available

Devlin, J. D., *Police Procedure, Administration and Organisation*, Butterworth, 1966.

Gilston and Podell, *The Practical Patrolman*, C. C. Thomas, 1959.

Gross, H., *Criminal Investigation*, 3 edn (adapted by Adam), Sweet & Maxwell, 1934.

Her Majesty's Stationery Office, London. *Field Service Pocketbook* 1914, David & Charles, 1971.

Jackson, Sir R., *Occupied with Crime*, Harrap, 1967.

Jones, E. W., *Police Pursuit Driving*, 4 edn, IACP, Washington DC, 1963.

Melville Lee, W. L., *A History of Police in England*, Methuen, 1901.

Morrish, R., *Criminal Law and Investigation*, 1 edn, Police Review Publishing Co. Ltd, 1942.

Parker, W. H., *Daily Training Bulletin of the Los Angeles Police* (volumes II, III and IV), C. C. Thomas, 1950–8.

Reed, Sir Andrew, *The Irish Constable's Guide*, HMSO, Dublin, 1918.

Rolph, C. H. (Editor), *Police and Public*, chapter 2, Heinemann, 1962.

Royal Irish Constabulary Code, HMSO, Dublin, 1911.

Schwartz, J. I., *Police Road Block Operation*, C. C. Thomas, 1962.

Soderman, H. L. and O'Connell, J., *Modern Criminal Investigation*, Bell, 1935.

Solnsson, A. & Wendell, O., *Crime Detection* (chapters VI and VII), Cleaver Hulme Press, 1955.

South African Police, *Instructions Regarding the Investigation of Crime and Aids to Investigation*, Government Printer, Pretoria, 1951.

Williams, W. J., *Moriarty's Police Law*, 20 edn, Butterworth, 1970.

Index